More House Specialties

Created by Deanna House

Book Design by Craig Minor

Interior Illustrations by Denise Chapman

[handwritten inscription:]

11/1/91

Karen—
I hope these
recipes always remind you
of the day we cooked together!
Real! Enjoy! Cook!
Deanna House

Third Printing, 20,000 copies in print

Published by Deanna House Specialties, Inc.
Library of Congress Catalog Card Number 86-72189
ISBN # 0-9610752-1-X

Printed in the USA by
WIMMER BROTHERS
A Wimmer Company
Memphis • Dallas

Introduction

Welcome to *More House Specialties ...*

This cookbook can aptly be described as a second serving of favorite proven recipes as it has been created to be a companion to my successful first cookbook, *House Specialties*. Between these thoughtfully designed covers is another collection of tested recipes developed to encourage happy cooking experiences.

For those who already enjoy *House Specialties* recipes, you'll again notice clear concise directions with microwave adaptations. To those new to this format, I hope you'll find the recipes easy to follow with satisfying results.

A select group of recipes in this cookbook have been given a special code because they are fine examples of using less sugar, less salt, or less fat. Watch for this symbol ◁ as you search for recipe ideas with these requirements. Conscientious cooks are well aware that moderate use of sugar, salt, and fat is a key to healthful living.

Writing this cookbook has provided me a time to appreciatively reflect on those significant personal and professional experiences that have made a difference in my life. From my loving parents who gracefully nurtured my first twenty years on a farm in southern Wisconsin to students and friends who faithfully attend my Portage Community Education classes I am very grateful.

As with my cookbook, *House Specialties,* this book is not a one person effort. Special heartfelt thanks to my husband, George, who shares not only his business expertise, but is a constant source of encouragement and support. Thanks also to our son Paul and daughter Sara for their helpful contributions during a memorable recipe testing and cookbook writing summer.

Lots of appreciation goes to my good friends Mary Ellen Behm and Mary Koenig, who along with Jerry Behm and Paul House using their computer talent, helped proofread and edit all of these recipes one marathon weekend so a deadline was met.

Do take time to read, enjoy, and prepare recipes from this favorite collection. Soon family members and friends will be asking for a second serving of *More House Specialties.*

Happy Cooking!

Deanna House

Contents

Recipes highlighted with this symbol contain less sugar, less salt or less fat.

Microwave cooks
The microwave directions in this book are for use with units having 600–700 watts. If oven with lower wattage is used microwave cooking times need to be increased.

Tasty Beginnings

It seems very natural to begin this collection of favorite recipes with a selection of ideas designed to whet the appetite. From the impressive Appetizer Garden Pizza to the tasty Spicy-Perk-A-Punch, these are recipes that integrate beautifully into today's busy life style.

Here is a dynamic group of flavorful sparkling beverages. Notice that several recipes contain reduced amounts of sugar or are sugar-free. The variety of color as well as quantity offers creative cooks the opportunity to match color schemes yet serve any size crowd.

Team cold beverages with hot appetizers and vice versa, being certain to keep hot things hot and cold things cold. Remember to vary texture, color, flavor and ease of preparation so that each delicious morsel is a tasty beginning.

Contents

Appetizer Garden Pizza

Serves 12

Here is a first class way of serving fresh vegetables for the appetizer course. I've included a plan for arranging the top of the pizza, but actually you can create your own design. Cardboard circles, which can be purchased wherever cake decorating supplies are sold, work out very well for serving trays.

1	**(8 ounce) package refrigerator crescent dinner rolls**
1	**(8 ounce) package cream cheese, softened**
¼	**cup mayonnaise or salad dressing**
1	**tablespoon milk**
⅛	**teaspoon dill weed**
	Broccoli flowerettes
	Carrot slices, about ¼ inch thick
	Cucumber slices, about ¼ inch thick and cut in half
¾	**cup chopped celery**
⅓	**cup pitted ripe olives, sliced**
	Cherry tomatoes, halved

1. Separate crescent dough into 8 triangles, place triangles with elongated points toward center in a greased 12-inch pizza pan.

2. With fingertips press dough to form a crust, being certain to seal the perforations.

3. Bake in preheated 375 degree oven for 10-12 minutes or until browned. Cool. Place on serving tray or cardboard circle.

4. In small mixing bowl, beat together cream cheese, mayonnaise and milk until light and fluffy.

5. Spread cream cheese mixture over cooled crust. Sprinkle with dill weed.

6. Arrange broccoli flowerettes in the center forming a 4-inch diameter circle. Circle the broccoli with sliced carrots, then sliced cucumber half circles, the chopped celery and sliced ripe olives.

7. Trim the outside edge with halved cherry tomatoes. Chill.

Tropical Cheese Ball

Serves 10-12

If you'd like a change of pace from the traditional cheese ball, try this interesting tropical variation. Remember, you don't have to entertain at a luau to enjoy these marvelous flavors.

(Continued)

Tropical Cheese Ball (continued)

1   (8 ounce) package cream cheese, softened
1   (8 ounce) can crushed pineapple, drained well
2   cups (8 ounces) shredded sharp cheddar cheese
½   cup pecans
¼   cup chopped dried apricots
1   teaspoon finely chopped crystallized ginger
    Toasted Coconut

1. In medium mixing bowl, combine softened cream cheese and pineapple. Mix well.

2. Add cheddar cheese, pecans, apricots and ginger. Mix well.

3. Chill thoroughly.

4. Shape into ball; slightly flatten top.

5. Roll in toasted coconut.

6. Serve with assorted crackers.

Dilled Cauliflower

Makes 8-12 appetizer servings

When snowy white heads of cauliflower grace the produce counter, remember the appetizer table as well as the vegetable course. Guests will enjoy nibbling on these marinated flowerettes and thank you for remembering to cook light.

1   medium head cauliflower, broken into flowerettes (4 cups)
¾   cup reduced calorie Italian salad dressing
1   tablespoon chopped, canned pimiento
1   tablespoon finely chopped onion
½   teaspoon dried dill weed

1. In medium saucepan, cook cauliflower, covered, in small amount of boiling water just till crisp-tender, about 10 minutes.

2. Drain; place in shallow dish.

3. In 1 cup glass measurer, combine Italian salad dressing, pimiento, onion and dried dill weed; pour over warm cauliflower.

4. Cover; marinate in refrigerator several hours or overnight, stirring occasionally.

5. Before serving, drain cauliflower. Serve with frilly toothpicks.

Microwave

In step **1,** cook cauliflower, covered, in 2-quart microwave-safe casserole on 100% power for 8-10 minutes or until crisp tender, stirring once.

Giant Taco Appetizer

Serves 20

When my friend, Mary Kaye Merwin who lives in the Washington, D.C. area, gathers a group of favorite guests together, this great layered appetizer is a must. Remember to purchase avocados three or four days before they are needed so they can ripen at room temperature. Avocados are ready to use when they have lost their firm feel.

2   (10-½ ounce) cans jalapeno bean dip
3   ripe avocados
2   tablespoons lemon juice
1   teaspoon salt
1   cup cultured sour cream
½   cup mayonnaise
1   (1-¼ ounce) package taco seasoning mix
3   tomatoes, peeled and diced
1   bunch green onions, thinly sliced including 4 inches of green tops
1   (6 ounce) can of black olives, sliced
1-½ cups (6 ounces) shredded cheddar cheese
    Taco chips

1. Select a large serving platter approximately 16 inches in diameter or larger.

2. Spread the bean dip in a circle or follow the shape of the platter, leaving room around the edges to arrange taco chips. (If platter is not large enough, pass tacos in a wicker basket.)

3. In blender or food processor, blend or process the avocados, lemon juice and salt. Spread on top of bean dip.

4. In small bowl, combine sour cream, mayonnaise and taco seasoning mix. Spread on top of avocado layer.

5. Sprinkle tomatoes on top of sour cream layer.

6. Arrange green onions over tomatoes.

7. Put black olives over onions.

8. Top black olives with shredded cheddar cheese.

9. Cover tightly. Store in refrigerator no longer than 8-10 hours.

10. Serve with lots of taco chips and enjoy.

Popcorn Nibble-Ons

Makes 4-½ quarts

This tasty snacking mixture has good color contrast and an interesting combination of flavors. Store in airtight containers for nibbling whenever dinner isn't quite ready.

3   quarts popped corn
2   cups cheese snack crackers or nibblers
2   cups salted Spanish peanuts
2   cups pretzel sticks
⅓   cup butter or margarine, melted
½   teaspoon garlic salt
½   teaspoon onion salt
½   teaspoon curry powder
½   teaspoon bottled steak sauce

1. In large roasting pan, like an aluminum foil turkey roasting pan, combine popped corn, crackers, peanuts and pretzels. Gently toss together.

2. In small bowl, stir together melted butter, garlic salt, onion salt, curry powder and steak sauce.

3. Heat mixture in preheated very slow (250 degree) oven about 1 hour, stirring every 15 minutes. Cool.

4. Store in airtight container.

Savory Vegetable Dip

8-12 appetizer servings

Attractive fresh vegetables have become commonplace at many appetizer tables. Here is an easy, yet out of the ordinary, dip to serve the next time you prepare a relish tray.

1   cup mayonnaise
2   tablespoons chopped chives, fresh, freeze dried, or frozen
2   tablespoons grated onion
2   tablespoons chili sauce
2   teaspoons vinegar
¼   teaspoon curry powder
¼   teaspoon salt
⅛   teaspoon thyme leaves

1. In small mixing bowl, combine mayonnaise, chives, onion, chili sauce, vinegar, curry, salt and thyme. Stir to blend well.

2. Cover and refrigerate until serving time.

3. Serve with your favorite selection of fresh vegetables.

Mosaic Sandwiches

1-2 dozen mini-sandwiches

The clever part of this recipe is the novel use of cookie cutters. Use whole wheat shapes over white bread sandwiches and vice versa. I like the window effect that is created when you use two sizes of the same shaped cutter.

1   **(3 ounce) package cream cheese, softened**
1   **tablespoon milk**
1   **teaspoon Worcestershire sauce**
4   **slices bacon, crisp-cooked, drained, and crumbled**
     White sandwich bread
     Whole wheat sandwich bread

1. In small mixing bowl, blend together cream cheese, milk, and Worcestershire sauce. Stir in bacon.

2. With cookie cutter, cut an equal amount of white and whole wheat bread into shapes like bells or rectangles.

3. Spread half of the cutouts (use an equal number of white and whole wheat) with cheese mixture.

4. With small hors d'oeuvre cutters, cut shapes from centers of remaining bread cutouts; fit together contrasting bread cutouts.

5. If desired, garnish with snipped parsley or chopped canned pimiento.

6. Chill until serving time.

Italian Scramble

Makes 12 cups

Crunchy nibbles are always popular when family and friends gather together. This recipe uses the nippy flavor of Italian salad dressing mix to bring ordinary ingredients to new heights.

6   **cups chex cereal**
3   **cups pretzel sticks**
3   **cups (1 pound) mixed nuts**
¼   **cup melted margarine or butter**
¾   **cup grated Parmesan cheese**
1   **tablespoon dry Italian salad dressing mix**

1. Put cereal in a 9x13 inch baking pan. Heat in preheated 300 degree oven for 5 minutes until warm.

2. Stir in pretzel sticks and nuts.

3. Pour the melted margarine or butter over cereal mixture.

(Continued)

Italian Scramble (continued)

4. Mix together the Parmesan cheese and salad dressing mix. Sprinkle over cereal/nut mixture and stir thoroughly.

5. Return cereal mixture to 300 degree oven and heat 15-20 minutes more, stirring once.

6. Store in airtight container.

Tuna Mini Puffs

Makes 4-5 dozen

This curry tuna salad finds a special home when spooned into tiny cream puff shells. It's the type of appetizer that always disappears quickly from the serving tray. Treat your guests soon.

1	**cup water**
½	**cup butter or margarine**
1	**cup flour**
4	**eggs**
1	**(6-½ ounce) can water packed tuna, drained**
1-½	**teaspoons lemon juice**
½	**teaspoon minced onion**
¾	**teaspoon curry powder**
½	**cup diced water chestnuts**
½	**cup mayonnaise or salad dressing**
	Salt and pepper, if desired

1. In medium saucepan, heat water and butter to rolling boil.

2. Stir in flour. Stir vigorously over low heat about 1 minute or until mixture forms a ball.

3. Remove from heat. Beat in eggs, all at one time; continue beating until smooth.

4. Drop dough by slightly rounded teaspoonfuls onto ungreased or parchment lined baking sheet.

5. Bake in preheated 400 degree oven 25-30 minutes until puffed and golden. Cool away from draft. Cut off tops. Pull out any filaments of soft dough.

6. In small mixing bowl, combine tuna, lemon juice, onion, curry, water chestnuts and mayonnaise. Salt and pepper, if desired.

7. Fill miniature cream puffs. Top with cut off tops.

8. Serve with pleasure.

Deviled Eggs

Makes 12

I always like to watch the deviled egg plate at a potluck supper. In just no time the plate will be empty because everyone takes one. So if you're at the end of the line, it's not the day for a deviled egg.

6   **hard-cooked eggs, halved lengthwise**
¼   **cup mayonnaise or salad dressing (I use calorie-reduced)**
⅛   **teaspoon salt, if desired**
1   **tablespoon finely chopped onion**
1-½ **teaspoons prepared mustard**
1   **tablespoon finely chopped pimiento-stuffed green olives, if desired**

   1. Remove egg yolks from whites.

   2. In small mixing bowl, mash yolks with fork or put yolks in food processor work bowl and pulse to mash.

   3. Add mayonnaise, salt, onion, mustard and olives. Blend with fork or pulse food processor to combine.

   4. Refill whites. You may want to use a pastry tube to pipe yolk mixture into whites for a touch of class.

   5. Sprinkle with paprika if desired.

Lemon Marinated Mushrooms

Makes 8 appetizer servings

In this interesting recipe we find mushrooms "dressed" for a special occasion. The low calorie dressing perfectly matches the outstanding qualities of this vegetable. Use frilly toothpicks to spear the mushrooms for the perfect festive flair.

1   **pound small fresh mushrooms**
½   **cup lemon juice**
¼   **cup water**
2   **tablespoons minced fresh parsley**
2   **tablespoons dijon mustard**
1   **tablespoon olive oil**
1   **teaspoon dried oregano leaves**
2   **teaspoons Worcestershire sauce**
¼   **teaspoon garlic salt**
⅛   **teaspoon red pepper**

   1. Wipe mushrooms clean with mushroom brush or damp paper towel; place in shallow dish.

   2. In pint jar, combine lemon juice, water, parsley, mustard, olive oil, oregano, Worcestershire sauce, garlic salt and red pepper. Cover tightly and shake vigorously.

(Continued)

Lemon Marinated Mushrooms (continued)

3. Pour marinade over mushrooms, tossing to coat.

4. Cover mushrooms and refrigerate overnight, stirring occasionally.

5. Drain and serve on attractive platter, complete with frilly toothpicks.

Crab Dip

Serves 6-8

When guests are coming and food preparation time is limited, my friend, Mary Ellen Behm, quickly puts together this classy crab dip. She likes to use mayonnaise rather than salad dressing and selects quality crackers to use with this appetizer.

1	**(8 ounce) package cream cheese, softened**
½	**cup mayonnaise**
½	**cup chopped onion**
½	**cup finely chopped celery**
3	**tablespoons lemon juice**
4	**(1-½ ounce) sticks imitation crab, chopped or 1 (6 ounce) can of crab**

1. In medium mixing bowl, combine softened cream cheese and mayonnaise.

2. Add onion, celery, lemon juice and crab. Stir to combine.

3. Put into attractive serving dish. Garnish with fresh parsley.

4. Refrigerate until guests arrive.

Yogurt-Cucumber Dip

Serves 8

A few interesting ingredients added to yogurt can produce a tasty dip for crisp vegetable dippers. Include some of the traditional favorites like carrot sticks and broccoli flowerettes, but also remember turnip slices and zucchini strips.

1	**(8 ounce) carton plain yogurt (1 cup)**
¼	**cup well-drained, finely shredded cucumber**
1	**tablespoon snipped parsley**
½	**teaspoon grated onion**
¼	**teaspoon garlic salt**
¼	**teaspoon Worcestershire sauce**
	Vegetable dippers

1. In medium mixing bowl, combine yogurt, shredded cucumber, snipped parsley, grated onion, garlic salt and Worcestershire sauce.

2. Serve with assorted crisp vegetable dippers.

Triple Herbed Cheese

Makes 1-½ cups

When you're entertaining, small crocks of this herbed cheese spread can be placed around the room for friends to enjoy as they begin to arrive and start to visit. To help guests feel at ease, get things started by having a cracker or two all ready spread with cheese.

1	**(8 ounce) package cream cheese, softened**
¼	**cup butter or margarine, softened**
¼	**cup cultured sour cream**
⅛	**teaspoon garlic powder**
1	**teaspoon dried oregano, crumbled**
1	**teaspoon dried basil, crumbled**
1	**teaspoon dill weed**

1. In medium mixing bowl, beat together cream cheese and butter.

2. Stir in sour cream, garlic, oregano, basil and dill weed. Mix well.

3. Put into attractive crocks or containers. Cover tightly and chill at least 12 hours.

4. Let the cheese soften for 30 minutes before serving.

5. Serve with delicately flavored crackers.

Spiced Pineapple Chunks

Serves 8-10

Delicately spiced pineapple chunks are a welcome addition to any appetizer repertoire. Low in calories, bite-size in shape and extremely easy to create, this is a tasty beginning to remember.

1	**(20 ounce) can juice pack pineapple chunks**
1	**tablespoon sugar**
1	**tablespoon vinegar**
2	**(3-inch) sticks cinnamon**
6	**whole cloves**

1. Drain pineapple, reserving juice; set pineapple aside.

2. In small saucepan, combine reserved juice, sugar, vinegar, stick cinnamon and whole cloves.

3. Simmer mixture, uncovered, for 5 minutes.

4. Add pineapple chunks; heat thoroughly. Cool.

5. Store in covered container in refrigerator at least 48 hours.

6. Drain. Serve on wooden picks.

(Continued)

Spiced Pineapple Chunks (continued)

Microwave

In step **2,** combine reserved juice, sugar, vinegar, stick cinnamon and whole cloves
    in 1-quart microwave-safe measurer.
In step **3,** microwave on 100% power 5 minutes.
In step **4,** microwave on 100% power 4-6 minutes until thoroughly heated,
    stirring once.

Tarragon Vegetable Appetizer

Serves 6

Rather than the usual assorted fresh vegetables and dip, try this marinated
combination for an interesting appealing appetizer. Use reduced-calorie Italian
salad dressing to please those who think slim. Individual servings arranged attractively on lettuce lined salad plates is a thoughtful way to welcome guests.

2   small carrots, peeled and diagonally sliced
1   (6 ounce) package frozen Chinese pea pods, thawed and drained
6   cherry tomatoes
1   medium cucumber, thinly sliced
⅓   cup reduced-calorie Italian salad dressing
3   tablespoons tarragon vinegar
2   tablespoons water
¼   teaspoon dried whole tarragon
¼   teaspoon freshly ground pepper
¼   teaspoon garlic powder

1. In small saucepan, cook carrots in a small amount of boiling water 3 to 4
    minutes until crisp tender; drain.

2. In large shallow dish, combine carrots, pea pods, tomatoes and cucumber.

3. In small jar, combine Italian dressing, vinegar, water, tarragon, pepper
    and garlic powder. Cover tightly and shake vigorously.

4. Pour dressing over vegetables, tossing lightly to coat.

5. Cover and chill overnight.

6. At serving time, arrange vegetables on 6 lettuce lined pretty salad plates.

Microwave

In step **1,** put carrots in 2 cup microwave-safe measurer. Add 1 tablespoon water.
Cover with vented plastic wrap. Microwave on 100% power 2-3 minutes
until crisp tender, stirring once. Drain.

Impromptu Appetizers

Serves 8-10

The secret of an impromptu appetizer is to be organized and ready to cook when the situation may be disorganized and no one has time to cook. The base of this idea is a package of cream cheese that keeps well in the refrigerator. Add any of the toppings suggested and presto an appetizer has been created.

1	(8 ounce) package cream cheese
	with
¼	cup cocktail sauce
1	(4-½ ounce) can shrimp, rinsed and drained
	or
1	(9 ounce) jar chutney
	or
1	(2-¼ ounce) can deviled ham
1	tablespoon sweet pickle relish
	or
6	slices bacon, cooked crisply and crumbled
½	cup green onion slices

1. Place cream cheese on center of small rectangular serving tray.

2. Top with cocktail sauce and drained shrimp or top with chutney or top with a mixture of deviled ham and sweet pickle relish or top with bacon and green onions.

3. Serve with rye or wheat crackers or party rye refrigerated bread.

Food Processor Spring Garden Dip

Serves 8-10

The interesting twist to this dynamite dip is that the vegetables are combined with the cream cheese rather than served with the dip. Ever since my friend, Anne Reuther from Milwaukee, sent me this recipe it has been a popular appetizer in my food processor class. Try it and you'll understand why.

1	stalk celery, cut into 3 pieces
1	carrot, cut into 3 pieces
¼	green pepper, cut into chunks
2	radishes
1	sweet pickle, cut in chunks
3	sprigs parsley
2	green onions, cut in pieces
½	teaspoon salt
¼	teaspoon ground pepper
1	(8 ounce) package cream cheese, cut in chunks

(Continued)

Food Processor
Spring Garden Dip (continued)

1. Insert steel blade in food processor work bowl.

2. Put celery, carrot, green pepper, radishes, sweet pickle, parsley, green onions, salt and pepper in food processor work bowl.

3. Pulse chop until vegetables are finely chopped.

4. Add cream cheese to chopped vegetables.

5. Pulse just until mixture is well combined.

6. Serve with assorted crackers.

Curried Almonds

Makes 3 cups

These specially seasoned almonds are a thoughtful selection for any appetizer table. Serve these first-class almonds in a vertical container for added eye appeal. Remember to store the nuts in an airtight place out of sight until needed.

3   **cups blanched whole almonds**
1   **tablespoon butter or margarine, melted**
1   **teaspoon seasoned salt**
¾   **teaspoon curry powder**

1. Place almonds in a shallow roasting pan; brush butter over nuts and stir well.

2. Roast almonds in preheated 350 degree oven for 20 minutes or until golden.

3. In small dish, combine seasoned salt and curry; sprinkle over almonds, and stir until well coated.

4. Bake an additional 10 minutes.

5. Drain on paper towels; cool.

6. Store in airtight container.

Fiesta Cheese Spread

Makes 1 cup

Salsa gives this cheese mixture pizazz. Use your pastry tube to pipe this golden spread in celery stalks or on crackers. If it is easier for you, a knife works well too.

1   (3 ounce) package cream cheese, softened
1   cup shredded cheddar cheese (4 ounces)
2   tablespoons mild salsa

1. In small mixer bowl, combine cream cheese, cheddar cheese and salsa.

2. Beat with an electric mixer on medium speed until well mixed, scraping bowl often.

3. Pipe in celery stalks. Chill. Spread may be chilled and then spread on crackers, if desired.

Note: Salsa is found in the ethnic food section at the grocery store.

Hot Cheesy Clam Dip

Serves 10-12

Surprise your guests with this cheesy clam combination. Select a variety of interesting shaped crackers or melba rounds to surround the spicy hot mixture. Relax and enjoy the festivities.

½   cup chopped green pepper
¼   cup chopped onion
3   tablespoons butter or margarine
¼   teaspoon cayenne pepper
¼   cup catsup
1   tablespoon Worcestershire sauce
2   (6 ounce) cans minced clams, well drained
1   cup cubed processed American cheese (4 ounces)

1. In medium saucepan, saute green pepper and onion in butter until tender.

2. Stir in cayenne pepper, catsup, Worcestershire sauce and clams; cook over medium heat until hot and bubbly.

3. Add cheese, stirring constantly until melted.

4. Reduce heat; cover. Simmer 10-15 minutes or until mixture has slightly thickened.

5. Serve warm with assorted crackers.

(Continued)

Hot Cheesy Clam Dip (continued)

Microwave

In step **1,** combine green pepper, onion and butter in 2-quart microwave-safe
  bowl. Microwave on 100% power for 2-3 minutes until vegetables are
  tender, stirring once.
In step **2,** add cayenne pepper, catsup, Worcestershire sauce and clams. Microwave on 100% power 2-3 minutes until hot.
In step **3,** add cheese; stir until well blended. Microwave on 100% power 2-3
  minutes until cheese is hot, stirring once. Stir before serving.

Hot Beef Dip

Serves 12

Hot appetizers are especially appropriate with cold beverages as the temperature contrast is pleasing to the palate. However, it can be difficult at times to find
recipes that fit into busy time schedules. Here is a quick idea that goes together
easily and meets every criteria of a great hot dip.

¼	**cup chopped onion**
1	**tablespoon butter or margarine**
1	**(8 ounce) package cream cheese, cubed**
1	**cup milk**
1	**(4 ounce) can mushrooms, drained**
1	**(2-½ or 3 ounce) package smoked slender sliced beef, finely snipped**
¼	**cup grated Parmesan cheese**
2	**tablespoons chopped fresh parsley**

1. In medium saucepan, saute onion in butter.

2. Add cream cheese and milk; stir over low heat until cream cheese
   is melted.

3. Add drained mushrooms, snipped beef, Parmesan cheese and parsley;
   heat thoroughly.

4. Serve hot with crisp chips.

Microwave

In step **1,** put onion and butter in 2-quart microwave-safe measurer. Microwave
  on 100% power 2-3 minutes until onion is tender, stirring once.
In step **2,** add cream cheese and milk. Microwave on 100% power 4-6 minutes
  until cheese is melted, stirring twice.
In step **3,** add drained mushrooms, snipped beef, Parmesan cheese and parsley.
  Microwave on 100% power 2-4 minutes until piping hot, stirring once.

Shrimp Fondue

6 appetizer servings

Give shrimp the appetizer spotlight it deserves by bringing out the fondue pot for cooking and conversation. No hot oil in this calorie-reduced plan. Just a delicately seasoned broth for easy quick cooking. Savor the flavor.

1	**pound fresh or frozen shelled shrimp**
½	**cup calorie-reduced Thousand Island salad dressing**
2	**teaspoons lemon juice**
1	**teaspoon snipped chives, fresh, frozen, or freeze dried**
3	**cups water**
4	**teaspoons instant chicken bouillon granules or 4 chicken bouillon cubes**
1	**tablespoon lemon juice**
1	**teaspoon grated onion**

1. Thaw shrimp, if frozen. Arrange attractively on lettuce lined tray.

2. In small bowl, combine Thousand Island dressing, 2 teaspoons lemon juice and chives. Put in small serving dish to be served with shrimp.

3. In metal fondue cooker, combine water, chicken bouillon, 1 tablespoon lemon juice and onion. Heat to boiling over medium heat.

4. Transfer cooker to fondue burner.

5. Have shrimp at room temperature.

6. Spear shrimp with fondue fork. Cook in hot broth till done. Dip in dressing mixture.

Fancy Franks

Serves 8-10

Here is an easy economical appetizer that is certain to be popular with guests of all ages. The make-ahead cook can let the franks marinate in the sweet sour sauce and reheat just before serving.

½	**cup chili sauce**
½	**cup currant jelly**
1-½	**tablespoons lemon juice**
1-½	**teaspoons prepared mustard**
1	**pound fully cooked wieners, cut diagonally in 1-inch pieces**
1	**(8 ounce) can pineapple chunks, drained**

1. In small skillet or saucepan, combine chili sauce, currant jelly, lemon juice, and mustard. Heat until mixture is blended.

2. Add pieces of wieners and drained pineapple chunks.

(Continued)

Fancy Franks (continued)

3. Simmer together 15 minutes.

4. Serve hot with frilly topped toothpicks.

Microwave

In step **1**, combine chili sauce, currant jelly, lemon juice and mustard in 2-quart microwave-safe casserole. Microwave on 100% power 2-4 minutes, until melted, stirring once.
In step **3**, microwave on 100% power 5-8 minutes until piping hot, stirring once.

Hot Crabmeat Appetizer

6-8 appetizer servings

     Gather your guests together to enjoy this tasty seafood spread. Whether you provide a selection of fresh vegetables or assorted crackers, you will receive smiles of approval.

1   **(8 ounce) package cream cheese, softened**
2   **tablespoons milk**
1   **(6 ounce) can crabmeat, drained**
2   **tablespoons finely chopped onion**
½   **teaspoon cream style horseradish**
¼   **teaspoon salt, if desired**
     Dash of pepper
⅓   **cup toasted sliced or slivered almonds**

1. In small mixing bowl, combine softened cream cheese and milk. Beat until smooth.

2. Add crabmeat, onion, horseradish, salt and pepper. Thoroughly combine.

3. Spoon into 9-inch pie plate or oven proof dish.

4. Sprinkle with almonds. You could cover and refrigerate, if desired.

5. Bake in preheated 375 degree oven for 15 minutes.

Microwave

In step **3**, use microwave-safe dish.
In step **5**, heat mixture in microwave at 80% power for 3-5 minutes.

Cranberry Meatballs

Makes 80 small meatballs

Miniature meatballs are one of the most popular items any cook can present on an appetizer table. Make them ahead of time and store them in the freezer for care-free entertaining. Microwave users will find it quick and easy to brown meatballs in the microwave. At serving time, put meatballs in your crock pot for casual entertaining.

2	eggs
2	pounds lean ground beef
2	tablespoons soy sauce
2	tablespoons dried minced onion
⅓	cup dried parsley flakes
½	teaspoon garlic powder
1	cup cornflake crumbs
2	teaspoons salt
¼	teaspoon ground pepper
2	tablespoons vegetable oil
1	(16 ounce) can jellied cranberry sauce
1	(12 ounce) bottle chili sauce
⅓	cup catsup
2	tablespoons brown sugar
1	tablespoon lemon juice

1. Beat eggs with rotary beater in the bottom of a large mixing bowl.

2. Add ground beef, soy sauce, onion, parsley, garlic powder, cornflake crumbs, salt and pepper to eggs. Mix until well combined.

3. With moistened hands, shape into 1-inch meatballs.

4. Brown meatballs in oil in hot skillet.

5. In large saucepan, combine cranberry sauce, chili sauce, catsup, brown sugar and lemon juice. Stir and heat until thick.

6. Add meatballs and simmer until serving time.

Microwave

In step **4,** put 20-24 meatballs on microwave roasting rack. Omit vegetable oil. Microwave on 100% power 5-6 minutes or until meatballs are done, rotating rack once. Repeat procedure.

In step **5,** put cranberry sauce, chili sauce, catsup, brown sugar and lemon juice in 3-quart microwave-safe casserole. Microwave on 100% power 5-6 minutes until piping hot, stirring mixture twice.

In step **6,** add meatballs and microwave on 100% power 4-7 minutes, until hot, stirring once.

Swiss Sandwich Puffs

Makes 32

Hot miniature open face sandwiches are party fare that's hard to resist. Accept the offer of helpful persons and ask them to be in charge of broiling these rye slices to perfection.

32	miniature refrigerated rye bread slices
½	cup mayonnaise
¼	cup chopped onion
2	tablespoons snipped parsley
8	(¾ ounce) slices processed Swiss cheese

1. Put rye slices on cookie sheet. Broil until lightly toasted.

2. In small bowl, combine mayonnaise, onion and parsley.

3. Spread a small amount of the mayonnaise mixture on each toasted rye slice.

4. Cut Swiss cheese slices in quarters.

5. Put 1 quarter slice Swiss cheese on each miniature rye.

6. Broil 2 to 3 minutes until lightly browned.

7. Serve hot and enjoy.

Hot Cheese Dip

Serves 12-16

These three ingredients teamed together create a cheese dip that brings rave reviews. Corn chips are the traditional favorite dippers, but fresh vegetables would also be tasty fare. It's great for parties, ballgame watching and midnight snacks.

2	pounds pasteurized American cheese
1	(10 ounce) can tomatoes with green chilies, undrained
1	pound pork sausage, cooked, drained and crumbled

1. In top of double boiler over boiling water, melt cheese.

2. Stir in undrained tomatoes and chilies; blend well, breaking up tomatoes.

3. Stir in crumbled cooked sausage.

4. Heat thoroughly.

5. Serve hot with corn chips or assorted fresh vegetables.

Microwave

In step **1,** put cheese in 2-quart microwave-safe measurer. Microwave on 100% power 3-5 minutes until melted, stirring once or twice.

In step **4,** microwave on 100% power 4-6 minutes until heated thoroughly, stirring once or twice.

South of the Border Spread

Serves 12-15

If you are in need of an attractive appetizer for a crowd, here is the answer. Although a chafing dish is nice to use as a serving piece, any pretty 2 quart dish will work well. If convenient, you could even keep the mixture warm on a hot serving tray.

2 **(15 ounce) cans chili-with-meat**
2 **(15 ounce) cans refried beans**
2 **cups (8 ounces) grated sharp cheddar cheese**
2 **fresh tomatoes, diced**
5 **to 7 green onions, sliced**
¼ **cup sliced ripe olives**
2 **(10 ounce) packages tortilla or taco chips**

1. Mix chili and refried beans together in saucepan. Heat gently until hot.

2. Pour bean mixture into chafing dish or other attractive serving dish.

3. Arrange cheese on top of beans in a circle around outside of dish.

4. Put tomatoes in a circle inside cheese, then onion, finishing with olives in the middle.

5. Serve as dip with tortilla or taco chips.

Microwave

In step **1,** combine chili and refried beans in 2-quart microwave-safe bowl. Microwave on 100% power 8-10 minutes, stirring two or three times, until hot.

Sugar-Free Punch

Serves 32 (½ cup servings)

This delicious combination of flavors is dedicated to my many friends and students who require or prefer sugar free recipes. Remember the ease of preparing sugar free lemonade from purchased mixes. Freeze extra lemonade or juices in ice cube trays to keep the punch icy cold.

1 **quart sugar-free lemonade, chilled**
1 **quart unsweetened orange juice, chilled**
1 **quart unsweetened pineapple juice, chilled**
1 **liter sugar-free ginger ale, chilled**

1. In large punch bowl, combine chilled lemonade, orange juice, and pineapple juice.

2. Just before serving add chilled ginger ale. Garnish with fruit juice ice cubes or plain ice.

Sparkling Citrus Punch

Serves 25

Guests will gather round the punch bowl when they taste this delicious light juice combination highlighted with club soda. Have the lemon lime ice ring waiting in the freezer to gracefully garnish this lovely punch.

	Lemon Lime Ice Ring (directions follow)
1	**(6 ounce) can frozen orange juice concentrate**
1	**(6 ounce) can frozen grapefruit juice concentrate**
1	**(6 ounce) can frozen tangerine juice concentrate**
1	**(6 ounce) can frozen lemonade concentrate**
½	**cup lime juice**
6	**cups ice cold water**
2	**liters club soda, chilled**

1. Prepare Lemon Lime Ice Ring by pouring 1 cup water into a 6 cup ring mold. Freeze. Slice 3 lemons and 3 limes. Alternately arrange lemon and lime slices on top of ice overlapping edges. Add enough water to just barely cover fruit slices. Freeze until solid.

2. In very large punch bowl, combine orange juice concentrate, grapefruit juice concentrate, tangerine juice concentrate, lemonade concentrate, lime juice and water.

3. Resting bottle on rim of punch bowl, carefully add club soda.

4. To unmold ice ring, dip mold into hot water until ice ring slips out.

5. Float ring in punch for an attractive garnish.

Tropical Punch

Serves 30-35

This refreshing blend of fruit juices creates a delicious punch that could highlight any occasion. Guests will return to the punch bowl time and again giving their stamp of approval.

1	**(46 ounce) can red Hawaiian punch**
1	**(6 ounce) can frozen lemonade concentrate**
1	**(6 ounce) can frozen orange juice concentrate**
1	**(6 ounce) can frozen grape juice concentrate**
6	**cups cold water**
1	**liter ginger ale, chilled**

1. In large punch bowl, combine Hawaiian fruit punch, lemonade concentrate, orange juice concentrate, grape juice concentrate and water.

2. Resting bottle on rim of punch bowl, carefully pour in ginger ale.

3. Garnish with ice ring, if desired.

Polynesian Punch

Serves 32 (½ cup servings)

This lovely white punch could easily highlight a holiday open house or be featured as the refreshing beverage at a summertime poolside party. Most supermarkets stock the cans of cream of coconut in the gourmet food or ethnic food section of their stores.

1 (20 ounce) can crushed pineapple, undrained
1 (15 ounce) can cream of coconut
1 (46 ounce) can unsweetened pineapple juice, chilled
1 liter ginger ale

1. In blender or food processor, combine the undrained crushed pineapple and cream of coconut. Blend or process until smooth.

2. Pour coconut mixture into punch bowl. Add chilled pineapple juice and ginger ale.

3. Garnish with lots of ice and fresh mint, if available.

Citrus Cooler

25 (½ cup servings)

Here is a punch recipe that requires very little measuring and preparation, but is just as delicious as if it took hours to make. If you can't find frozen tangerine juice concentrate at your grocery store, just substitute frozen orange juice concentrate.

1 (6 ounce) can frozen lemonade concentrate, thawed
1 (6 ounce) can frozen orange juice concentrate, thawed
1 (6 ounce) can frozen tangerine juice concentrate, thawed
2 cups cold water
2 liters ginger ale, chilled

1. In punch bowl, combine lemonade concentrate, orange juice concentrate, tangerine juice concentrate and water. Stir to combine.

2. Slowly add chilled ginger ale. Garnish with lots of ice and fresh orange slices, if desired.

Tomato Frappe

Serves 6-8

It's hard to believe that flavored frozen tomato juice, could be so refreshingly frothy and delicious. This frosty frappe could be served while guests wait for brunch or sipped at the pool on a warm summer afternoon. Easy on the calories, here's a winner.

(Continued)

Tomato Frappe (continued)

1	**tablespoon butter**
3	**tablespoons finely chopped onion**
1	**teaspoon sugar**
1	**tablespoon lemon juice**
⅛	**teaspoon Worcestershire sauce**
4	**cups tomato juice**
	Lemon wedges for garnish

1. In small frying pan, melt butter and saute onion until golden.

2. Place the sauteed onion, sugar, lemon juice, Worcestershire sauce and tomato juice in blender.

3. Blend 1 minute, or until smooth.

4. Pour into 6-cup freezer-safe container. Freeze.

5. Half an hour before serving, remove the pan from the freezer.

6. Break the tomato mixture into chunks with a fork and put a small amount in the blender container.

7. Blend just until smooth, don't let it melt.

8. Serve in stemmed glasses with lemon wedges and straws.

Microwave

In step **1,** put butter and onion in 1 cup microwave-safe measurer. For even fewer calories substitute 1 tablespoon water for 1 tablespoon butter. Microwave on 100% power 1-2 minutes, stirring once.
In step **5,** remember mixture may be defrosted in the microwave oven.

Strawberry Banana Cooler

Serves 3 or 4

This cool drink is nutritious, delicious, and sugar-free. What a great idea for an after school snack on a warm day. Add a Tuna Pocket sandwich using the recipe on page 88 to complete your treat.

2	**cups unsweetened orange juice**
½	**cup whole frozen strawberries**
1	**large banana, sliced**
3-4	**ice cubes**

1. In blender container, put orange juice, frozen strawberries, sliced banana and ice cubes. Cover tightly.

2. Blend until smooth and serve immediately.

Spiced Pineapple Sparkle

Serves 12

Here is an excellent example of mulled spices used to extend and build deep bodied flavor in a calorie reduced beverage. One sip and you'll know the few minutes it took to brew the spices has a tasty reward.

1-½ cups water
2 (3-inch) pieces stick cinnamon
12 whole cloves
Sugar substitute equal to ½ cup sugar
1 (46 ounce) can unsweetened pineapple juice
1-½ cups orange juice
½ cup lemon juice
1 liter sugar free lemon-lime carbonated beverage, chilled

1. In saucepan, combine water, cinnamon and cloves.

2. Cover and simmer 15 minutes. Strain and cool.

3. Add sugar substitute, pineapple juice, orange juice and lemon juice to spice water. Chill.

4. Just before serving, slowly pour carbonated beverage into chilled juices.

5. Serve with lots of ice.

Microwave

In step 1, combine water, cinnamon and cloves in 1-quart microwave-safe measurer.
In step 2, microwave on 100% power 3 minutes; reduce to 50% power and microwave 8-10 minutes. Strain and cool.

Cranberry Apple Punch

Serves 8

Here is a quick punch recipe that's just right for an informal impromptu gathering. Frozen lemonade concentrate provides the perfect flavor base for this cranberry apple combination.

2 cups cranberry juice cocktail, chilled
2 cups apple juice, chilled
1 (6 ounce) can frozen lemonade concentrate, thawed
½ liter ginger ale, chilled

1. In pretty punch bowl or large pitcher, mix chilled cranberry juice, apple juice and frozen lemonade concentrate.

2. Add ginger ale.

3. Serve immediately over crushed ice or float ice molds in punch bowl.

4. To make ice molds: fill fluted individual gelatin molds with water, freeze, unmold and float in punch.

Mint Lemonade

Serves 10-12

Homemade lemonade is a great summertime treat. Our son. Paul, likes to make this variation using fresh mint to add depth of flavor. In many places mint grows profusely and those who grow it share generously with those who need mint for recipes like this one.

2-½ cups water
2 cups sugar
Grated peel of 1 orange
Juice of 2 oranges
Juice of 6 lemons
1 cup fresh mint leaves

1. In medium saucepan, cook water and sugar for 5 minutes. Cool.

2. Add orange peel, orange juice, and lemon juice to sugar water.

3. Pour over mint leaves; cover and let stand 1 hour.

4. Strain into jar; keep in refrigerator.

5. Use ⅓ cup syrup for each glass; fill with ice cubes and water.

6. Garnish with lemon slices and fresh mint leaves.

Microwave

In step **1,** combine water and sugar in 2 quart microwave-safe measurer. Microwave on 100% power 6-8 minutes, stirring once. Cool.

Hawaiian Lemonade

Makes 2 quarts

Here is a punch recipe designed to serve a small casual group. Actually it can be easily prepared in a large pitcher or any 2 quart container. I think you'll like the sparkling fruit flavor.

1 (6 ounce) can frozen lemonade concentrate
1 (12 ounce) can apricot nectar (1-½ cups)
1-½ cups unsweetened pineapple juice
2 cups water
1 (16 ounce) bottle lemon-lime carbonated beverage (2 cups)

1. In large pitcher or 2 quart container, combine lemonade concentrate, apricot nectar, pineapple juice and water. Chill thoroughly.

2. Just before serving add carbonated beverage.

3. Add lots of ice and enjoy.

Rhubarb Punch

Serves 24 (½ cup servings)

This delicate pink punch is perfect for a spring bridal shower. Cook tender red rhubarb stalks when convenient and either refrigerate or freeze the punch base to use when needed.

6   **cups finely chopped fresh rhubarb stalks**
6   **cups water**
1   **(12 ounce) can frozen lemonade concentrate**
1   **cup sugar**
1   **liter lemon-lime carbonated beverage, chilled**

1. In large saucepan, combine rhubarb, water, lemonade concentrate and sugar.

2. Cover and cook about 20 minutes, or until rhubarb is very soft.

3. Strain to remove pulp. Chill liquid.

4. Just before serving, pour rhubarb mixture over ice cubes in punch bowl.

5. Resting bottle on rim of bowl, carefully pour in chilled carbonated beverage. Garnish with additional ice cubes or an ice ring.

Floating Island Punch

Serves 24

Frosty fruit sherbet floating in the punch bowl announces to everyone that this occasion is special. One clue to complete success is to have all ingredients well chilled before mixing. Remember this lovely combination the next time you're searching for the perfect punch recipe.

4   **cups apricot nectar, chilled**
2   **cups unsweetened pineapple juice, chilled**
2   **cups orange juice, chilled**
1   **liter lemon-lime carbonated beverage, chilled**
1   **pint pineapple sherbet**
1   **pint orange sherbet**

1. Combine apricot nectar, pineapple juice and orange juice in punch bowl.

2. Slowly add lemon-lime carbonated beverage. Stir gently.

3. Float scoops of pineapple and orange sherbet on punch.

4. Serve immediately.

Cider Frost

Serves 8-10

Cool, refreshing apple cider is a favorite beverage at our house. We are especially partial to the cider that comes from Grandpa House's southern Wisconsin apple orchard. Sometimes I add this frosty top to each glass for interest and eye appeal.

2   **quarts chilled apple cider**
1   **pint lemon sherbet**

1. Fill attractive glasses or mugs with cold cider.

2. Float small scoops of lemon sherbet on top of each glass.

Johnny Appleseed Tea

Serves 6-8

Hot mugs of this cider tea would be warm and wonderful on a crisp autumn afternoon. It would be equally delicious in as practical a situation as a snack break from leaf raking or in as festive an occasion as a tailgate party.

1   **(12 ounce) can frozen apple cider concentrate**
2   **tablespoons instant tea powder**
1   **tablespoon honey**
½   **teaspoon ground cinnamon**

1. In medium saucepan, reconstitute apple cider concentrate according to package directions.

2. Add instant tea powder, honey and cinnamon. Stir to blend.

3. Heat until piping hot.

4. Serve in mugs with cinnamon stick stirrers.

Microwave

In step 1, reconstitute apple cider concentrate according to package directions in 2 quart microwave-safe measurer.
In step 3, microwave on 100% power 7-9 minutes until piping hot.

Herbed Vegetable Cocktail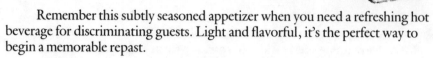

Serves 6

Remember this subtly seasoned appetizer when you need a refreshing hot beverage for discriminating guests. Light and flavorful, it's the perfect way to begin a memorable repast.

1	**(12 ounce) can vegetable juice cocktail (1-½ cups)**
1	**(13-½ ounce) can chicken broth (1-½ cups)**
1	**or 2 drops bottled hot pepper sauce**
¼	**teaspoon basil leaves, crushed**

1. In medium saucepan, combine vegetable juice cocktail, chicken broth, hot pepper sauce and basil.

2. Bring to boiling, reduce heat and simmer 10 minutes.

3. Serve hot and enjoy.

Microwave

In step **1,** combine vegetable juice cocktail, chicken broth, hot pepper sauce and basil in 2 quart microwave-safe measurer.
In step **2,** microwave on 100% power 8-12 minutes, stirring once.

Pineapple-Apricot Wassail

Serves 20 (½ cup servings)

Midwest winters and simmering hot beverages seem to go hand in hand. Here is a sugar-free combination of mulled flavors that will entice any guest.

1	**quart unsweetened pineapple juice**
1	**quart apple cider**
1-½	**cups apricot nectar (12 ounce can)**
1	**cup unsweetened orange juice**
2	**(3 inch) sticks cinnamon**
2	**teaspoons whole cloves**
½	**teaspoon ground nutmeg**

1. Combine pineapple juice, apple cider, apricot nectar, and orange juice in dutch oven.

2. Tie cinnamon and cloves in small bag or piece of cheesecloth. Add tied spices and nutmeg to fruit juices.

3. Bring mixture to a boil and simmer about 30 minutes.

4. Remove spice bag and serve piping hot.

Grape Steamer

Serves 24 (½ cup servings)

Get out the crock pot and create a simmering hot beverage for card club friends, winter sports enthusiasts, or the after school bunch. Just keep the plugged-in crock pot on the counter so friends and family can help themselves. An attractive plate of orange and/or lemon slices would be nice for fixing your own garnish.

6   cups water
1   quart unsweetened grape juice
1   (6 ounce) can frozen lemonade concentrate
1   (6 ounce) can frozen orange juice concentrate
1   cup sugar
    Orange and/or lemon slices for garnish

1. In crockpot or large saucepan, combine water, grape juice, lemonade concentrate, orange juice concentrate and sugar.

2. Stir to thoroughly combine.

3. Heat until very warm and sugar is dissolved.

4. Serve in mugs garnished with fruit slices, if desired.

Hot Cranberry Swizzle

Serves 25 (½ cup servings)

Guests love to mingle and chat as they sip this delicious cranberry brew. Another time, fill thermos bottles with cranberry swizzle to keep toasty warm at the football game.

4   cups fresh or frozen cranberries
3-½   quarts water
12   whole cloves
4   (3 inch) sticks cinnamon
¾   cup orange juice
⅔   cup lemon juice
2   cups sugar

1. Combine cranberries, water and spices in dutch oven or large kettle. Bring to a boil. Cover, reduce heat, and simmer 12-15 minutes.

2. Strain juice mixture through fine sieve or cheese cloth, squeezing gently.

3. Add lemon juice, orange juice and sugar; stir until sugar dissolves.

4. Serve piping hot.

Spicy Perk-A-Punch

Serves 25-30

Hot punch brewing in a coffee maker is a wonderful carefree way to entertain guests. This cranberry-pineapple combination could be served in the morning for brunch as well as after the evening's bridge game.

2	**quarts cranberry juice**
2	**quarts unsweetened pineapple juice**
1	**quart water**
⅔	**cup brown sugar**
1	**tablespoon whole cloves**
1	**tablespoon whole allspice**
2	**(2-inch) sticks cinnamon**
2	**lemons, sliced and quartered**

1. In 30-cup electric coffee maker, combine cranberry juice, pineapple juice and water.

2. Insert stem and put basket in place.

3. In basket, put brown sugar, cloves, allspice, cinnamon sticks and lemons.

4. Allow coffee maker to complete the perking cycle.

5. Serve directly from the coffee maker.

Note: If your coffee maker needs cleaning follow these directions:

1. Fill coffee maker with 1 quart each water and white distilled vinegar.

2. Put stem and empty basket in place, lock cover onto coffee maker and plug into socket.

3. Allow the coffee maker to complete the perking cycle and then let stand 10-15 minutes.

4. Empty and rinse out well.

Entrees

The focal point of many interesting menus is an exciting entree. Whether the occasion calls for an easy Cheese Strata or Cranberry-Stuffed Cornish Hens, this chapter provides a spectrum of wonderful main dish ideas.

There are soups that satisfy like the hearty Sausage Chowder to special soups like zesty Gazpacho. Family members will race to the table when Breakfast Pizza is served.

Traditionally beef and pork have been popular stars in the world of entrees. From Sauerbraten Round Steak to Savory Sausage Rice Bake, these recipes are designed to please both family and friends.

You'll find an especially thoughtful collection of recipes that extol the healthy virtues of poultry and fish. Entree styles vary from Sesame Chicken Kabobs to Oven Fried Fish Fillets.

Main dish salads like Crab Salad and sandwiches such as Pecan Chicken Croissants complete this interesting entree effort.

Contents

38

Oriental Spinach Soup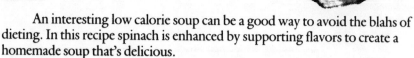

Serves 6

An interesting low calorie soup can be a good way to avoid the blahs of dieting. In this recipe spinach is enhanced by supporting flavors to create a homemade soup that's delicious.

1   (10 ounce) package frozen chopped spinach
1   tablespoon cornstarch
1-½ cups water, divided
2   (10-½ ounce) cans chicken broth, undiluted
½   cup diagonally sliced celery
2   tablespoons sliced green onion
2   teaspoons soy sauce

1. Cook spinach according to package directions, omitting salt; drain well.

2. Dissolve cornstarch in ¼ cup water; add to remaining 1 and ¼ cups water. Combine cornstarch mixture and chicken broth in a saucepan.

3. Add spinach, celery, green onions and soy sauce; bring to a boil. Reduce heat and simmer 5 minutes.

Microwave

In step **1**, remove foil wrapper from package, if present. Puncture package with fork 2-3 times to let steam escape. Place package on microwave-safe plate. Microwave on 100% power 5 minutes, turning package over halfway through cooking time. Drain well by pressing out excess liquid.
In step **2**, combine cornstarch mixture and chicken broth in microwave-safe soup tureen or large casserole.
In step **3**, add spinach, celery, green onion and soy sauce. Microwave on 100% power 10-15 minutes until boiling.

Tomato-Clam Chowder

Serves 8-10

This creative soup could be served either as an appealing appetizer or an exciting entree. The tomato clam flavor combination has traditionally been popular, so don't hesitate getting into the soup making mood.

4   slices bacon
3   medium onions, chopped
4   medium potatoes, peeled and diced
6   cups water
4   (8 ounce) bottles clam juice
1   (28 ounce) can tomatoes, undrained and chopped,
     or 1 quart home canned tomatoes
2   (6-½ ounce) cans minced clams, undrained

(Continued)

Tomato-Clam Chowder (continued)

¼ teaspoon ground pepper
⅛ teaspoon ground red pepper

1. In large dutch oven, cook bacon until crisp; remove bacon, reserving drippings. When cool, crumble bacon, and set aside.

2. Add onions to drippings; saute until tender.

3. Add potatoes, onion, bacon, water, clam juice, tomatoes, undrained clams and both kinds of pepper.

4. Bring to a boil; reduce heat and simmer, uncovered, for 1 to 2 hours.

Sausage Chowder

Serves 4-6

Hot bowls of this hearty chowder are certain to take the chill out of any cold winter day. Add hot corn bread, fresh fruit and icy cold glasses of milk for a nutritious delicious supper. Oh yes, this recipe doubles easily and freezes well.

1 pound ground sausage
1 (16 ounce) can kidney beans, drained
1 (16 ounce) can tomatoes, cut up or 1 pint home canned tomatoes
2 cups water
1 small onion, chopped
¼ cup chopped green pepper
½ teaspoon salt
1 bay leaf
¼ teaspoon thyme leaves, crushed
¼ teaspoon garlic powder
¼ teaspoon ground pepper
1 cup diced potatoes

1. Brown sausage in skillet and drain off grease.

2. In large soup kettle, combine drained browned sausage, kidney beans, tomatoes, water, onion, green pepper, salt, bay leaf, thyme, garlic powder, pepper and potatoes.

3. Cook over medium heat for 45 minutes until potatoes are tender. Chowder may then be allowed to simmmer on low heat until ready to serve.

Microwave

In step 1, brown sausage using the colander method described on page 238.
In step 2, combine browned sausage, kidney beans, tomatoes, water, onion, green pepper, salt, bay leaf, thyme, garlic powder, pepper and potatoes in microwave-safe soup tureen or 3-quart casserole.
In step 3, microwave on 100% power for 25-30 minutes, stirring 2-3 times.

Fresh Mushroom Soup

Serves 4-6

Here is an excellent example when "fresh is best". What a great feeling you'll experience as you transform one pound of fresh mushrooms into this perfectly wonderful soup. Treat your family and friends soon.

½   **cup butter or margarine**
1-½   **cups chopped green onions with tops**
1   **pound fresh mushrooms, sliced**
¼   **cup plus 2 tablespoons flour**
¼   **teaspoon white pepper**
3   **cups water**
3   **cups milk**
4   **teaspoons instant chicken bouillon or 4 chicken bouillon cubes, crushed**

1. In dutch oven, melt butter. Saute onion in butter until tender, 3 or 4 minutes.

2. Add mushrooms, and saute 2 or 3 minutes.

3. Stir in flour and white pepper; cook over medium heat, stirring constantly, 2 minutes.

4. Gradually add water, milk, and chicken bouillon, stirring until smooth; bring mixture just to a boil over low heat, stirring constantly.

Microwave

In step **1,** put butter in microwave-safe soup tureen or 3 quart casserole. Microwave on 100% power for 30-40 seconds. Add onions and microwave on 100% power 3-4 minutes, stirring once.
In step **2,** add mushrooms and microwave on 100% power 4-6 minutes, stirring once.
In step **3,** add flour, pepper, water, milk, and chicken bouillon. Stir thoroughly.
In step **4,** microwave on 100% power 12-15 minutes or until thickened, stirring 3 or 4 times.

Gazpacho

Serves 12

I first tasted this marvelous classic cold vegetable soup at the home of Sheila and Gary Bigelow. Ice cubes kept the gazpacho chilled in a punch bowl while a variety of accompaniments were available for guests to select their own topping. If you're looking for a splashy idea for a summer gathering, let me suggest a dynamite Gazpacho Party.

½   **pound day old French or Italian bread or hard rolls, cubed (2 quarts)**
1-½   **cups water**
3   **cups cubed cucumber, pared and seeded (2 large)**
2   **medium green peppers, seeded and cut up**
3   **cloves garlic, halved**
4   **teaspoons salt**
¼   **cup olive oil**
½   **cup red wine vinegar**
4   **pounds fresh ripe tomatoes, peeled and quartered**

Accompaniments: sliced pimiento-stuffed olives, diced cucumber, chopped green onions, diced tomatoes, chopped green pepper, croutons, crisp crumbled bacon, sliced toasted almonds and/or chopped hard-cooked egg.

1. Place bread in shallow dish; add water. Let bread soak, stirring once.

2. In electric blender container or food processor work bowl, place half of the cucumber, green pepper, garlic, salt, oil and vinegar. Cover and blend or process until smooth.

3. Pour into large bowl. Repeat procedure with remaining half of the above ingredients.

4. Blend or process half of soaked bread and half of tomatoes in blender or food processor; add to vegetables in large bowl. Repeat procedure with remaining half of bread and tomatoes.

5. Stir mixture to thoroughly combine.

6. Chill completely before serving. Serve in bowls with ice cubes and pass assorted accompaniments.

Note: Freezes very well.

Country Inn Corn Soup

Serves 8

This creamy rich soup reminds me of delicious dinners our family has enjoyed on summer vacations when we stayed at Country Inns. The amazing part is the extreme simplicity not only in procedure, but in the ingredient list.

¼   **cup butter or margarine**
1   **medium-size onion, chopped**
¼   **cup flour**
2-½ **cups milk**
2   **cups half and half coffee cream**
1-½ **teaspoons salt**
1   **teaspoon instant chicken bouillon or 1 chicken bouillon cube, crushed**
⅛   **teaspoon white pepper**
2   **(16 ounce) cans cream-style corn**
¼   **cup chopped fresh parsley, if desired**

1. Melt the butter in large saucepan and saute the chopped onion until tender.

2. Stir in the flour. Add milk and cream; cook over medium heat until smooth and thickened, stirring constantly.

3. Add salt, chicken bouillon, pepper and corn. Heat just to the simmering point, do not boil.

4. Ladle into soup bowls and garnish with fresh parsley, if desired.

Microwave

In step 1, put butter and onion in 3 quart microwave-safe casserole or soup tureen. Microwave on 100% power 3-4 minutes, stirring once.
In step 2, stir in flour. Add milk and cream. Microwave on 100% power 10-12 minutes, stirring 2-3 times, until thickened.
In step 3, add salt, chicken bouillon, pepper and corn. Microwave on 100% power 3-4 minutes, until hot or probe to 180 degrees.

Midwest Ham Chowder

Serves 6-8

Homemade soup is one of those simple pleasures that get lost in the whirl of everyday life. This nutritious recipe is an easy way to introduce that homemade goodness to your family and friends. Remember extra servings of soup store well in the freezer all ready for a quick meal on a busy day.

2	cups boiling water
2	cups diced potatoes
½	cup sliced carrots
½	cup diced celery
¼	cup chopped onion
1	to 1-½ teaspoons salt, depending on ham
¼	teaspoon ground pepper
¼	cup butter or margarine
¼	cup flour
2	cups milk
2-½	cups shredded sharp cheddar cheese (10 ounces)
1	(17 ounce) can cream style corn
2	cups cubed ham

1. In large dutch oven, combine water, potatoes, carrots, celery, onion, salt and pepper. Cover; simmer 10 minutes. Do not drain.

2. In another saucepan, melt butter and stir in flour. Add milk. Stir mixture constantly with a wire whisk over medium heat until thickened. Add cheese and stir until cheese melts.

3. Add cheese sauce, corn and ham to cooked vegetables. Heat until hot, but not boiling.

Microwave

In step **1**, use a microwave-safe soup tureen or 3-quart microwave safe casserole. Microwave on 100% power 10-15 minutes, stirring once.

In step **2**, microwave butter in 2-quart microwave-safe measurer for 30 seconds on 100% power. Blend in flour with wire whisk. Stir in milk. Microwave on 100% power 6-8 minutes, stirring every 2 minutes until thickened.

In step **3**, probe to 180 degrees or microwave on 100% power 3-5 minutes.

Cream of Cucumber Soup

Serves 4-6

Magnificent is the word my husband, George, uses to describe this delicious soup. We first tasted this creation when my sister-in-law, Mary Howell, served it chilled on a hot summer day. Actually it is equally as lovely served hot. Garnish with fresh or dried thyme leaves.

6   **green onions**
1   **tablespoon butter or margarine**
2   **medium cucumbers, peeled, seeded, and cubed**
2   **(13-¾ ounce) cans chicken broth (3-½ cups)**
½   **teaspoon dried thyme leaves or 1 tablespoon snipped fresh thyme**
1-½ **tablespoons lemon juice**
1   **teaspoon sugar**
½   **teaspoon salt**
1   **cup whipping cream**

1. Slice green onions using 4 inches of the green stems.

2. In large saucepan, combine onions and butter. Saute over medium heat for about 5 minutes until tender.

3. Add cucumbers; cook and stir 5 minutes longer.

4. Add broth, thyme, lemon juice, sugar and salt. Bring to a boil. Reduce heat to medium. Cover, cook 20 minutes or until vegetables are tender.

5. Cool for a few minutes and puree a portion at a time in blender or food processor. (At this point the mixture may be refrigerated.)

6. Add whipping cream and heat just to boiling. Serve hot or chill and serve cold.

Microwave

In step **2,** combine onions and butter in 2-quart microwave-safe casserole. Microwave on 100% power for 3-4 minutes, stirring once.

In step **3,** add cucumber and microwave on 100% power 4-5 minutes, stirring once.

In step **4,** add broth, thyme, lemon juice, sugar and salt. Cover. Microwave on 100% power for 15-20 minutes, stirring twice, until vegetables are tender.

Surprise Chowder
Serves 6-8

The "surprise" in this full bodied chowder is bite-size cubes of fish fillets. Family and friends may not guess the secret ingredient, but they will agree the flavor is marvelous. It's a nice change of pace for the homemade soup crowd.

2	tablespoons butter or margarine
⅓	cup chopped onion
⅓	cup chopped celery
1	cup shredded carrot
2	cups diced potatoes
¼	cup flour
4	teaspoons instant chicken bouillon or 4 chicken bouillon cubes, crushed
¼	teaspoon salt
1-¼	teaspoons seafood seasoning, if desired
	Dash of paprika
3	cups milk
2-¼	cups water
1	pound fish fillets, fresh or frozen, thawed, cut in 1-inch cubes
1	cup shredded cheddar cheese

1. In large saucepan, melt butter. Add onion, celery, carrot and potatoes.

2. Cook, stirring frequently, until onion is transparent.

3. Blend in flour, bouillon, salt, seafood seasoning and paprika.

4. Add milk and water. Cook stirring constantly, until thickened.

5. Add fish; simmer 5-10 minutes until fish flakes easily.

6. Add cheese; stir until melted.

7. Serve piping hot. Enjoy.

Microwave

In step **1,** put butter in microwave-safe soup tureen or 3 quart casserole. Microwave on 100% power 20-30 seconds until melted. Add onion, celery, carrots and potatoes.

In step **2,** microwave on 100% power 5-7 minutes until onion is transparent, stirring twice.

In step **4,** add milk and water. Microwave on 100% power 15-17 minutes until thickened, stirring three or four times.

In step **5,** add fish; microwave on 100% power 5-10 minutes until fish flakes easily, stirring twice.

In step **6,** add cheese; microwave on 100% power 2-4 minutes until cheese melts, stirring once.

Sausage Breakfast Pizza

6-8 servings

This dynamite breakfast creation is guaranteed to win the hearts and the taste buds of young people everywhere. The added bonus is that older folks love it too. If you are short on preparation time, brown the sausage the night before or store cooked and drained sausage in the freezer. Remember, too, slices of cooked pizza reheat well in the microwave at 80% power.

1	**pound bulk pork sausage**
1	**(8 ounce) package refrigerated crescent rolls**
1	**cup frozen loose-pack hash brown potatoes, thawed**
1	**cup (4 ounces) shredded sharp Cheddar cheese**
5	**eggs**
¼	**cup milk**
½	**teaspoon salt**
⅛	**teaspoon ground pepper**
3	**tablespoons grated Parmesan cheese**

1. Cook sausage in medium skillet until browned; drain. Set aside.

2. Separate crescent dough into 8 triangles; place triangles with elongated points toward center in a greased 12-inch pizza pan.

3. Press bottom and sides to form a crust; seal perforations.

4. Spoon sausage over dough; sprinkle with hash brown potatoes and Cheddar cheese.

5. Beat together eggs, milk, salt and pepper with rotary beater; pour over sausage mixture.

6. Bake in preheated 375 degree oven for 25 minutes.

7. Sprinkle with Parmesan cheese, and bake an additional 5-10 minutes.

8. Let stand about 5 minutes before cutting into pizza slices.

Cheese Strata

Serves 6

This classic cheese entree sometimes is forgotten and yet it has many qualities that make recipes popular today. It's a make-ahead cook's dream as strata can be prepared when convenient, then refrigerated until baking time.

8	**slices day-old bread**
1	**(8 ounce) package sliced sharp process cheddar cheese**
4	**eggs**
2-½	**cups milk**
½	**teaspoon prepared mustard**

(Continued)

Cheese Strata (continued)

1   **tablespoon chopped onion**
1   **teaspoon salt**
       Dash ground pepper

1. Trim crusts from 5 slices of the bread; cut each trimmed slice in half diagonally.

2. Cover the bottom of an 8 or 9-inch square baking dish with the trimmings from the 5 slices of bread and the remaining 3 slices of bread.

3. Layer cheese over bread.

4. Arrange the 10 trimmed "triangles" in 2 rows on top of cheese. (Points should overlap bases of preceding "triangles.")

5. In medium mixing bowl, beat eggs; blend in milk, mustard, onion, salt and pepper.

6. Pour milk mixture over bread and cheese.

7. Cover and refrigerate at least 4 hours or overnight.

8. Uncover. Bake in preheated 325 degree oven 1 hour or until knife inserted halfway between center and edge comes out clean.

9. Let stand 5 minutes before serving.

Oven Cheese Puff

Serves 1

This wonderful combination of very ordinary ingredients makes a perfect individual serving. However, you could easily multiply each measurement to serve more than one. Add a crisp green salad and fresh fruit for a quick light meal.

1   **slice bread, buttered and cut into sixths**
1   **egg**
½   **cup milk**
¼   **cup shredded cheddar cheese**
¼   **teaspoon salt, if desired**
⅛   **teaspoon onion salt**
6   **to 8 drops red pepper sauce**

1. Line bottom and/or sides of ungreased 10-12 ounce casserole with bread slices buttered side down.

2. Beat together egg, milk, cheese and seasonings with hand beater or fork until well blended; pour over bread.

3. Bake uncovered in preheated 350 degree oven until puffy and golden brown, about 35 minutes.

Bacon/Egg Bake

Serves 6-8

Bacon and eggs are traditional breakfast fare here in the Midwest. However, never have they been so easy to prepare and serve to a crowd as in this winning recipe.

¼   **cup butter or margarine**
4   **cups unseasoned croutons**
2   **cups (8 ounces) shredded Cheddar cheese**
2   **cups milk**
8   **eggs**
½   **teaspoon dry mustard**
1   **(12 ounce) package bacon, cooked, drained, and crumbled**

1. Place butter in a 2-quart flat baking dish. Heat butter in a preheated 325 degree oven 5 minutes or until butter is melted. Remove from oven. Tilt dish to coat with butter.

2. Put croutons over butter; sprinkle cheese over croutons, and set aside.

3. In medium mixing bowl, beat together milk, eggs and mustard with rotary beater. Pour egg mixture over cheese, and sprinkle with bacon.

4. Bake in preheated 325 degree oven for 40-50 minutes until set.

5. Let casserole stand at room temperature 5-10 minutes before serving, if time permits.

Colorful Egg Squares

Serves 12

Here is a wonderful brunch entree filled with exciting ingredients that result in superior flavor. Serve with lots of luscious fresh fruit and an assortment of fancy quick breads for a morning to remember.

1   **pound bulk pork sausage, cooked and drained**
4   **ounces fresh mushrooms, sliced**
½   **cup sliced green onions**
2   **medium tomatoes, peeled and chopped**
2   **cups (8 ounces) shredded mozzarella cheese**
1-¼ **cups buttermilk baking mix**
12   **eggs**
1   **cup milk**
1-½ **teaspoons salt**
½   **teaspoon ground pepper**
½   **teaspoon dried oregano leaves**

(Continued)

Colorful Egg Squares (continued)

1. In 9x13 inch greased baking dish, layer sausage, mushrooms, green onions, tomatoes and cheese.

2. In medium mixing bowl, beat together baking mix, eggs, milk, salt, pepper and oregano.

3. Pour over sausage mixture.

4. Bake uncovered in preheated 350 degree oven until golden brown and set, about 30 minutes.

5. Cut into twelve 3-inch squares.

Oven Swiss Steak

Serves 6

This delicious swiss style steak could easily be baking in the oven while other tasks are being accomplished. Add mashed potatoes to the menu for those who are meat and potato fans. It's great country fare.

2	pounds round steak, ½ inch thick, cut in serving-size portions
¼	cup flour
2	teaspoons salt
¼	teaspoon ground pepper
¼	cup salad oil
2	medium onions, sliced
½	cup chopped celery
¾	cup chili sauce
¾	cup water
⅛	teaspoon garlic powder
1	medium green pepper, seeded and sliced in rings

1. In 2 quart plastic bag, combine flour, salt and pepper. Shake steak pieces in flour mixture until well coated.

2. Brown in hot oil in skillet, removing meat as it browns. Add onion and saute until lightly browned.

3. In small bowl combine celery, chili sauce, water and garlic powder.

4. In 2 quart serving dish, layer meat, sauteed onions, green pepper rings and chili sauce mixture. Cover with lid or aluminum foil.

5. Bake in preheated 350 degree oven 1 to 1-½ hours until meat is tender.

Sauerbraten Round Steak

Serves 4-6

The robust flavor and aroma of sauerbraten is quickly created in this clever recipe using round steak. Your family and friends will flash smiles of approval as they ask for second servings.

1-½ **pounds round steak, ½ inch thick**
1   **tablespoon vegetable oil**
1   **(.87 ounce) envelope brown gravy mix**
2   **cups water**
1   **tablespoon instant minced onion**
2   **tablespoons white wine vinegar**
2   **tablespoons brown sugar**
½   **teaspoon salt**
¼   **teaspoon ground pepper**
½   **teaspoon ground ginger**
1   **teaspoon Worcestershire sauce**
1   **bay leaf**
     Hot buttered noodles

1. Cut meat in 1-inch squares.

2. In a large skillet, brown meat on all sides in hot vegetable oil.

3. Add gravy mix and water. Bring to boiling, stirring constantly.

4. Stir in onion, vinegar, brown sugar, salt, pepper, ginger, Worcestershire sauce and bay leaf.

5. Cover and simmer over very low heat 1 to 1-½ hours, stirring occasionally, until meat is tender. Remove bay leaf.

6. Serve meat over hot buttered noodles.

Spaghetti and Meatballs

Serves 6

This traditional Italian specialty is our daughter Sara's favorite meal. Quite often we share the preparation tasks. Sara will make the meatballs using the microwave oven and I cook the spaghetti conventionally and make the sauce. Remember that cooked spaghetti reheats marvelously in the microwave, thus eliminating that last minute hassle. When you coordinate microwave and conventional cooking like this, you're experiencing the best of both cooking worlds.

¾	cup chopped onion
1	garlic clove, minced or ⅛ teaspoon garlic powder
3	tablespoons vegetable oil
2	(16 ounce) cans tomatoes, cut up or 1 quart home canned tomatoes
2	(6 ounce) cans tomato paste
2	cups water
1	teaspoon sugar
1-½	teaspoons salt
1-½	teaspoons dried oregano leaves, crushed
½	teaspoon ground pepper
1	bay leaf
	Italian Meatballs (recipe follows)
	Hot cooked spaghetti
	Grated Parmesan cheese

1. In dutch oven, cook onion and garlic in oil till tender, but not brown.

2. Add tomatoes, tomato paste, water, sugar, salt, oregano, pepper and bay leaf.

3. Simmer, uncovered, 30 minutes; remove bay leaf.

4. Add meatballs. Loosely cover and cook 30 minutes.

5. Serve over hot spaghetti.

6. Pass grated Parmesan cheese.

Italian Meatballs

Serves 6

These flavor packed meatballs go into the preceding spaghetti sauce recipe to complete the Spaghetti and Meatball entree. If you have a microwave, I urge you to cook the meatballs the quick and easy microwave way.

4	slices of bread
½	cup water
2	eggs
1	pound ground beef
¼	cup grated Parmesan cheese
2	tablespoons snipped parsley
1	teaspoon salt
¼	teaspoon dried oregano leaves, crushed
	Dash of pepper
2	tablespoons vegetable oil

1. In large mixing bowl, tear bread into small pieces. Add water and let soak for 2 to 3 minutes.

2. Add eggs and mix well.

3. Add ground beef, Parmesan cheese, snipped parsley, salt, oregano leaves and pepper. Mix thoroughly.

4. With wet hands, form meat into approximately 24 small balls.

5. Heat oil in skillet and slowly brown meatballs.

6. Drain meatballs and add to spaghetti sauce.

Microwave

In step **5,** omit oil. Put half of the meatballs on a microwave roasting rack or in 9-inch glass pie dish. Cover with waxed paper.
Microwave on 100% power 4-6 minutes or until meat is set, rotating rack once. Repeat procedure with remaining meatballs.

Italian Steak

Serves 5-6

This delicious way to transform round steak into an Italian flavored entree is a treasured family recipe of my friend and neighbor, Mary Koenig. The beauty of this recipe is not only in the tasty ingredients but in the carefree oven baking.

1-½   **pounds round steak, cut ¾-inch thick**
2   **tablespoons butter or margarine**
1   **(4 ounce) can mushroom stems and pieces, drained or ½ pound sliced fresh mushrooms**
½   **cup chopped onion**
2   **tablespoons chopped green pepper**
⅓   **cup chili sauce**
¼   **cup water**
1   **teaspoon salt**
⅛   **teaspoon ground pepper**
⅛   **teaspoon garlic salt**
½   **teaspoon Worcestershire sauce**
¼   **cup sliced ripe olives, if desired**

1. Cut steak in serving-size pieces and place in 2 quart casserole.

2. Melt butter in small skillet. Add mushrooms, onion and green pepper.

3. Saute about 5 minutes until vegetables are tender.

4. Blend in chili sauce, water, salt, pepper, garlic salt, Worcestershire sauce and olives.

5. Pour sauce mixture over steak in casserole.

6. Cover and bake in preheated 300 degree oven 1-½ to 2 hours, until meat is tender.

Meat and Potato Pie

Serves 4-6

Hearty stew mixtures are favorite supper fare at our house. This variation features oven browned mashed potatoes on top of the bubbling meat and vegetables. This recipe will require a repeat performance.

2	**pounds round steak, cut into 1-inch cubes**
¼	**cup flour**
1	**teaspoon salt**
¼	**teaspoon ground pepper**
¼	**cup vegetable oil**
½	**cup chopped celery**
1	**cup sliced carrots**
4	**ounces fresh mushrooms, sliced**
½	**cup chopped onion**
2	**cups water**
½	**cup frozen peas**
1	**teaspoon browning for gravy sauce**
1	**teaspoon chopped fresh parsley**
3	**cups hot cooked mashed potatoes**
	Paprika

1. Combine flour, salt and pepper in 2-quart plastic bag. Shake steak cubes in flour mixture.

2. In large skillet, brown meat in hot vegetable oil.

3. Add celery, carrots, mushrooms, onion and water. Cover and simmer 1 hour or until tender. Add peas and browning for gravy sauce.

4. Pour meat mixture into 8x12-inch baking dish. Sprinkle with parsley.

5. Spoon mashed potatoes around outside edge of meat mixture. Sprinkle with paprika.

6. Bake in preheated 425 degree oven for 20 minutes until hot.

Note: For 3 cups mashed potatoes you'll need 1-½ lb. potatoes, cooked and drained. Prepare as usual. Instant mashed potatoes could be used.

Slim Line Marinated Pot Roast

Serves 8-10

If you're hungry for beef, yet concerned about total calorie intake, this marinated eye-of-round roast is the answer to your craving. This very lean cut of beef becomes tender and delicious when marinated overnight and then cooked slowly.

1	**(3 pound) boneless eye-of-round beef roast**
1	**cup unsweetened pineapple juice**
½	**cup red wine vinegar**
½	**cup water**
2	**teaspoons Worcestershire sauce**
1	**medium onion, thinly sliced**
⅛	**teaspoon garlic powder**
1	**bay leaf**
¼	**teaspoon freshly ground pepper**

1. Trim excess fat from roast; set aside.

2. In medium mixing bowl, combine pineapple juice, vinegar, water, Worcestershire sauce, onion, garlic powder, bay leaf and pepper.

3. Put roast in 2 quart plastic bag. Pour marinade over roast. Close bag with metal twist tie. Set in bowl or pan.

4. Refrigerate overnight, turning meat occasionally.

5. Place meat and marinade in a Dutch oven.

6. Cover and simmer 1-½ to 2 hours or until desired degree of doneness.

7. To serve, thinly slice roast.

Spaghetti Pizza
Serves 12

The basic idea for this crowd pleasing pizza style one-dish meal comes from my friend, Jo Ann Burt, and her daughter Sarah of Salem, Oregon. If you have lots of hungry family and friends gathering, then this is the recipe for you. It could easily be covered and refrigerated after step #8; just add a few extra minutes of baking time before serving.

1   (16 ounce) package spaghetti
2   eggs
½   cup milk
1   cup shredded mozzarella cheese
¾   teaspoon garlic powder
1   teaspoon salt
1   (32 ounce) jar spaghetti sauce
1-½ pounds ground beef, browned and drained
1   (8 ounce) can mushroom stems and pieces, drained
½   teaspoon oregano leaves, crushed
½   teaspoon basil leaves, crushed
3   cups shredded mozzarella cheese, divided

1. Break spaghetti into thirds and cook according to package directions. Rinse with cold water and drain thoroughly.

2. In large mixing bowl, beat together eggs and milk.

3. Add cooked spaghetti, 1 cup mozzarella cheese, garlic powder and salt. Mix thoroughly.

4. Pour spaghetti mixture into lightly greased 10-½ x 15-½ inch jelly roll pan.

5. Bake in preheated 400 degree oven for 15 minutes. This forms the crust.

6. In large mixing bowl, combine spaghetti sauce, cooked and drained ground beef, drained mushrooms, oregano, basil and 1 cup of the mozzarella cheese.

7. Spread meat mixture on cooked spaghetti crust.

8. Sprinkle with remaining 2 cups mozzarella cheese.

9. Bake in preheated 350 degree oven 30 minutes until piping hot.

Barbecued Pot Roast

Serves 6-8

Family members will race to the table when this barbecued pot roast head-lines the menu. Although the ingredient list may look long, it's worth the effort. Let pot roast simmer on the stove on a day when you're accomplishing lots of household tasks.

1	(3-4 pound) beef chuck or shoulder roast
3	tablespoons vegetable oil
1	(8 ounce) can tomato sauce
½	cup water
3	medium onions, thinly sliced
2	cloves garlic, minced or ¼ teaspoon garlic powder
2	teaspoons salt
¼	teaspoon ground pepper
2	tablespoons brown sugar
½	teaspoon dry mustard
¼	cup lemon juice
¼	cup catsup
¼	cup cider vinegar
1	tablespoon Worcestershire sauce

1. Brown roast on all sides in hot oil in a large dutch oven.

2. Drain off excess oil.

3. In small mixing bowl, combine tomato sauce, water, onion, garlic, salt and pepper, mixing well.

4. Pour over roast: reduce heat, cover and simmer 1-2 hours.

5. In small mixing bowl, combine brown sugar, dry mustard, lemon juice, catsup, vinegar and Worcestershire sauce.

6. Pour over roast.

7. Cover and simmer 1 hour or until tender.

8. Lift meat out of sauce and place on heated platter.

Enchilada Bake

Serves 6-8

Family and friends are certain to give this enchilada casserole their seal of approval. It's just the right combination of seasoned meat wrapped up in flour tortillas topped with lots of cheese. Make ahead cooks can refrigerate the completed casserole to be baked when needed.

1   **pound ground beef**
1   **(15 ounce) can tomato sauce**
1   **(1-¼ ounce) package taco seasoning mix**
12 **soft regular-size flour tortillas**
1   **(10-¾ ounce) can cream of mushroom soup**
1   **cup cultured sour cream**
1   **(4 ounce) can chopped green chilies**
2   **cups grated sharp cheddar cheese (8 ounces)**

1. In medium skillet, brown ground beef, drain well.

2. Return drained ground beef to skillet.

3. Add tomato sauce and taco mix. Stir to combine.

4. Simmer 15 minutes to develop flavors, stirring occasionally.

5. Spoon meat mixture on tortillas. Roll and place filled tortillas in greased 9x13-inch baking pan.

6. In medium mixing bowl, combine mushroom soup, sour cream and chilies.

7. Spread sour cream mixture over tortillas.

8. Sprinkle with grated cheese.

9. Bake in preheated 350 degree oven for 25-30 minutes until bubbly hot.

Microwave

In step **1,** put ground beef in hard plastic colander that rests in microwave-safe dish. Microwave on 100% power 5-7 minutes, stirring once with fork to break up meat.

In step **2,** put drained browned ground beef in 2 quart microwave-safe dish.

In step **3,** add tomato sauce and taco mix. Microwave on 100% power 6-10 minutes, stirring once or twice.

In step **5,** divide tortillas in two 8-inch square microwave-safe baking dishes.

In step **9,** microwave each 8-inch square dish on 80% power 10-15 minutes, until bubbly, rotating dish once or twice.

German Cabbage Rolls

Makes 18-24

The last time Gramma and Grandpa Behm came from Montana to visit their Michigan relatives, we were invited over to Mary Ellen and Harley's home to enjoy these delicious cabbage rolls that Gramma made for us. Never before had I experienced the German tradition of cabbage rolls tucked inside yeast rolls. To the preservation of this family tradition, I share this recipe with you.

1   **small head cabbage, shredded or finely sliced**
2   **or 3 medium onions, chopped**
½   **cup water**
2   **pounds ground beef, browned and drained**
     Salt and pepper to taste
     Yeast bread or roll dough, ready for shaping

1. In medium skillet, combine cabbage, onions and water. Simmer until cabbage is tender, drain completely.

2. Add drained brown ground beef to cabbage.

3. Salt and pepper to taste.

4. Cool cabbage-meat mixture thoroughly.

5. On floured surface, roll bread dough ¼-½ inch thick. Cut into 6-inch squares.

6. Put 2 tablespoons or more of cabbage-meat mixture in center of dough.

7. Bring the 4 corners of dough up to the center together; pressing edges together tightly to make a tight seal.

8. Place on greased or parchment lined baking sheet. Brush lightly with melted butter. Cover with oiled plastic wrap.

9. Let raise until doubled in bulk and puffed.

10. Remove plastic wrap. Bake in preheated 375 degree oven for 40-45 minutes until rolls are brown.

11. Brush again with melted butter and put on rack.

12. Delicious both hot and cold.

Microwave

In step **1,** combine cabbage, onions and water in 2-quart microwave-safe casserole. Cover with lid or vented plastic wrap. Microwave on 100% power 7-9 minutes, until tender, stirring twice, drain completely.

Chinese Beef Stir-Fry

Serves 6

My family likes this beef and vegetable combination so much I could serve it once a week. It's a great way to enjoy beef and keep the calorie count under control. The oyster-flavored sauce which adds a full bodied flavor can be found in the oriental food section of the grocery store.

1	**pound boneless flank or sirloin steak**
½	**cup water**
¼	**cup soy sauce**
1	**tablespoon cornstarch**
1-½	**teaspoons sugar**
2	**tablespoons oyster-flavored sauce**
1	**medium onion**
	Vegetable cooking spray
3	**stalks celery, diagonally sliced**
½	**pound fresh mushrooms, sliced**
1	**(8 ounce) can sliced water chestnuts, drained**
1	**(6 ounce) package frozen Chinese pea pods, thawed and rinsed or ½ pound fresh snow peas**

1. Slice partially frozen steak across grain into 2-¼-inch strips or ask the butcher at the meat market to do the slicing for you.

2. In 1 cup glass measurer, combine water, soy sauce, cornstarch, sugar and oyster flavored sauce; set aside.

3. Peel onion and cut into ¼-inch slices; quarter each slice. Set aside.

4. Coat wok or skillet well with cooking spray; allow to heat at medium high (325 degrees) for 2 minutes. Add steak and stir-fry about 3 minutes until cooked. Remove meat from wok. Leave drippings in wok.

5. Add onion, celery, mushrooms, and water chestnuts to wok; stir-fry 2-3 minutes. Add meat and peas; cover and reduce heat to medium (275 degrees). Simmer 2 to 3 minutes.

6. Stir in soy sauce mixture. Cook over medium high heat (325 degrees) stirring constantly until thickened and bubbly. Serve over rice.

Make Ahead Mexican Chicken

Serves 8-10

My friend, Mary Kaye Merwin, likes to have this yummy casserole tucked in the refrigerator or freezer for expected or unexpected guests. It assures a degree of calmness only appropriate for the well organized person.

1	**chicken, cooked, skinned, deboned and chopped; yields 3 to 4 cups**
2	**tablespoons butter or margarine**
1	**large onion, chopped**
2	**(4 ounce) cans chopped green chilies**
1	**(10-¾ ounce) can cream of chicken soup**
1	**(10-¾ ounce) can cream of mushroom soup**
1	**cup milk**
1-½	**dozen corn tortillas, cut into eight pieces each**
4	**cups shredded mozzarella cheese (1 pound)**

1. Cook chicken conventionally or in the microwave. Skin, debone, and cut into bite-size pieces.

2. In 2 quart saucepan, melt butter. Add onion and saute until onion is transparent. Add chopped chilies, chicken soup, mushroom soup, milk and chopped chicken.

3. Cook over low heat until mixture is hot.

4. Butter 3 quart casserole. Starting with the cut tortillas, layer ⅓ of the tortillas, then ⅓ chicken mixture and then ⅓ of the shredded cheese.

5. Repeat this layering process 2 more times ending with cheese.

6. Casserole may now be covered and refrigerated up to 24 hours or frozen.

7. Bake in preheated 350 degree oven 30-40 minutes (longer if frozen) until cheese is melted and mixture is bubbly.

Microwave

In step **1,** cook chicken according to directions on page 238.
In step **2,** melt butter in 2 quart microwave-safe casserole on 100% power for 20-30 seconds. Add onion and microwave on 100% power for 2-3 minutes, stirring once. Add chopped chilies, chicken soup, mushroom soup, milk and chopped chicken.
In step **3,** microwave on 100% power 4-5 minutes, stirring once.
In step **4,** use microwave-safe casserole.
In step **7,** microwave on 80% power 20-30 minutes until hot and bubbly.

Chicken-Vegetable Stir-Fry

Serves 6

Stir-frying is a great way to combine chicken and vegetables in an easy and creative way. Serve on a bed of fluffy rice with an assortment of fresh fruit for a delightful light meal.

3	whole chicken breasts, skinned and boned
	Vegetable cooking spray
¼	cup plus 1 tablespoon soy sauce
1	(4 ounce) can sliced mushrooms, undrained
1	large onion, coarsely chopped
2	small green peppers, cut into 1-inch strips
1	(8 ounce) can sliced water chestnuts, drained
1	teaspoon cornstarch
½	teaspoon sugar
⅛	teaspoon red pepper

1. Cut chicken breasts into 1-½ inch cubes.

2. Coat wok or skillet well with cooking spray; allow to heat at medium high (325 degrees) for 1 to 2 minutes.

3. Put chicken and soy sauce in hot wok or skillet. Stir-fry 3 to 4 minutes or until lightly browned. Remove chicken from wok or skillet. Leave drippings in wok or skillet.

4. Drain mushrooms, reserving the liquid; set aside.

5. Add onion and green pepper to wok or skillet; stir-fry 4 minutes or until vegetables are crisp-tender.

6. Return chicken to wok. Stir in mushrooms and water chestnuts.

7. In small bowl, combine reserved mushroom liquid, cornstarch, sugar and red pepper; mix well. Pour over chicken and vegetables, stirring well. Reduce heat to low (225 degrees), simmer 2 or 3 minutes or until slightly thickened. Serve over rice.

Turkey Broccoli Casserole

Serves 4-6

When the occasion calls for a casserole with special flair, here is a combination that is a real winner. Add your favorite cranberry salad and hot French bread to complete the menu.

(Continued)

Turkey Broccoli Casserole (continued)

1   (16 ounce) bag frozen broccoli cuts
1   tablespoon lemon juice
3   cups cubed cooked turkey or chicken
6   slices process American cheese
1   (10-¾ ounce) can condensed cream of chicken soup
½   cup milk
1   (3 ounce) can French fried onion rings

1. Spread broccoli in ungreased 12x8-inch baking dish; drizzle with lemon juice.

2. Top broccoli with turkey and cheese slices.

3. Mix soup and milk in small mixing bowl. Pour over turkey and cheese.

4. Bake uncovered in preheated 350 degree oven until hot and bubbly, about 30 minutes.

5. Sprinkle with onion rings; bake 5 minutes longer. Serve.

Chicken Crunch

Serves 8

When the occasion calls for a chicken casserole, here is a crunchy possibility. The surprise ingredient is a can of tuna which adds a hidden full bodied flavor everyone will enjoy.

2   (10-¾ ounce) cans condensed cream of mushroom soup
½   cup milk
1   teaspoon instant chicken bouillon or 1 chicken bouillon cube, crushed
3   cups diced cooked chicken
1   (6-½ ounce) can tuna, drained and flaked
¼   cup finely chopped onion
1   cup diced celery
1   (8 ounce) can sliced water chestnuts, drained
1   (3 ounce) can chow mein noodles (1-½ cups)
⅓   cup toasted slivered or sliced almonds

1. In large mixing bowl, blend soup, milk and bouillon.

2. Add chicken, tuna, onion, celery, water chestnuts and chow mein noodles.

3. Pour mixture into 2 quart casserole. Top with toasted almonds.

4. Bake in preheated 350 degree oven 40-45 minutes, until bubbly hot.

Microwave

In step **3,** use microwave-safe casserole.
In step **4,** microwave at 80% power 20-30 minutes until bubbly hot or probe to 160 degrees.

Sesame Chicken Kabobs

Serves 4

These colorful kabobs are a great way to serve low calorie chicken with real flair. It works equally well to cook kabobs under the broiler or on a grill. Efficient cooks like to have the skewers filled before guests arrive all ready to cook before serving.

2	**whole chicken breasts, skinned and boned**
¼	**cup soy sauce**
¼	**cup reduced calorie French salad dressing**
1	**tablespoon sesame seeds**
2	**tablespoons lemon juice**
¼	**teaspoon ground ginger**
¼	**teaspoon garlic powder**
1	**large green pepper, cut into 1 inch pieces**
12	**cherry tomatoes**
1	**(8 ounce) can pineapple chunks packed in own juice, drained**

1. Cut chicken breasts into 1-inch pieces; place chicken in a shallow container and set aside.

2. In a glass jar, combine soy sauce, French dressing, sesame seeds, lemon juice, ginger and garlic powder. Cover tightly. Shake vigorously.

3. Pour mixture over chicken; cover and marinate in the refrigerator at least two hours.

4. Remove chicken from marinade, reserving marinade. Alternate chicken with pepper squares, tomatoes and pineapple chunks on skewer.

5. Broil or grill kabobs until chicken is done, turning often and basting frequently with marinade.

Orange Chicken

Serves 8

The flavors of orange and herbs grace these chicken breasts in a wonderful slim line way. Add bright green asparagus spears and fluffy rice for an eye catching main course.

4	**whole chicken breasts, boned, skinned and cut in half**
2	**tablespoons reduced-calorie margarine, melted**
1	**teaspoon paprika**
⅛	**teaspoon ground pepper**
1	**(6 ounce) can frozen orange juice concentrate, thawed and undiluted**
1	**teaspoon dried rosemary leaves, crushed**
½	**teaspoon dried thyme-leaves, crushed**

1. Brush chicken with melted margarine; place on rack of broiler pan. Broil 3 to 5 minutes on each side or until light golden brown.

2. Remove from oven and place chicken in 9x13x2-inch baking pan. Sprinkle with paprika and pepper.

3. Pour orange juice concentrate over chicken; sprinkle with rosemary and thyme.

4. Bake uncovered in preheated 350 degree oven for about 30 minutes, do not overbake.

5. Garnish with fresh parsley and orange slices, if desired.

Microwave

In step **2,** put chicken in 8x12-inch microwave-safe baking dish.
In step **4,** microwave on 100% power 5 minutes per pound or 12-18 minutes, rotating dish once.

Hawaiian Chicken Breasts

Serves 6

When the "What should I serve for dinner?" thought crosses your mind, try these delicious chicken breasts. They are festive enough to serve to guests, yet easy enough to treat your family. The lovely sauce is not complicated and oh so tasty.

¾	cup unsweetened pineapple juice
⅓	cup catsup
¼	cup firmly packed brown sugar
¼	cup butter or margarine
¼	cup vinegar
2	tablespoons cornstarch
1	teaspoon salt
1	teaspoon chili powder
1	teaspoon soy sauce
½	teaspoon Worcestershire sauce
3	whole chicken breasts, cut in half and skinned

1. Combine the pineapple juice, catsup, brown sugar, butter, vinegar, cornstarch, salt, chili powder, soy sauce and Worcestershire sauce in small saucepan. Bring to a boil; cook 1 minute, stirring constantly.

2. Place chicken in 9x13-inch baking dish; pour sauce over chicken. Cover with foil and bake in preheated 350 degree oven for 45 minutes.

3. Uncover and bake an additional 30 minutes, basting occasionally if needed.

Microwave

In step **1,** combine pineapple juice, catsup, brown sugar, butter, vinegar, cornstarch, salt, chili powder, soy sauce and Worcestershire sauce in 2-quart microwave-safe measurer. Microwave on 100% power 3-4 minutes, stirring every minute.

In step **2,** use microwave-safe baking dish. Cover with waxed paper and microwave on 100% power 7 minutes for each pound of chicken.

Turkey and Vegetable Stir Fry

Serves 3-4

This flavorful entree idea is a marvelous way to disguise a bit of leftover turkey or chicken. If you do not have this meat available, cooked turkey breast can usually be easily found at the grocery store.

2	tablespoons cornstarch
1	tablespoon sugar
½	teaspoon ground ginger
3	tablespoons soy sauce
2	cups cooked turkey or chicken, cut in slender strips
1	cup water
1	teaspoon instant chicken bouillon or 1 chicken bouillon cube
1	cup thinly sliced carrots
2	cups diagonally sliced fresh broccoli or 2 cups frozen broccoli cuts
1	medium onion, thinly sliced
1	cup sliced fresh mushrooms or 1 (4 ounce) can mushroom pieces, drained
	Cooked rice or chow mein noodles

1. In medium bowl, combine cornstarch, sugar, ginger and soy sauce; Mix well. Add turkey and stir to coat. Let stand 10-15 minutes.

2. In wok or large skillet, place water and bouillon. Bring to a boil.

3. Add carrots and broccoli if using fresh broccoli. Cover and steam 2 or 3 minutes. If using frozen broccoli, let carrots cook for a short time before adding broccoli.

4. Add turkey and soy sauce mixture, onion and mushrooms. Stir fry 2 or 3 minutes until mixture is thickened and piping hot.

5. Serve over hot cooked rice or chow mein noodles.

Asparagus-Chicken Casserole

12 servings

If asparagus and chicken sound like a wonderful combination and if you need an easy make ahead entree for a crowd, look no further. This recipe meets those qualifications and would be lovely served with assorted fresh fruit and attractive whole wheat rolls.

2   (10 ounce) packages frozen asparagus cuts or 2 pounds fresh aspar-
     agus cut into inch-long pieces or 1 quart home frozen asparagus cuts
2   cups dry egg noodles, cooked according to package directions,
     drain well
6   cups cooked, boned and diced chicken or turkey
1   (8 ounce) can mushroom stems and pieces, drained
1   (8 ounce) can sliced water chestnuts, drained
2   (10-½ ounce) cans cream of chicken soup
1   cup mayonnaise
1   teaspoon lemon juice
1   cup soft bread crumbs
1   cup shredded sharp cheddar cheese

1. Cook asparagus in boiling water just until tender. Drain well.

2. Arrange asparagus in 9x13 inch buttered casserole.

3. In large mixing bowl, combine cooked noodles, chicken, mushrooms and water chestnuts.

4. In smaller mixing bowl, combine soup, mayonnaise and lemon juice.

5. Pour soup mixture over chicken mixture and thoroughly combine.

6. Carefully cover the asparagus with the chicken/soup mixture.

7. Toss together bread crumbs and shredded cheese. Sprinkle over chicken.

8. Cover and refrigerate overnight, if time permits.

9. To bake, uncover and bake in preheated 350 degree oven 45-60 minutes until hot and bubbly.

10. Garnish and serve.

Microwave

In step **1,** put frozen asparagus in 2-quart microwave-safe casserole. Cover with lid or vented plastic wrap. Microwave 7-10 minutes, just until tender, stirring once. Drain well.

Cranberry-Stuffed Cornish Hens

Serves 4

When the occasion calls for a special entree, these lovely hens are perfect. They work out especially well for times when turkey might be served if the group were larger. For years we have enjoyed cranberries with poultry. Here it is featured all in one recipe.

⅔	cup chopped cranberries
2	tablespoons sugar
1	teaspoon grated orange peel
⅛	teaspoon ground cinnamon
¼	teaspoon of salt
3	cups toasted raisin bread cubes
2	tablespoons butter or margarine, melted
4	teaspoons orange juice
4	(1 to 1-½ lb.) Cornish game hens, thawed
	Salad oil
¼	cup orange juice
2	tablespoons butter, melted

1. Combine chopped cranberries, sugar, orange peel, cinnamon and salt in medium mixing bowl.

2. Add toasted raisin bread cubes, 2 tablespoons melted butter and 4 teaspoons of orange juice. Toss lightly to mix.

3. Rinse hen cavities; pat dry with paper towel. Season cavities lightly with salt.

4. Lightly stuff birds with cranberry mixture. Pull neck skin to back of each bird and fasten securely with round toothpick. Tie legs to tail; twist wing tips under back.

5. Place hens, breast side up, on a rack in shallow roasting pan. Brush with salad oil; cover loosely with foil.

6. Roast in preheated 375 degree oven for 30 minutes.

7. Combine orange juice and 2 tablespoons melted butter or margarine.

8. Uncover birds; baste with orange juice-butter mixture.

9. Roast, uncovered, about 1 hour longer or until done, basting once or twice with orange juice-butter mixture.

Microwave

In step **5,** place hens breast side down on microwave roasting rack. Brush with salad oil; cover loosely with greased waxed paper.

In step **6,** microwave on 100% power for 16-18 minutes.

In step **8,** turn hens breast side-up.

In step **9,** microwave on 100% power for 16-18 minutes. When done, brush Cornish hens with orange juice-butter mixture. Cover tightly with foil and let set 5-10 minutes.

Leg of Lamb with Plum Sauce

Serves 8-10

Leg of lamb is the favored entree for special occasions and holidays at the family farm in Wisconsin. Family members from the youngest to the oldest are all happy when the platter of roast leg of lamb is passed for the second time. The lovely plum sauce gives a festive flair to this very special cut of meat.

1	**5-6 pound leg of lamb**
	Salt and pepper, if desired
1	**(16 ounce) can purple plums**
2	**tablespoons lemon juice**
1	**tablespoon soy sauce**
1	**teaspoon Worcestershire sauce**
½	**teaspoon basil leaves, crushed**
	Dash of garlic powder

1. Place lamb, fat side up, on rack in shallow roasting pan.

2. Season with salt and pepper, if desired. (Salt only goes into the roast ¼ to ½ inch.)

3. Roast in preheated 325 degree oven 2-½ to 3 hours or until meat thermometer reads 175 degrees.

4. Meanwhile, drain plums, reserving ¼ cup of the syrup.

5. Pit and sieve plums.

6. In small saucepan, combine reserved syrup, plums, lemon juice, soy sauce, Worcestershire, basil and garlic powder.

7. Baste lamb with plum sauce 4 times during last hour of roasting.

8. Simmer remaining sauce 5 minutes; pass with meat.

9. How fortunate we are that both my husband, George, and my brother, Rich, are expert meat carvers.

10. Carve the leg of lamb and enjoy the family gathering.

Barbecued Spare Ribs

Serves 4-6

When my friend and neighbor, Mary Koenig, shared this finger-licking-good recipe with me, I knew it was a winner. The barbecue sauce, made from ingredients found in many kitchens, can simmer on the stove or in the microwave while the ribs are pre-roasting in the hot oven.

¼   **cup chopped onion**
1   **tablespoon vegetable oil**
½   **cup water**
2   **tablespoons vinegar**
1   **tablespoon Worcestershire sauce**
¼   **cup lemon juice**
2   **tablespoons brown sugar**
1   **cup chili sauce**
½   **teaspoon salt**
¼   **teaspoon paprika**
2   **pounds pork spareribs, cut into serving size pieces**

1. In medium saucepan, saute onion in vegetable oil until tender.

2. Add water, vinegar, Worcestershire, lemon juice, brown sugar, chili sauce, salt and paprika.

3. Simmer for 20 minutes to develop flavors.

4. Place spareribs in roasting pan. Cover them lightly with aluminum foil.

5. Bake ribs in preheated hot 450 degree oven for 15 minutes.

6. Reduce oven temperature to 350 degrees.

7. Remove foil and pour sauce over the meat.

8. Continue to bake ribs for 1 hour longer, basting frequently with barbecue pan juices.

Microwave

In step **1,** put onion and vegetable oil in 2-quart microwave-safe measurer.
Microwave on 100% power for 1-2 minutes, until onion is tender.
In step **3,** microwave on 80% power for 15-20 minutes, stirring twice.

Rosy Ham Rings

Serves 12-15

I like to shape this moist ham loaf mixture into rings with indented centers. At serving time, brightly colored cooked vegetables can be nestled in each ham ring for a picture pretty entree.

2	eggs
½	teaspoon ground allspice
3	pounds ground smoked ham
1	pound ground pork
1-½	cups milk
1-¾	cups graham cracker crumbs
1	(10-¾ ounce) can tomato soup
½	cup brown sugar
½	cup vinegar
1-½	teaspoons prepared mustard

1. In very large mixing bowl, beat eggs and allspice with rotary beater.

2. Add ham, pork, milk and graham cracker crumbs. Mix thoroughly with wooden spoon and then clean hands.

3. Shape ham mixture into serving size rings. Place on aluminum foil or parchment lined 10-½ by 15-½-inch baking pan. Leave an indentation in center of each ring, if desired.

4. In medium mixing bowl, combine tomato soup, brown sugar, vinegar and mustard. Mix ingredients together to create a tomato basting sauce.

5. Baste ham rings with approximately half of the sauce.

6. Bake in preheated 350 degree oven for 30-45 minutes; continue to baste with sauce and bake 30-45 minutes more.

7. Carefully lift cooked ham rings from baking sheet to serving platter. Fill with colorful cooked vegetables, like green peas, if desired.

Ham/Broccoli Roll-Ups

Serves 8

This tasty combination of ham and broccoli was developed when I needed an easy, yet attractive brunch main dish idea. The rolled ham slices seem more festive than chunks of ham and is certainly not difficult if you purchase the slices of ham at your favorite delicatessen or grocery store. The completed dish could be refrigerated overnight before heating, if convenient.

1	**(20 ounce) package frozen broccoli cuts**
16	**thin slices of boiled ham**
¼	**cup butter or margarine**
¼	**cup flour**
½	**teaspoon salt**
¼	**teaspoon dry mustard**
2	**cups milk**
1	**cup (4 ounces) shredded sharp cheddar cheese**
3	**slices fresh bread**
1	**tablespoon butter or margarine, melted**

1. Cook broccoli in boiling water just until thawed and crisp-tender. Drain.

2. Place a row of drained broccoli on each ham slice. Roll up and place seam side down in an 8x12-inch baking dish.

3. Melt ¼ cup butter in saucepan over low heat. Blend in flour, salt and mustard. Cook gently, stirring until mixture is smooth and bubbly.

4. Add milk. Heat to boiling, stirring constantly. Boil and stir one minute. Remove from heat; add cheese; stir until melted.

5. Pour cheese sauce over ham rolls in baking dish.

6. Make fresh bread crumbs using a food processor, blender, or by hand. Toss gently with 1 tablespoon melted butter. Sprinkle over ham rolls.

7. Bake uncovered in preheated 350 degree oven 25-30 minutes until lightly browned.

Microwave

In step **1,** put broccoli in microwave-safe casserole. Cover with lid or with vented plastic wrap. Microwave on 100% power 4-6 minutes until broccoli is crisp tender and thawed. Drain.

In step **3,** put butter in 1-quart microwave-safe measurer. Microwave on 100% power, 30-45 seconds until melted. Stir in flour, salt and mustard.

In step **4,** stir in milk with wire whisk. Microwave on 100% power 4-6 minutes until thick, stirring every minute or two. Add cheese and stir until melted.

In step **6,** use whole wheat bread for added color.

In step **7,** microwave uncovered at 80% power for 15-20 minutes, rotating dish once.

Roast Pork Orange

Serves 6 to 8

Few special entrees are easier to prepare than slowly roasting a fragrant pork loin in the oven. Glazed with a lovely orange juice mixture, this roast is certain to become a favorite. If your family is like mine, they'll not only appreciate, but ask for applesauce to be served with roast pork.

1   3-4 pound boneless pork loin roast
1   teaspoon dried marjoram leaves, crushed
1   teaspoon dry mustard
1   teaspoon salt, if desired (some pork roasts are seasoned at the meat market)
2   teaspoons grated orange peel
½   cup orange juice
1   tablespoon brown sugar

1. Place pork roast on rack in shallow baking pan.

2. Combine marjoram, mustard and salt; rub on surface of meat.

3. Insert meat thermometer. Roast in preheated 325 degree oven for 2-½ to 3 hours.

4. In small bowl, combine orange peel, orange juice, and brown sugar. Spoon over roast.

5. Return meat to oven and roast about 30 minutes more, till meat thermometer registers 170 degrees.

6. Slice and arrange attractively on serving platter.

Apple-Currant Stuffed Pork Chops

Serves 6

One of the great flavor mates of all time is pork served with applesauce, so you can imagine how delicious apple stuffing tucked in a pork chop pocket could be. These chops gently bake in the oven for a wonderful carefree entree.

¾   cup applesauce
2   tablespoons brown sugar
1   cup herb flavored package stuffing mix
1   tablespoon lemon juice
¼   cup currants or raisins
6   thick pork chops, cut with pockets
½   teaspoon salt
2   tablespoons vegetable oil
½   cup hot water

(Continued)

Apple-Currant Stuffed Pork Chops (continued)

1. In small mixing bowl, combine applesauce, brown sugar. stuffing mix, lemon juice and currants.

2. Salt inside pockets of pork chops.

3. Fill each pork chop with stuffing mixture. Close opening with round natural colored toothpick.

4. In skillet, brown pork chops in hot vegetable oil, turning to brown both sides.

5. Place browned chops in 8x12-inch baking dish.

6. Add hot water. Cover with aluminum foil.

7. Bake in preheated 350 degree oven 1 to 1-½ hours.

Kids' Supper Skillet

Serves 4-6

Kids will be anxious for supper time when this quick and easy recipe is the featured attraction. Serve with apple slices and ice cold glasses of milk for a nutritious meal that's lots of fun.

2	tablespoons margarine or butter
¼	cup chopped onion
1	pound wieners, sliced crosswise into ½-inch pieces
1	(10-¾ ounce) can condensed tomato soup
1	cup (4 ounces) shredded Cheddar cheese
½	cup water
2	cups cooked macaroni

1. In large skillet, melt margarine. Saute onions and wieners in melted margarine.

2. Stir in soup, cheese and water. Cook over low heat, stirring constantly until cheese is melted.

3. Stir in cooked macaroni. Heat thoroughly.

4. Serve to hungry kids.

Microwave

In step **1,** put margarine in 1-½ or 2-quart microwave-safe casserole. Melt margarine using 100% power for 20-30 seconds. Add onions and wieners. Cook on 100% power 4-6 minutes, stirring once until cooked.

In step **2,** stir in soup, cheese and water. Cook on 100% power 3-5 minutes, stirring once, until hot.

In step **3,** add cooked macaroni. Heat 4-6 minutes at 80% power, stirring once, until piping hot.

Smoked Sausage Skillet dinner

Serves 6

One way to add variety to menus is to serve basic ingredients in interesting ways. Here is a delicious supper dish that features sausage with wonderful supporting flavors. Just add a crisp tossed salad, bread sticks, and icy cold glasses of milk to complete the meal.

1	**pound smoked sausage, cut into ¼-inch slices**
1	**medium onion, chopped**
½	**cup chopped green pepper**
½	**cup sliced celery**
2	**tablespoons butter or margarine**
4	**cups cooked elbow macaroni**
2	**(8 ounce) cans tomato sauce**
1	**teaspoon chili powder**
⅛	**teaspoon ground pepper**
½	**cup shredded cheddar cheese (2 ounces)**

1. Saute sausage, onion, green pepper and celery in butter in large skillet until vegetables are tender.

2. Stir in cooked macaroni, tomato sauce, chili powder and pepper. Cook over low heat, stirring frequently, until thoroughly heated.

3. Sprinkle with cheese and heat until cheese melts. Serve.

Orange-Glazed Pork Chops

Serves 4

Here's an easy way to add exciting character to everyday pork chops. Orange juice is the creative base for the orange glaze. Simmer gently as flavors develop slowly to perfection.

4	**(¾ inch-thick) pork chops**
	Salt and pepper to taste
	Flour
1	**tablespoon vegetable oil**
½	**cup orange juice**
2	**tablespoons brown sugar**
2	**tablespoons orange marmalade**
1	**tablespoon vinegar**

(Continued)

Orange-Glazed Pork Chops (continued)

1. Sprinkle pork chops lightly with salt and pepper; dredge in flour.

2. Heat oil in heavy skillet; brown pork chops on both sides.

3. In 1 cup glass measurer, combine orange juice, brown sugar, orange marmalade and vinegar. Mix well.

4. Pour orange juice mixture over pork chops.

5. Reduce heat; cover and simmer 40-45 minutes.

Pork Chops Kraut Style

Serves 6

Hearty pork chops and sauerkraut have been flavor companions for such a long time that often they are a forgotten duo. No longer will that need to be true when you try this easy oven dinner. With just one bite, you'll agree that subtly seasoned sauerkraut is the perfect partner for pork.

6	(¾-inch) pork chops
1	teaspoon salt
	Dash of pepper
2	tablespoons vegetable oil
1	(1 pound 11 ounce) can sauerkraut, drained
1	(16 ounce) can tomatoes, cut into pieces
1	teaspoon instant minced onion
1	teaspoon caraway seed

1. Trim all fat from pork chops.

2. Season pork chops with salt and pepper.

3. In large skillet, heat oil. Brown chops on both sides in hot oil.

4. In 8x12-inch baking dish, combine drained sauerkraut, tomatoes, onion and caraway seed. Spread evenly in baking dish.

5. Arrange browned pork chops on top of sauerkraut mixture.

6. Cover tightly with foil.

7. Bake in preheated 350 degree oven for 1 hour.

8. Remove foil and continue baking 30 minutes or until meat is done.

Food Processor Sausage

Serves 8-10

Meat grinding is a task that is easily accomplished with the aid of a food processor. The beauty of this recipe is that the cook is in complete control of the added ingredients. This sausage could be created for the low sodium diet as well as the preservative free diet. Because pork loins are quite lean, these sausage patties are almost fat free.

2-½ **pounds lean pork loin end roast**
2 **teaspoons salt, if desired**
1 **teaspoon ground pepper**
½ **teaspoon ground ginger**
½ **teaspoon poultry seasoning**
½ **teaspoon sugar**
¼ **teaspoon ground cloves**

1. Cut pork into 1-inch pieces. There should be about 4 cups.

2. In small bowl, combine salt, pepper, ginger, poultry seasoning, sugar and cloves.

3. Put pork cubes in large mixing bowl. Sprinkle spice mixture over meat and toss mixture to coat.

4. Cover and refrigerate one or two days to blend flavors.

5. When ready to make sausage, insert steel blade in food processor work bowl.

6. Put about 1 cup pork pieces in work bowl. Use pulsing motion to grind meat (Meat hitting the blade makes a smooth sound when it is uniformly ground and seems to form a ball. If you should notice a loud sound, stop processor. Check blades for small pieces of bone or cartilage.)

7. Transfer ground pork to a mixing bowl.

8. Repeat procedure until all pork is ground.

9. Shape meat into sausage patties.

10. Spray skillet with vegetable spray. Brown sausage patties using medium high heat. If patties seem dry, add a small amount of water.

Savory Sausage Rice Bake

Serves 10

    For years, condensed soups have been used in casserole mixtures. In this interesting recipe dry chicken noodle soup mix is used to enhance the flavors of the sausage and rice. Compliments are guaranteed when you serve this wonderful combination to family and friends.

2	pounds ground sausage
2-½	cups chopped celery
1	cup chopped green pepper
¾	cup chopped onion
1	box (3.5 ounce) chicken noodle soup mix (Use both envelopes)
4-½	cups boiling water
1	cup regular rice
1	cup sliced or slivered almonds
2	tablespoons butter or margarine, melted

1. Lightly brown sausage in large skillet or Dutch oven; drain well.

2. Add celery, green pepper and onion to drained sausage; saute until tender.

3. Combine soup mix and boiling water in 3-quart saucepan. Stir in rice. Cover and simmer 15-20 minutes until rice is tender.

4. Add sausage mixture to rice; thoroughly combine.

5. Pour into lightly greased 2-3 quart baking dish or casserole.

6. Sprinkle with almonds; drizzle with melted butter.

7. Bake uncovered in preheated 375 degree oven 20-30 minutes until piping hot.

Microwave

In step **1,** brown sausage in large hard plastic colander in microwave on 100% power for 8-10 minutes, stirring twice.

In step **2,** put drained sausage, celery, green pepper and onion in 2 quart microwave-safe casserole. Microwave on 100% power 4-6 minutes, stirring twice.

In step **5,** put mixture in 2-3 quart microwave baking dish or casserole.

In step **7,** microwave at 80% power for 10-15 minutes until piping hot or probe to 150 degrees at 80% power.

Salmon Loaf

Serves 8

Thyme leaves, lemon juice and fresh parsley help give pizazz to this salmon loaf. Create an old fashioned oven meal by popping scrubbed potatoes in the oven too. All that's needed at serving time is a bright green vegetable and gelatin fruit salad for a praise worthy menu.

2	**(16 ounce) cans salmon**
¼	**cup finely chopped onion**
¼	**cup minced fresh parsley**
¼	**cup lemon juice**
½	**teaspoon salt**
¼	**teaspoon ground pepper**
½	**teaspoon thyme leaves, crushed**
2	**cups coarse soda cracker crumbs**
	Milk
4	**eggs, well beaten**
¼	**cup butter or margarine, melted**

1. Drain salmon, reserving liquid.

2. Flake salmon in large mixing bowl.

3. Add onion, parsley, lemon juice, salt, pepper, thyme and cracker crumbs. Mix lightly.

4. Add enough milk to reserved salmon liquid to make 1 cup. Add this liquid, beaten eggs and melted butter to salmon; mix lightly.

5. Spoon mixture into greased 8x4-inch loaf pan or 2-quart casserole.

6. Bake in preheated 350 degree oven 1 hour or until loaf is set in center.

7. Garnish with lots of fresh parsley. Serve.

Ross' Jambalaya

Serves 4-6

This first class recipe is my brother-in-law's, Ross House's, all-time favorite recipe. I'll agree it's hard to surpass this Creole dish starring fresh shrimp and oysters. Top off the menu with a crisp tossed salad and hot French bread for a meal to remember.

⅓	**cup butter or margarine**
½	**cup sliced green onion**
½	**cup chopped white onion**
½	**cup chopped celery with a few leaves**
1	**large green pepper, cut in strips**

(Continued)

Ross' Jambalaya (continued)

sausage

1	garlic clove, minced
½	to 1 pound raw shrimp, peeled and deveined
2	dozen raw oysters
1	(16 ounce) can tomatoes, cut up or 1 pint home canned tomatoes
1	cup chicken broth
1	cup long grain uncooked rice
½	teaspoon salt
⅛	teaspoon cayenne pepper

1. In large skillet, melt butter. Saute both types of onion, celery, pepper and garlic in butter until tender.

2. Add shrimp and oysters and cook approximately 5 minutes.

3. Stir in tomatoes, broth, rice, salt and pepper.

4. Cover and cook 25-30 minutes over low heat until rice is done.

5. Enjoy. Enjoy.

Potato Fish Fry

Serves 3-4

One way to introduce fish to family members is to combine it with an often used food. In this recipe instant mashed potatoes are used as part of the coating, thus producing a fish and potato entree.

½	cup instant mashed potato flakes
2	tablespoons sesame seeds
1	egg, slightly beaten
1	tablespoon lemon juice
1	teaspoon salt
⅛	teaspoon ground pepper
1	pound frozen fish fillets, thawed (sole, orange roughy, cod, haddock, etc.)
2	tablespoons butter or margarine

1. In shallow dish, combine instant mashed potato flakes and sesame seeds.

2. In another shallow dish, combine egg, lemon juice, salt and pepper. Mix well.

3. Dip fish in egg mixture and then in potato flake sesame seed combination.

4. Melt butter in large skillet over medium heat; fry fish until golden brown on both sides.

5. Garnish with lemon wedges, if desired.

Oven Fried Fish Fillets

Serves 4

This fish recipe is so easy and so delicious that very soon you'll have the ingredients memorized. Use your favorite fish fillets, remembering that orange roughy and sole are two of the mildest choices.

1	pound orange roughy, sole, perch, cod or flounder fillets
1	tablespoon reduced-calorie mayonnaise
6	tablespoons fine dry bread crumbs
2	tablespoons minced fresh parsley
½	teaspoon paprika
	Lemon wedges for garnish, if desired

1. Coat fillets with mayonnaise.

2. On flat plate, combine bread crumbs, parsley and paprika. Dredge coated fillets in bread crumb mixture.

3. Arrange fillets on baking sheet lined with parchment paper or coated lightly with cooking spray.

4. Bake in preheated 450 degree oven for 12 minutes or until fillets flake easily with a fork.

5. Serve with lemon wedges.

Microwave

In step **2**, use whole wheat bread crumbs.
In step **3**, put coated fish fillets on microwave-safe platter.
In step **4**, microwave fish uncovered on 100% power 5-6 minutes, rotating dish halfway through cooking time.

Grilled Barbecued Shrimp

Serves 3-4

These mouth watering shrimp will put your next grilling experience in a class by itself. Marinated overnight, they would be equally spectacular served as the entree or offered during the appetizer course.

1	cup barbecue sauce
3	tablespoons lemon juice
1	tablespoon Worcestershire sauce
1	teaspoon dill weed
1	pound large fresh shrimp, peeled and deveined

(Continued)

Grilled Barbecued Shrimp (continued)

1. In 2 cup glass measurer, combine barbecue sauce, lemon juice, Worcestershire sauce and dill weed for marinade.

2. Pour over shrimp; cover and let stand at least 6 hours or overnight in the refrigerator, stirring occasionally.

3. Cook shrimp on fine wire grill or on cake rack on grill over hot coals about 6 to 8 minutes or till done, turning once and brushing often with marinade. Be careful not to over-cook.

4. Heat remaining marinade in small metal pan on edge of grill and serve with shrimp.

5. Enjoy. Enjoy.

Cashew Tuna Casserole

Serves 8

Here is a tuna casserole all dressed up for a special occasion. Whether it graces a summer poolside luncheon or is quickly carried off to a pot luck supper, you'll be glad Doris Schuring shared this recipe with me.

2 (6-½ ounce) cans water packed white albacore tuna, drained
1 (8 ounce) can sliced water chestnuts, drained
1 (16 ounce) can chop suey vegetables, drained
1 (16 ounce) can bean sprouts, drained
1 cup chopped celery
½ cup chopped onion
1 (5 ounce) can chow mein noodles (3 cups)
2 (10-¾ ounce) cans cream of chicken soup
½ cup salad dressing
½ teaspoon curry powder
½ teaspoon lemon juice
1 cup cashews, whole or broken

1. In large mixing bowl, combine tuna, water chestnuts, chop suey vegetables, bean sprouts, celery, onion and chow mein noodles.

2. In medium mixing bowl, combine chicken soup, salad dressing, curry and lemon juice. Stir well.

3. Add soup mixture to tuna and vegetables. Stir well to combine.

4. Pour into greased 2-½-quart casserole.

5. Top with cashews.

6. Cover and refrigerate up to 12 hours, if desired.

7. Uncover. Bake in preheated 350 degree oven 45-60 minutes, until hot and bubbly.

Grilled Scallop Kabobs

Serves 6

Whenever I see fresh scallops at the fish market, I think of kabobs because their size and shape are perfect for threading on a skewer. Add pineapple, mushrooms and green pepper with bacon for extra flavor and you have a first class grilling experience.

1	**pound scallops, fresh or frozen, thawed**
¼	**cup olive oil or vegetable oil**
⅛	**teaspoon garlic powder**
¼	**cup lemon juice**
¼	**cup finely chopped parsley**
¼	**cup soy sauce**
½	**teaspoon salt**
	Freshly ground pepper
1	**(20 ounce) can pineapple chunks, drained**
1	**(4 ounce) can button mushrooms, drained**
1	**green pepper, cut in 1-inch squares**
12	**slices bacon**

1. Rinse scallops with cold water to remove any pieces of shell; drain on paper towel. Cut large scallops into small pieces, if desired.

2. In large mixing bowl, combine oil, garlic powder, lemon juice, parsley, soy sauce, salt and pepper. Mix thoroughly.

3. Add scallops, pineapple chunks, mushrooms and green pepper pieces. Toss to coat ingredients with the marinade. Set aside at least 30 minutes, tossing several times.

4. Meanwhile, panbroil bacon until cooked but still soft. Cut the slices in half.

5. Using long thin skewers, thread each with a scallop, pineapple chunk, mushroom cap, green pepper piece and bacon piece; repeat to fill skewer.

6. Brush kabobs with some of the leftover marinade and place on grill about 4 inches from hot coals. (Kabobs could be broiled)

7. Cook until bacon is crisp and browned, 10-12 minutes. Turn kabobs several times while cooking and brush with the marinade.

Microwave

In step **4,** place bacon on microwave bacon rack and microwave on 100% power 6-8 minutes until bacon is slightly underdone.

Salmon/Rice Casserole

Serves 8

Casserole fans are always on the outlook for easy recipes that will perk up mundane menus. In this interesting combination, pink salmon takes the spotlight when teamed with rice and broccoli. Enjoy at home or carry to a potluck gathering.

1   (10-¾ ounce) can condensed cream of chicken soup
1   (15-½ ounce) can pink salmon, drain, flake; reserve liquid
2   teaspoons prepared mustard
½   to 1 teaspoon seasoned ground pepper
1   (10 ounce) package frozen chopped broccoli, thawed
3   cups cooked rice
1   cup (4 ounces) grated cheddar cheese
     Paprika

1. In small mixing bowl, combine soup and ½ cup salmon liquid, mustard and pepper.

2. In medium mixing bowl, toss together drained broccoli and rice. Stir in half the soup mixture.

3. Spoon rice mixture into buttered 2-quart shallow casserole.

4. Top with drained flaked salmon.

5. Pour remaining soup mixture over salmon; sprinkle with cheese. Dust with paprika.

6. Bake in preheated 350 degree oven for 25 minutes or until hot and bubbly.

Microwave

In step **3,** use microwave-safe casserole.
In step **5,** do not sprinkle with cheese and paprika.
In step **6,** microwave on 80% power 15-20 minutes until piping hot. Sprinkle with cheese and dust with paprika. Microwave 1-2 minutes more on 80% until cheese melts.

Marinated Shrimp Kabobs

Serves 4-6

These spectacular shrimp kabobs are light, elegant and easy. Calorie conscious friends and families will appreciate your trip to the fresh fish market as they savor each scrumptious morsel.

1	**pound large fresh shrimp**
1	**(8 ounce) can unsweetened pineapple chunks, undrained**
2	**tablespoons sesame oil**
2	**tablespoons soy sauce**
¼	**teaspoon white pepper**
⅛	**teaspoon garlic powder**
⅛	**teaspoon ground ginger**
12	**cherry tomatoes**
1	**green pepper, cut into 1-inch chunks**

1. Peel shrimp, leaving tails on; devein shrimp. Set aside.

2. Drain pineapple, reserving juice; set pineapple aside.

3. In shallow dish, combine reserved pineapple juice, sesame oil, soy sauce, white pepper, garlic powder and ground ginger. Mix well.

4. Add shrimp to marinade, tossing gently to coat. Cover and marinate at least 1 hour in the refrigerator, stirring occasionally.

5. Remove shrimp from marinade, reserving marinade.

6. Alternate cherry tomatoes, green pepper squares, pineapple chunks, and shrimp on kabob skewers.

7. Broil or grill 4 or 5 inches from heat 2 to 3 minutes on each side or until shrimp are done, basting frequently with marinade.

8. Serve over hot cooked rice, if desired.

Note: Sesame oil can be found at oriental food shops or in the oriental food section at the grocery store.

Turkey-Mushroom Salad

Serves 6

How fortunate we are that cooked turkey breast is available year round at the grocery store. In just a few minutes, this hearty salad can be created for a warm weather menu. Fresh mushrooms add just the right elegance to these delicious chunks of turkey.

(Continued)

Turkey-Mushroom Salad (continued)

2-½ cups cubed cooked turkey
1-½ cups sliced fresh mushrooms
1 cup chopped celery
2 tablespoons sliced stuffed green olives
⅓ cup mayonnaise or salad dressing
1 tablespoon lemon juice
1 teaspoon finely chopped onion
½ teaspoon salt

1. In large mixing bowl, combine cubed turkey, sliced mushrooms, celery and olives; toss together.

2. In small mixing bowl, blend together mayonnaise, lemon juice, onion and salt.

3. Add dressing to turkey mixture; mix lightly. Chill thoroughly.

4. Serve in bowl lined with fresh salad greens.

Fruited Chicken Salad

Serves 6

When it comes to main dish salads, I'm sure chicken is one of the most popular and well-liked. Microwave cooks will want to follow the directions on page 238 for an easy quick method to prepare the chicken. Then add the other interesting ingredients for an excellent entree.

3 cups cubed cooked chicken
1 cup diced celery
1 (11 ounce) can mandarin oranges, drained
1 (8 ounce) can pineapple tidbits, drained
½ cup toasted slivered almonds
¾ cup mayonnaise or salad dressing
½ teaspoon salt
¼ teaspoon marjoram leaves, crushed

1. In large mixing bowl, combine chicken, celery, oranges, pineapple and almonds. Chill well.

2. In small mixing bowl, blend together mayonnaise, salt and marjoram.

3. Add mayonnaise dressing to chicken mixture. Toss together lightly to coat all ingredients. Chill, if time permits.

4. Serve in an attractive serving dish, garnished with extra oranges, if desired.

Tuna Pockets

Serves 2-4

If you need a way to dress up tuna salad, just pop it in a pocket of pita bread and voila you've created a special sandwich. I usually use water packed tuna and reduced calorie salad dressing or mayonnaise to cut calories.

1   (6-½ ounce) can tuna, drained
2   tablespoons sliced green onion
2   tablespoons sweet pickle relish
¼   cup chopped celery
¼   cup salad dressing or mayonnaise
    Leaf lettuce
2   pita pockets

1. In small mixing bowl, combine drained tuna, green onion, pickle relish, celery and salad dressing.

2. Slice pita pockets in half; line with small piece of leaf lettuce and fill with tuna salad mixture.

3. Serve with ice cold glasses of milk.

Crab Salad

Serves 3-4

An attractive serving of this seafood salad would be a very tasteful luncheon entree. I like to present individual servings in crisp curved lettuce leaves garnished with hard cooked egg slices and ripe olives.

1   (6 ounce) can crab meat, well drained, flaked, with cartilage removed
½   cup sliced celery
2   tablespoons sliced ripe olives
1   tablespoon sliced green onion
¼   teaspoon salt
¼   teaspoon monosodium glutamate
    Dash pepper
⅓   cup mayonnaise or salad dressing
3   hard cooked eggs, sliced

1. In medium mixing bowl, combine crab, celery, olives, onion, salt, mono-sodium glutamate and pepper. Toss gently.

2. Fold in mayonnaise and two of the hard cooked eggs, reserving third egg for garnish. Chill.

3. Serve in crisp lettuce leaves garnished with egg slices and ripe olives.

Salad Bowl Puff

Serves 6

Cream puffs can be baked in many sizes and shapes. One of the easiest and most interesting ways is to create a bowl in which a salad or dessert mixture could be served. Believe me, you'll be glad you tried this suggestion.

½   cup water
¼   cup margarine or butter
½   cup flour
⅛   teaspoon salt
2   eggs
    Meat salad mixture like Ham Salad Filling found on page 90.

1. In medium saucepan, heat water and margarine to a rolling boil.

2. Stir in flour and salt. Stir vigorously over low heat until mixture forms a ball, about 30 seconds.

3. Remove from heat; cool 10 minutes, if time allows.

4. Beat in eggs, one at a time; beating mixture smooth each time.

5. Grease 9-inch pie plate. Spread dough evenly in pie plate, building up edge slightly.

6. Bake in preheated 400 degree oven 45-60 minutes until puffed and dry in the center. Cool.

7. Just before serving, fill with Ham Salad Filling or meat filling of your choice.

Ham Salad Filling

Serves 6

It's fun to serve this hearty salad in the cream puff salad bowl on page 89. However, it's just as delicious served in a crisp lettuce leaf. Use leftover ham or purchase just the amount of cooked ham that you need at the meat or delicatessen counter at the grocery store.

1   (10 ounce) package frozen green peas
2   cups cubed fully cooked smoked ham
1   cup shredded sharp Cheddar cheese
2   tablespoons chopped onion
¾   cup mayonnaise or salad dressing
1-½ teaspoons prepared mustard

   1. Rinse frozen peas under running cold water to separate; drain.

   2. In medium mixing bowl, combine peas, ham, cheese, onion, mayonnaise and mustard.

   3. Gently stir to combine.

   4. Cover and refrigerate at least 2 hours.

   5. Serve in salad bowl puff, if desired.

Dieter's Tuna Salad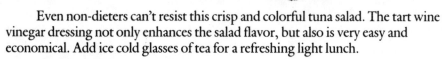

Serves 8

Even non-dieters can't resist this crisp and colorful tuna salad. The tart wine vinegar dressing not only enhances the salad flavor, but also is very easy and economical. Add ice cold glasses of tea for a refreshing light lunch.

¾   cup wine vinegar
2   teaspoons sugar
1-½ teaspoons dried basil leaves, crushed
     Dash of pepper
8   cups torn lettuce
2   (6-½ ounce) cans water-pack tuna, drained and flaked
1-½ cups cherry tomatoes, halved
½   medium onion, thinly sliced and separated into rings
1   medium cucumber, sliced
½   cup sliced celery

   1. In medium glass jar, combine vinegar, sugar, basil leaves and pepper. Shake until blended. Chill.

   2. In large salad bowl, toss together lettuce, tuna, cherry tomatoes, onion rings, cucumber and celery.

   3. Add chilled dressing; toss lightly.

   4. Bon Appetit.

Chicken Pecan Croissants

Serves 4

This lovely luncheon entree idea comes to me from my friend, Bev Hoffman, who lives in Vicksburg, Michigan. She adds a fresh fruit cup and lemon buttered asparagus spears to complete her "welcome to my home" menu.

1	**cup diced cooked chicken**
½	**cup chopped pecans**
½	**cup mayonnaise**
1-½	**cups finely shredded lettuce**
4	**croissants, warmed to freshen**

1. In medium mixing bowl, combine chicken, pecans and mayonnaise. Mix gently.

2. Just before serving, gently stir in lettuce.

3. Split croissants and fill with chicken filling.

4. Serve attractively on each guest's plate.

5. Enjoy the conversation.

Hero Sandwich

Serves 8

If you need a splashy sandwich for a poolside party, tailgate picnic or midnight snack, here is a great plan. Believe me, it will look like you have the talent of a great gourmet chef. Only you will know how very easy it is to put this hero together.

1   (14-inch) loaf Vienna or French Bread, unsliced
½   cup mayonnaise or salad dressing
1   tablespoon prepared mustard
1   teaspoon prepared horseradish
6-8 ounces thinly sliced Swiss Cheese
6-8 ounces thinly sliced turkey breast
6-8 ounces thinly sliced boiled ham
1   green pepper, thinly sliced
1   large tomato, thinly sliced
1   large sweet onion, thinly sliced
    Leaf lettuce leaves
    Alfalfa sprouts, if desired

1. Cut bread loaf in half lengthwise.

2. In small bowl, combine mayonnaise, mustard and horseradish. Spread bread slices with mayonnaise mixture.

3. Arrange slices of cheese, meat, green pepper, tomato, onion and lettuce on bottom half of loaf. Garnish with alfalfa sprouts, if desired.

4. Replace top half of loaf; secure with long toothpicks, if desired.

5. Wrap in aluminum foil and refrigerate until served. Slice diagonally and serve to happy guests.

Baked Chicken Sandwiches

Serves 8

This attractive hot sandwich idea came from the recipe file of my sister-in-law Betsey House. I'm sure you'll enjoy the tasty chicken mixture hidden inside these crispy tender triangles. Add crisp relishes, cold beverages and fruit topped sundaes for a wonderful quick meal.

1   (3 ounce) package cream cheese, softened
2   tablespoons milk
2   cups finely chopped cooked chicken (Use food processor)
½   teaspoon salt
¼   teaspoon ground pepper
2   (8 ounce) cans crescent dinner rolls
¼   cup butter or margarine, melted
½   cup crushed seasoned croutons

(Continued)

Baked Chicken Sandwiches (continued)

1. In medium mixing bowl, beat together cream cheese and milk until smooth.

2. Stir in chicken, salt and pepper.

3. Separate roll dough into triangles. Place 8 triangles on ungreased or parchment lined cookie sheet.

4. Divide chicken mixture equally on the 8 triangles. Spread chicken to within ½ inch of the edge of the dough.

5. Moisten dough edges with water. Place remaining 8 triangles on top of chicken. Press edges with finger tips or fork to seal.

6. Brush each sandwich with melted butter.

7. Sprinkle with crushed croutons.

8. Bake in preheated 350 degree oven 20-25 minutes until lightly browned.

Fresh Vegetable and Egg Salad Sandwiches

Serves 6

Fresh vegetables add quite a splash when teamed with the popular flavors of egg salad. Add whole wheat bread and crisp lettuce leaves for a sandwich to remember.

12 slices whole wheat bread, buttered
8   hard-cooked eggs, chopped
1   cup chopped fresh spinach
⅔   cup grated carrots
½   cup chopped celery
2   tablespoons finely chopped onion
1   tablespoon chopped pimiento
½   cup mayonnaise or salad dressing
1   teaspoon salt
¼   teaspoon white pepper
    Crisp lettuce leaves

1. Butter one side of each bread slice.

2. In medium mixing bowl, combine eggs, spinach, carrots, celery, onion, pimiento, mayonnaise, salt and pepper.

3. Divide salad mixture on six slices of bread and spread evenly to the edge.

4. Top with lettuce leaves and remaining bread slices, buttered side down.

5. Cut sandwiches in half or quarters for serving.

Monte Cristo Just For One

Serves 1

    Lots of times it is difficult to gear down to cooking for one or two after years of preparing meals for an entire family. Recipes designed for one can be very helpful. This delicious sandwich is easy to fix after a stop at the delicatessen or meat counter where you can specifically ask for just the desired amount of meat and cheese.

2	slices bread
1	slice Swiss cheese
1	slice boiled ham
1	slice cooked turkey breast
1	egg
1	tablespoon milk
1	teaspoon butter or margarine

1. Place cheese and meats between bread slices.

2. Beat egg with milk.

3. Melt butter in skillet over medium heat.

4. Dip sandwich in egg mixture to coat both sides.

5. Brown sandwich, pressing down with spatula after turning.

Cottage Cheese Topped Rice Cakes

Serves 6

    Open-faced sandwiches are a lovely light lunch entree. This recipe features caraway seasoned cottage cheese presented on a 100% all natural whole grain rice cake. Carry the cottage cheese, lettuce leaves and rice cakes separately to create this idea for lunch at the office.

1-½	cups small curd cream-style cottage cheese
½	cup diced celery
¼	cup shredded carrot
¼	cup chopped radish
½	teaspoon caraway seed
6	rice cakes
6	leaf lettuce leaves, washed and dried thoroughly

1. In small mixing bowl, mash cottage cheese with a fork.

2. Stir in celery, carrot, radish, and caraway seed. Chill.

3. At serving time, place a lettuce leaf on rice cake.

4. Put ⅓ cup cottage cheese mixture on top of each leaf.

5. Garnish with additional radish slices.

3

Accompaniments

Most folks have experienced a situation where supporting factors enhance the main event. That's also true in menus when interesting recipes are selected to accompany the entree. Thus, this chapter of marvelous ideas for breads, salads and vegetables was created.

Add snap to meals by keeping Potato Refrigerator Roll dough chilled ready to shape and bake. If time is short, why not opt for French Fried Onion Bread hot from the oven. Loaves of tasty quick breads like Pumpkin Date Bread can be stored in the freezer until needed.

Select a salad that fits into your meal preparation time schedule and compliments the menu. Remember that gelatin salads, like the Red Raspberry Ribbon Salad, add both delicious flavor and lovely color to the mealtime experience. There are occasions when a combination fruit idea such as Fruit Salad Extraordinaire or vegetable creation like low calorie Marinated Asparagus or tossed salad such as Romaine Walnut Toss will be the perfect selection.

Variety in vegetable recipes is one key to dynamic menus. Here is an interesting collection ranging from attractive Asparagus AuGratin to zesty Zucchini Julienne. Do stretch your vegetable repertoire by trying the Ratatouille, a wonderful vegetable stew mixture.

Contents

Coconut Bread

1 loaf

This delicious coconut filled quick bread provides an interesting flavor and color contrast when served with an assortment of home baked breads. Look in the spice section at the grocery store for coconut extract.

1-¼   cups flaked coconut
2-¾   cups flour
1   cup sugar
1   tablespoon plus 1 teaspoon baking powder
1   teaspoon salt
1   egg
1-½   cups milk
2   tablespoons vegetable oil
1   teaspoon coconut extract

1. Spread coconut in shallow baking pan. Toast coconut in preheated 350 degree oven 5-10 minutes, stirring occasionally for even toasting. Cool.

2. In large mixing bowl, sift together flour, sugar, baking powder and salt. Stir in toasted coconut. Make a well in center of mixture.

3. In medium bowl, beat together egg, milk, vegetable oil and coconut extract.

4. Add liquid ingredients to dry mixture, stirring just until moistened.

5. Spoon mixture into greased and floured or parchment lined 9x5x3 inch loaf pan.

6. Bake in preheated 350 degree oven for 1 hour or until wooden pick inserted in center comes out clean.

7. Cool in pan about 10 minutes. Remove from pan, and cool completely on a wire rack.

Apple/Granola Bread

1 loaf

Applesauce gets the credit for keeping this hearty quick bread moist, while granola adds an extra splash of good nutrition. Serve with chunks of cheese for a great after-school snack or spread with cream cheese for morning coffee.

1-¾	**cups flour**
⅔	**cup sugar**
2	**teaspoons baking powder**
½	**teaspoon baking soda**
1	**teaspoon salt**
1	**teaspoon ground cinnamon**
½	**teaspoon ground nutmeg**
½	**cup margarine or butter, chilled**
1	**cup granola cereal**
2	**eggs**
1	**cup applesauce**

1. In large mixing bowl, sift together flour, sugar, baking powder, soda, salt, cinnamon and nutmeg. Cut in chilled margarine with pastry blender or fork. Mixture should resemble coarse crumbs.

2. Stir in granola cereal.

3. In small mixing bowl beat eggs with rotary beater. Stir in applesauce.

4. Fold egg mixture into dry ingredients just until moistened.

5. Pour into greased and floured or parchment lined 8x4 inch baking pan.

6. Bake in preheated 350 degree oven 50-60 minutes or until inserted wooden pick comes out clean.

7. Remove from pan and cool on rack.

Zucchini-Carrot Bread

2 loaves

Zucchini and carrots are new found partners in this interesting quick bread. It would be a great idea to keep several loaves stored in the freezer for morning coffee breaks, after-school treats, or midnight snacks.

2-½ cups flour
1   teaspoon baking powder
1   teaspoon baking soda
1   teaspoon salt
1   tablespoon ground cinnamon
3   eggs
¾   cup vegetable oil
1-½ cups packed brown sugar
2   teaspoons vanilla extract
1   cup unpeeled shredded zucchini
1   cup shredded carrots
1   cup chopped pecans or walnuts
½   cup crushed bran flakes cereal

1. In medium mixing bowl, sift together flour, baking powder, soda, salt, and cinnamon. Set aside.

2. In large mixing bowl beat together eggs and oil. Stir in brown sugar and vanilla. Beat well. Stir in zucchini and carrots.

3. Add flour mixture to liquid ingredients, stirring just until moistened.

4. Stir in the pecans and cereal.

5. Pour batter into 2 greased and floured or parchment lined 8x4x3 inch baking pans.

6. Bake in preheated 350 degree oven for 1 hour or until a wooden pick inserted in center comes out clean.

7. Cool loaves 10 minutes in pans; remove to wire racks and cool completely.

Blueberry-Oatmeal Bread

1 loaf

If you'd like a change of pace from the usual blueberry bread recipe, try this moist oatmeal variation. It's a delicious snack when served with chunks of cheese and fresh fruit. This loaf slices best if allowed to "mellow" overnight before cutting.

2	**cups flour**
1	**cup quick cooking oats, uncooked**
½	**cup sugar**
1	**tablespoon baking powder**
½	**teaspoon baking soda**
½	**teaspoon salt**
½	**teaspoon ground cinnamon**
6	**tablespoons butter or margarine, softened**
2	**eggs**
1	**cup milk**
¼	**cup light corn syrup**
1	**cup fresh or frozen blueberries**

1. In large mixing bowl, combine flour, oats, sugar, baking powder, baking soda, salt and cinnamon.

2. Cut in butter with a pastry blender or fork until mixture resembles coarse crumbs.

3. In small mixing bowl, beat together eggs, milk and corn syrup.

4. Add milk mixture to dry ingredients, stirring just until moistened.

5. Fold in blueberries.

6. Pour batter into a well-greased and floured or parchment lined 9x5x3-inch baking pan.

7. Bake in preheated 350 degree oven for 1 hour and 10 minutes or until a wooden pick inserted in center comes out clean.

8. Cool loaf in pan 10 minutes; remove from pan, and cool completely on a wire rack.

Pumpkin Date Bread

1 loaf

My recipe files seem to have always contained a pumpkin bread recipe and a date bread recipe. Now I present to you a combination of the two flavors which I think is extraordinarily good. Our family likes this bread when served with a variety of natural cheese from a favorite cheese factory in Green County, Wisconsin.

½   cup butter or margarine, softened
1-½ cups sugar
2   eggs
1   cup pumpkin
⅓   cup water
1-⅔ cups flour
1   teaspoon baking soda
½   teaspoon baking powder
¾   teaspoon salt
½   teaspoon ground cinnamon
½   teaspoon ground cloves
1   cup dates, cut up
½   cup walnuts, chopped

1. In large mixing bowl, cream together butter and sugar. Add eggs, one at a time, beating well after each addition.

2. Stir in pumpkin and water.

3. Sift together flour, baking soda, baking powder, salt, cinnamon and cloves. Add dry ingredients to pumpkin mixture and stir just until moistened.

4. Gently add dates and walnuts.

5. Pour into greased and floured or parchment lined 9x5x3-inch loaf pan.

6. Bake in preheated 350 degree oven 60-70 minutes until inserted wooden pick comes out clean. Remove from pan and cool on rack.

Cranberry Banana Loaf

1 loaf

This festive quick bread blends the tangy flavor of cranberries with the mild taste of banana. Be sure to save time and energy by using your food processor to chop the cranberries and mash the bananas.

¾   **cup fresh or frozen cranberries, chopped**
1   **cup sugar, divided**
1   **teaspoon grated orange peel**
1-¾ **cups flour**
2   **teaspoons baking powder**
½   **teaspoon baking soda**
½   **teaspoon salt**
2   **eggs**
¾   **cup (2 small) mashed bananas**
⅓   **cup salad oil**
½   **cup chopped walnuts**

1. In small mixing bowl, combine cranberries, ½ cup of the sugar, and orange peel; set aside.

2. In large mixing bowl, sift together flour, remaining ½ cup sugar, baking powder, baking soda and salt.

3. In medium mixing bowl, combine eggs, bananas and oil; stir well with fork to combine.

4. Add banana mixture to dry ingredients, stirring just enough to moisten.

5. Stir in cranberry mixture and walnuts.

6. Pour into well greased and floured or parchment lined 9x5x3-inch loaf pan.

7. Bake in preheated 350 degree oven for 1 hour or until golden brown and inserted wooden pick comes out clean. Remove from pan and cool on rack.

Favorite Popovers

8-10 popovers

My friend, Nan Banks from Chetek, Wisconsin, makes these crusty pop-overs as a favorite after-school treat for her crew. Hot from the oven son Adam prefers them entirely plain while son Joshua and husband John smother their warm popovers with butter and jam.

4   eggs
2   cups milk
2   cups flour
1   teaspoon salt

1. In medium mixing bowl, beat eggs slightly with rotary beater.

2. Add milk, flour and salt to eggs. Beat just until smooth. DO NOT OVER BEAT.

3. Fill 8-12 well-greased popover cups or custard cups ¾ full of popover batter.

4. Bake 25 minutes in preheated 450 degree oven.

5. Reduce oven temperature to 350 degrees.

6. Bake 15-20 minutes longer or until a deep golden brown.

7. Immediately remove from pan onto cooling rack.

8. Serve hot.

Big Puffed Pancake

Serves 6

This impressive puffy pancake is not only quick and easy, but uses common ingredients usually found in most kitchens. Bake this rendition of a popover in a heavy skillet; then dust with powdered sugar, fill with fresh fruit, enjoy with jam, or drizzle with syrup.

4   eggs
1   cup flour
1   cup milk
1   tablespoon sugar
½   teaspoon ground cinnamon
¼   teaspoon salt
1-½ tablespoons butter or margarine
2   tablespoons sifted confectioners' sugar, if desired
½   teaspoon ground cinnamon, if desired

(Continued)

Big Puffed Pancake (continued)

1. In large mixing bowl, combine eggs, flour, milk, sugar, cinnamon and salt. Beat until smooth at medium-high speed of an electric mixer.

2. Place the batter in freezer while skillet is heating.

3. Place butter in a 10-inch oven-proof skillet (cast iron works best); place in preheated 425 degree oven for 4 minutes or until butter sizzles and skillet is hot.

4. Pour batter immediately into skillet.

5. Bake 27-30 minutes or until puffed and golden, do not open oven before pancake has baked at least 25 minutes.

6. Combine confectioners' sugar and cinnamon; sift over hot pancake, if desired.

7. Serve immediately.

Yogurt Waffles

Serves 4-6

Chuck full of good nutrition these crispy waffles will stick to your ribs all morning long. Top with fruit flavored yogurt or the traditional maple syrup. Extra waffles can be refrigerated or frozen and then heated in the toaster.

2   **eggs separated**
3   **teaspoons sugar**
1   **cup (8 ounces) plain yogurt**
1   **cup flour**
½   **cup wheat germ**
1   **teaspoon baking powder**
½   **teaspoon baking soda**
½   **teaspoon salt**
3   **tablespoons vegetable oil**

1. In small mixing bowl, beat egg whites until soft peaks form. Gradually add sugar, one teaspoon at a time, beating until stiff peaks form. Set aside.

2. In large mixing bowl, combine egg yolks, yogurt, flour, wheat germ, baking powder, baking soda, salt and oil; beat until smooth.

3. Fold one-fourth of egg whites into egg yolk mixture until blended; fold remaining whites into yolk mixture, blending well.

4. Cook in waffle iron according to manufacturer's instructions. Serve hot.

Angel Biscuits

2 dozen biscuits

"These biscuits make such lovely dinner rolls you will rate hugs and kisses from the whole family," wrote Mae Saunders when she gave me this recipe. I'm so glad she shared this part of her southern heritage with me for now my midwest family often requests those wonderful "angel rolls". Little do they know how efficient I can be when the dough is already in the refrigerator.

¼ **cup warm water (110-115 degrees)**
1 **package active dry yeast**
2-½ **cups flour**
2 **tablespoons sugar**
1 **teaspoon baking powder**
½ **teaspoon baking soda**
1 **teaspoon salt**
½ **cup vegetable shortening**
1 **cup buttermilk**

1. In 1 cup glass measurer, add yeast to warm water. Stir to dissolve.

2. In large mixing bowl, combine flour, sugar, baking powder, soda and salt.

3. Cut in shortening with pastry blender or fork until mixture resembles coarse crumbs. (Use food processor, if you wish.)

4. Add dissolved yeast and buttermilk. Thoroughly combine.

5. Refrigerate dough well covered up to 3 days, if desired.

6. Dough may be rolled immediately, if desired.

7. Roll dough ¼ to ½ inch thick on lightly floured surface.

8. Cut with biscuit cutter and place on greased or parchment lined baking sheet. Cover with oiled plastic wrap.

9. Let dough rise in a warm place for a short period of time. If dough is chilled, allow a little longer time.

10. Remove plastic wrap. Bake in preheated 400 degree oven 12-15 minutes until lightly browned.

Mini-Chocolate Chip Muffins

1 dozen muffins

If you'd like to add a very special ingredient to an otherwise plain batch of muffins, then try adding mini-chocolate chips. Chocolate lovers will appreciate your thoughtfulness.

(Continued)

Mini-Chocolate Chip Muffins (continued)

1-½ cups flour
½ cup sugar
3 teaspoons baking powder
¼ teaspoon salt
1 cup miniature chocolate chips
1 cup milk
⅓ cup melted butter or margarine, melted
1 egg

1. In large mixing bowl, sift together flour, sugar, baking powder and salt. Add chocolate chips.

2. Beat together milk, melted butter and egg with rotary beater.

3. Add liquid ingredients to flour mixture. Stir just to combine. Do NOT over stir.

4. Put into lightly greased or paper lined muffin cups.

5. Bake in preheated 375 degree oven for about 20 minutes until lightly browned.

Orange Granola Muffins

1 dozen muffins

These hearty nutritious muffins are a great way to start the day full of vim and vigor. If there are some extras, the moist wholesome qualities of these muffins make them a good lunch box choice.

1-½ cups flour
1-½ cups granola-style cereal
½ cup sugar
1 teaspoon baking soda
½ teaspoon salt
½ cup orange juice
2 eggs
½ cup butter or margarine, melted
1 teaspoon grated orange peel

1. In medium mixing bowl, combine flour, cereal, sugar, soda and salt.

2. In small mixing bowl, beat together with rotary beater orange juice, eggs and melted butter. Stir in orange peel.

3. Add liquid ingredients to dry ingredients. Stir just enough to moisten.

4. Fill 12 greased muffin cups ⅔ full.

5. Bake for 15-20 minutes in preheated 375 degree oven until light golden brown.

Fresh Lemon Muffins

1 dozen muffins

When your menu calls for an interesting light bread product, let me suggest these mouthwatering lemon muffins. Tucked in a cloth lined roll basket, these lemon jewels will please even your most discriminating guest.

½   cup butter or margarine, softened
½   cup sugar
2   egg yolks
1   cup flour
1   teaspoon baking powder
¼   teaspoon salt
3   tablespoons lemon juice
2   egg whites
1   tablespoon grated lemon peel
2   tablespoons sugar
¼   teaspoon ground cinnamon

1. Cream together butter or margarine and ½ cup sugar. Beat until light and fluffy.

2. Beat in egg yolks.

3. Sift together flour, baking powder and salt.

4. Add dry ingredients alternately with lemon juice, mixing just until combined.

5. Beat egg whites until stiff; gently stir in lemon peel.

6. Fold egg whites with lemon peel into muffin mixture.

7. Spoon batter into well greased muffin tins, filling three-fourths full.

8. In small mixing bowl, combine 2 tablespoons sugar and cinnamon. Sprinkle top of each muffin with ½ teaspoon cinnamon-sugar mixture.

9. Bake in preheated 375 degree oven 20-25 minutes or until done.

Pecan Cinnamon Muffins

1 dozen muffins

Muffins are just as delicious for lunch or supper as they are for breakfast. Tuck this tasty recipe idea in the back of your mind for the next time you need a quick homemade bread product. You'll be glad you did.

1-½   cups flour
¼   cup sugar
2   teaspoons baking powder
½   teaspoon salt

(Continued)

Pecan Cinnamon Muffins (continued)

½   **teaspoon ground cinnamon**
¼   **cup brown sugar**
1   **egg**
⅓   **cup salad oil**
½   **cup milk**
½   **cup chopped pecans**

1. In large mixing bowl, sift together flour, sugar, baking powder, salt and cinnamon. Stir in brown sugar.

2. In medium mixing bowl, beat together egg, salad oil, and milk.

3. Add liquid ingredients all at once to dry ingredients, stirring just until flour begins to disappear. Gently stir in pecans.

4. Spoon batter into greased or paper lined muffin cups, filling ⅔ full.

5. Bake in preheated 400 degree oven 20 minutes or until golden brown.

6. Remove from pans and serve warm.

Golden Corn Bread

Serves 6-8

Hot corn bread can add pizazz to many entrees. It takes just a matter of minutes to combine these ingredients and pop them in the oven. Serve with generous amounts of butter and honey.

1-½ **cups yellow cornmeal**
½   **cup flour**
4   **teaspoons baking powder**
½   **teaspoon salt**
1   **egg**
⅓   **cup honey**
¼   **cup melted butter or margarine, cooled**
⅔   **cup milk**

1. In large mixing bowl, combine cornmeal, flour, baking powder and salt.

2. In medium mixing bowl, beat together egg and honey. Add melted butter and milk. Beat together.

3. Pour the liquid ingredients into the dry ones and stir to blend. Do not beat.

4. Pour batter into greased and floured 8-inch square baking pan.

5. Bake in preheated 375 degree oven for 20-25 minutes.

6. Remove from oven and serve hot.

Banana Coffee Cake

One 10-inch cake

When it's your turn to take a coffee cake to the office for someone's birthday, here's a great recipe. Subtly seasoned with yummy mellow bananas, this moist cake will be enjoyed all day, unless it's totally devoured in the morning.

½   cup butter or margarine, softened
1   (8 ounce) package cream cheese, softened
1-¼ cups sugar
2   eggs
1   cup mashed banana
1   teaspoon vanilla
2-¼ cups flour
1-½ teaspoons baking powder
½   teaspoon baking soda
¼   teaspoon salt
¾   cup chopped pecans
2   tablespoons sugar
1   teaspoon ground cinnamon

1. In large mixing bowl, cream butter and cream cheese together. Gradually add 1-¼ cups sugar, beating until light and fluffy.

2. Add eggs, one at a time, beating well after each addition.

3. Stir in bananas and vanilla.

4. Sift together flour, baking powder, baking soda and salt; gradually add to banana mixture, stirring well.

5. In small bowl, combine pecans, 2 tablespoons sugar and cinnamon; stir half of pecan mixture into batter.

6. Pour half of batter into well greased and floured 10-inch bundt pan; sprinkle with remaining nut mixture.

7. Pour remaining batter into pan.

8. Bake in preheated 350 degree oven 40-45 minutes or until wooden pick inserted in center comes out clean. Cool in pan 10 minutes.

9. Remove from pan; cool on rack. Sprinkle with confectioners' sugar.

Overnight Cinnamon Coffee Cake

Serves 15

What a great morning it will be when you transfer this coffee cake from the refrigerator to the oven for baking. Family and friends are certain to enjoy hot homemade coffee cake and only you will know the secret of night before preparation.

¾   cup butter or margarine, softened
1   cup sugar
2   eggs
1   cup (8 ounces) cultured sour cream
2   cups flour
1   teaspoon baking powder
1   teaspoon baking soda
½   teaspoon salt
1   teaspoon ground nutmeg
¾   cup firmly packed brown sugar
½   cup chopped walnuts
1   teaspoon ground cinnamon

1. In large mixing bowl, cream together butter and sugar until light and fluffy.

2. Add eggs, one at a time, beating after each addition.

3. Beat in sour cream.

4. Sift together flour, baking powder, soda, salt and nutmeg. Add to creamed mixture and mix well.

5. Pour batter into greased and floured 9x13-inch baking pan.

6. Combine brown sugar, walnuts and cinnamon; mix well, and sprinkle over batter. Cover and chill overnight.

7. Uncover and bake in preheated 350 degree oven for 35-40 minutes or until inserted wooden pick comes out clean.

Almond-Blueberry Coffee Cake

Serves 12

Toasted almonds add a wonderful flavor dimension to this tasty blueberry coffee cake. To toast almonds, just spread them on a shallow pan, bake uncovered in a 350 degree oven, stirring frequently, until delicately browned, 6-10 minutes. Watch carefully to avoid burning.

¾   **cup butter or margarine, softened**
1   **cup sugar**
4   **eggs**
2   **teaspoons lemon juice**
1-¾ **cups flour**
2   **teaspoons baking powder**
¼   **teaspoon salt**
2   **cups fresh or frozen blueberries**
2   **teaspoons lemon juice**

Almond Topping:
1   **cup flour**
¼   **cup sugar**
½   **cup slivered almonds, toasted**
¼   **cup butter or margarine**

1. In a large mixing bowl, cream together butter and sugar until light and fluffy. Add eggs, one a time, beating well after each addition. Stir in 2 teaspoons lemon juice.

2. Sift together flour, baking powder and salt. Add to creamed mixture and mix well.

3. Spread batter evenly in a greased and floured 9x13-inch baking pan; sprinkle with blueberries and 2 teaspoons lemon juice.

4. For topping, combine flour, sugar and almonds; cut in butter until mixture resembles coarse crumbs.

5. Sprinkle almond topping on blueberries.

6. Bake in preheated 325 degree oven for 40-45 minutes or until lightly browned.

Banana-Blueberry Bread

1 loaf

If your quick bread repertoire needs a suggestion, try this nice flavor combination. It doesn't take long to pop this loaf in the oven, especially if you use a food processor to mash the bananas.

½   **cup shortening**
1   **cup sugar**
2   **eggs**
1   **cup mashed bananas**
½   **cup quick cooking oats**
½   **cup chopped pecans or walnuts**
1-½ **cups flour**
1   **teaspoon baking soda**
¼   **teaspoon salt**
½   **cup fresh or frozen blueberries**

1. In large mixing bowl, cream shortening and sugar, beating until light and fluffy.

2. Add eggs, one at a time, beating well after each addition. Stir in bananas.

3. In medium mixing bowl, combine oats, pecans, flour, soda, salt and blueberries, stirring gently.

4. Add blueberry mixture to creamed mixture; stir just until moistened.

5. Pour into well greased and floured or parchment lined 9x5x3-inch baking pan.

6. Bake in preheated 350 degree oven for 50-55 minutes or until wooden pick inserted in center comes out clean.

7. Cool in pan 10 minutes; remove from pan, and cool completely on a wire rack.

Whole Wheat Yeast Rolls

Makes 3 dozen

Instant mashed potato flakes are the surprise convenient ingredient in these wonderful moist yeast rolls. Actually the starch in potatoes helps to feed the yeast and causes the cells to multiply quickly. Potatoes also act as a natural preservative in yeast dough.

2	packages active dry yeast
½	cup lukewarm water (110 degrees)
1	cup milk, scalded
⅓	cup butter or margarine, softened
1	cup instant potato flakes
½	cup brown sugar
1	teaspoon salt
2	eggs
2	cups stirred whole-wheat flour
2	cups flour
1	egg yolk
1	tablespoon water

1. In 1 cup glass measurer, dissolve yeast in lukewarm water.

2. In large mixing bowl, combine milk, butter, potato flakes, brown sugar and salt. Cool mixture to lukewarm.

3. Add yeast mixture, eggs, and whole-wheat flour to milk mixture. Beat until smooth, using electric mixer.

4. Stir in enough of the flour to make a soft dough.

5. Knead on floured surface until smooth and elastic.

6. Place in greased bowl. Cover with greased plastic wrap. Let rise in warm place until doubled, about 1 hour.

7. Punch dough down. Make pan rolls by shaping dough into 2-inch balls and placing them in well greased baking pans. Balls should just barely touch each other in baking pan.

8. Cover shaped rolls with greased plastic wrap and let rise until double in bulk.

9. In small dish, combine egg yolk and 1 tablespoon water. Brush egg mixture on rolls just before baking.

10. Bake rolls in preheated 375 degree oven 15-20 minutes until golden brown.

11. Remove rolls from pan and cool on rack.

Dark Rye Bread

2 loaves

If you're in the mood for a wonderful sampling of "old world" flavor, then bake this yeast bread. Unsweetened cocoa powder assures the deep dark color while the addition of molasses and caraway seeds adds to the great taste.

3	**cups flour**
¼	**cup unsweetened cocoa powder**
2	**packages active dry yeast**
1	**tablespoon caraway seed**
2	**cups water**
½	**cup molasses**
2	**tablespoons butter or margarine, softened**
1	**tablespoon sugar**
1	**tablespoon salt**
3	**to 3-½ cups rye flour**

1. In large mixing bowl, combine flour, cocoa, yeast and caraway seeds.

2. In medium saucepan, heat water, molasses, butter, sugar and salt until warm (115-120 degrees)

3. Add heated liquid to flour mixture. Beat on low speed of electric mixer for ½ minute, scraping sides of bowl.

4. Beat mixture with electric mixer on high speed for 3 minutes.

5. By hand, stir in enough rye flour to make a soft dough.

6. Turn dough out onto floured surface. Knead until smooth.

7. Put in large greased bowl. Cover with oiled plastic wrap.

8. Let rise in warm draft-free place until double in bulk.

9. Punch down dough, divide dough in half. Shape into two round loaves.

10. Place loaves on opposite corners of a large greased or parchment lined baking sheet. Slash top of loaves two or three times with sharp knife.

11. Cover with oiled plastic wrap. Let rise in warm place until double.

12. Bake in preheated 375 degree oven 40-45 minutes, until loaves sound hollow when tapped. Cool on wire rack.

114

Low-Sodium Refrigerator Rolls

3 dozen rolls with about 4 milligrams of sodium per roll

When these rolls were taste tested in a Cooking Light class which I taught, we found that even those students who were not searching for low sodium recipes liked these easy to make rolls. There is something magical about homemade yeast rolls...no one can resist them.

2   **packages dry yeast**
¼   **cup warm water (105-115 degrees)**
1   **tablespoon sugar**
1   **cup boiling water**
¾   **cup vegetable shortening**
¾   **cup cold water**
¼   **cup sugar**
2   **eggs**
6   **cups flour**

1. Dissolve yeast in warm water; add 1 tablespoon sugar and set aside.

2. Pour boiling water over shortening in a large bowl, stirring to melt shortening. Stir in cold water and ¼ cup sugar. Add eggs and dissolved yeast mixture. Beat with electric mixer until well combined.

3. Add 3 cups flour. Beat until smooth with electric mixer. Using a wooden spoon, gradually stir in remaining 3 cups flour, mixing well.

4. Put dough in clean greased bowl; cover and chill well.

5. Turn dough out onto a lightly floured surface and knead 2 or 3 minutes.

6. Shape into 1-½ inch balls and place in greased baking pan or on parchment lined or greased baking sheets. Cover with oiled plastic wrap.

7. Let rise in warm place until double in bulk.

8. Bake rolls in preheated 400 degree oven for 20-25 minutes or until lightly browned.

9. Remove from baking pan and brush with unsalted margarine. Cool on rack.

Potato Refrigerator Rolls

3 dozen rolls

   Refrigerated yeast doughs are perfectly designed for the busy cook who would like hot fresh rolls straight from the oven, but doesn't have three or four consecutive hours in the kitchen. With this method roll dough can be mixed up, refrigerated, shaped and baked at your convenience.

1	**package active dry yeast**
1-½	**cups warm water (105 to 115 degrees)**
⅔	**cup sugar**
1-½	**teaspoons salt**
⅔	**cup vegetable oil**
2	**eggs**
1	**cup lukewarm mashed potatoes (2 servings of instant mashed potatoes)**
7	**to 7-½ cups flour**

1. In large mixing bowl, dissolve yeast in warm water. Stir in sugar, salt, oil, eggs and potatoes. Beat to combine.

2. Add 4 cups flour. Beat until smooth.

3. Mix in enough remaining flour to make dough easy to handle.

4. Turn dough onto lightly floured surface; knead until smooth and elastic, about 5 minutes.

5. Place in greased bowl; turn greased side up. Cover bowl tightly; refrigerate at least 8 hours but no longer than 5 days.

6. Punch dough down. Form in desired shapes. Cover with greased plastic wrap. Let rise until double in size. Gently remove plastic wrap.

7. Bake in preheated 400 degree oven 15-25 minutes until golden brown.

Note: Here are easy directions for two possible roll shapes:

Cloverleaf Rolls: Shape bits of dough into 1-inch balls. Place 3 balls in each greased muffin cup.

Crescents: Roll dough into 12-inch circle, about ¼-inch thick. Spread with softened butter. Cut into 16 wedges. Roll up beginning at rounded edge. Place rolls with point underneath on greased or parchment lined baking sheet.

Orange-Carrot Yeast Bread

2 loaves

Those of us that enjoy making a good loaf of yeast bread are always looking for interesting new recipes. Here is a creative flavor suggestion featuring an orange-carrot combination complete with tasty raisins. As with many breads, it is delicious when toasted.

2	packages dry yeast
1	cup warm water (110-115 degrees)
2	tablespoons sugar
2	teaspoons salt
½	teaspoon ground cinnamon
¼	teaspoon ground nutmeg
¼	teaspoon ground allspice
1	egg
3	tablespoons butter or margarine, softened
⅔	cup lukewarm orange juice
2	tablespoons grated orange peel
6	to 6-½ cups flour, divided
1	cup seedless raisins
1-½	cups grated carrots, at room temperature

1. In large mixing bowl, sprinkle yeast on warm water, stir until dissolved.

2. Add sugar, salt, cinnamon, nutmeg, allspice, egg, butter, orange juice and orange peel. Beat with electric mixer to thoroughly combine.

3. Stir in 3 cups of the flour. Beat until smooth.

4. Add raisins and carrots, blend well.

5. Gradually add enough remaining flour to make a soft dough. Turn out on lightly floured board or pastry cloth. Knead until smooth.

6. Place dough in greased bowl, turning to grease top. Cover with greased plastic wrap and let rise in warm place until double in bulk.

7. Divide dough in half; shape each half into a loaf.

8. Place each loaf in well greased 9x5x3-inch baking pan.

9. Cover with greased plastic wrap; let rise in warm place until double in bulk.

10. Bake in preheated 400 degree oven about 35-40 minutes or until done.

11. Remove from pans, cool on racks.

English Muffin Loaves

2 loaves

Here is one dynamite recipe. Just think, home baked bread with a plan so easy that the dough goes straight from the mixing bowl to the prepared baking pan. Just look, there are no eggs or shortening for those on restricted diets. Savor this delicious bread which tastes even better toasted.

6	cups flour, divided
2	packages dry yeast
1	tablespoon sugar
1-½	teaspoons salt
¼	teaspoon baking soda
2	cups milk
½	cup water
	Cornmeal

1. In large mixing bowl, combine 3 cups flour, yeast, sugar, salt and soda. Stir to combine.

2. In small saucepan, combine milk and water. Heat until very warm (120-130 degrees).

3. Gradually add milk mixture to dry ingredients, mixing on low speed of electric mixer 2 to 3 minutes.

4. Stir in the remaining 3 cups of flour to make a soft dough.

5. Turn dough out onto lightly floured surface. Form into a smooth ball and divide in half. Shape each half into a loaf.

6. Grease two 8x4-inch baking pans, sprinkle bottom and sides with cornmeal.

7. Place dough into prepared pans and sprinkle tops with cornmeal.

8. Cover with oiled plastic wrap and let rise in warm place until double in bulk, about 45-60 minutes.

9. Bake in preheated 400 degree oven 25 minutes.

10. Remove from pan and cool on rack.

Microwave

In step **2**, put milk and water in 1-quart microwave-safe measurer. Probe to 120 degrees.

Italian Breadsticks

3 dozen breadsticks

Homemade breadsticks can lift an ordinary meal into a special event. Just follow these easy directions for an outstanding bread product. It's lots of fun when family members join in the breadstick shaping procedure.

1	**package active dry yeast**
⅔	**cup warm water (105-115 degrees)**
1	**tablespoon sugar**
1	**teaspoon salt**
¼	**cup vegetable oil**
2	**to 2-¼ cups flour**
	Vegetable oil
1	**egg white**
1	**tablespoon water**
	Toasted sesame seed or poppy seed, if desired

1. Dissolve yeast in warm water in large mixing bowl.

2. Stir in sugar, salt, ¼ cup oil and 1 cup of the flour. Beat until smooth.

3. Mix in enough remaining flour to make dough easy to handle.

4. Turn dough onto lightly floured surface; knead until smooth and elastic.

5. Divide dough in half. Divide each half in thirds. Divide each third into six small pieces of dough. Roll each piece into a rope 6-8 inches long.

6. Place about 1-inch apart on a parchment lined or greased cookie sheet.

7. Brush each piece with oil. Cover with plastic wrap; let rise in warm place about 20-30 minutes.

8. Preheat oven to 350 degrees. Beat egg white and 1 tablespoon water slightly; brush over breadsticks and sprinkle with sesame seed or poppy seed, if desired.

9. Bake until golden brown, about 20-25 minutes.

Easy Overnight Caramel Rolls

Serves 10-12

When family and friends bite into these luscious rolls, no one will ever guess that you started with two loaves of frozen bread dough. All of the preparation is done the night before so that the morning is free for you to receive compliments on your baking skills.

2	**(1 pound) loaves frozen bread dough, thawed**
1	**cup firmly packed brown sugar**
1	**(4-¾ ounce) package regular vanilla pudding and pie filling mix**

(Continued)

Easy Overnight Caramel Rolls (continued)

½   **cup butter or margarine, melted**
¼   **cup milk**
1   **cup chopped pecans or walnuts, divided**

1. Thoroughly grease a 9x13x2-inch baking pan.

2. Cut 1 loaf of dough into small pieces; place dough pieces in greased pan.

3. In small bowl, combine brown sugar, pudding mix, butter and milk; mix well.

4. Drizzle half of the brown sugar mixture over dough pieces; sprinkle with ½ cup nuts.

5. Cut remaining loaf of dough into small pieces; place dough pieces over first layer.

6. Drizzle remaining brown sugar mixture over dough pieces; sprinkle with remaining nuts.

7. Cover and refrigerate several hours or overnight.

8. Uncover. Bake in preheated 325 degree oven 50-60 minutes until golden brown.

9. Immediately invert pan on heat-proof serving tray. Let pan remain a minute so caramel drizzles over rolls.

10. Serve with pride and pleasure.

Herb Buttered Bread

Serves 8-10

Everyone seems to enjoy slices of hot buttered bread seasoned with herbs. When busy families gather, have the seasoned butter, bread and serrated knife waiting for the first person that utters, "What can I do to help?"

½   **cup butter or margarine, softened**
½   **teaspoon Worcestershire sauce**
½   **teaspoon dried basil leaves, crushed**
½   **teaspoon dried marjoram leaves, crushed**
1   **(16 ounce) loaf French or Vienna Bread**

1. In small mixing bowl, combine butter, Worcestershire sauce, crushed basil and marjoram.

2. With serrated knife, slice bread into slices as thick or thin as desired.

3. Spread one side of each slice with butter mixture.

4. Place buttered slices on aluminum foil to reshape the loaf. Wrap tightly.

5. Bake in preheated 350 degree oven 15-20 minutes.

Hot Garlic Bread

Serves as many as desired

This is a "guideline" recipe for wonderful hot garlic bread. I've included a specific plan for storing loaves in the freezer to use at your convenience. One word of caution: even mini-appetites have been known to devour several pieces. Yum. Yum.

Garlic butter
Loaf of Italian or French bread
Dried basil leaves
Paprika
Olive or vegetable oil

1. In small mixing bowl, blend softened butter or margarine with minced garlic or garlic powder, using the guideline of 1 clove minced garlic or ⅛ teaspoon garlic powder per ½ cup butter or margarine.

2. Slice bread in half lengthwise with serrated knife.

3. Spread butter/garlic mixture on both cut sides of bread. Sprinkle lightly with basil, then paprika.

4. Close up loaf. Brush outside of loaf lightly with oil.

5. Wrap loaves in foil and bake in preheated 350 degree oven about 20 minutes or until inside of bread is hot.

6. For an informal atmosphere, allow guests to rip off hunks according to appetite.

Freezer Directions:

1. Wrap loaves in a double thickness of aluminum foil; seal completely and fit back into the plastic bag the bread came in when purchased. Freeze.

2. When ready to bake, remove bread from plastic bag.

3. Bake frozen loaves in preheated 350 degree oven about 30 minutes. Remove foil and raise temperature to 375 degrees. Return bread to oven for a few minutes to crisp.

French Fried Onion French Bread

Serves 8

Hot loaves of this crispy onion flavored bread are certain to be favorite fare at casual suppers and picnics. Remember that the food processor would be glad to do the onion crushing work.

1   (16 ounce) loaf French bread
½   cup butter or margarine, softened
1   (2.8 ounce) can French fried onions, crushed

1. Slice French bread horizontally.

2. In small mixing bowl, mix together softened butter and crushed onions.

3. Generously butter slices of bread.

4. Wrap loaf in foil.

5. Bake in preheated 350 degree oven for 15 or 20 minutes.

Microwave

In step **4,** wrap bread in cloth or paper napkin. Place in wicker basket, without staples.
In step **5,** microwave at 50% power 2-3 minutes until warm, rotating basket once.

Delicious Pumpernickel

Serves 8-12

One of my favorite ways to serve bakery bread is to cut it in thick slices, spread with seasoned butter, wrap in foil and heat until hot. In this recipe, I've selected delicious pumpernickel that will add interest, flair and flavor to any menu.

1   (16 ounce) loaf pumpernickel bread
½   cup butter or margarine, softened
1   tablespoon prepared mustard
½   cup grated Parmesan cheese
¼   cup snipped fresh parsley

1. Cut pumpernickel bread in ½-inch thick slices.

2. In small mixing bowl, mix butter, mustard, Parmesan cheese and parsley until well blended.

3. Spread slices with butter mixture.

4. Wrap well in heavy duty foil.

5. Heat in preheated 350 degree oven for 15-20 minutes.

6. Serve hot.

Red Raspberry Ribbon Salad

Serves 9

This bright red delicious salad would be lovely for a Christmas menu or equally attractive to honor St. Valentine. In fact, it has been known to draw rave reviews at other times of year too.

2   (3 ounce) packages raspberry flavored gelatin
1-½ cups boiling water
1   (10 ounce) package frozen red raspberries
1   (20 ounce) can crushed pineapple packed in juice, undrained
1   cup cultured sour cream

1. In large mixing bowl, dissolve gelatin in boiling water.

2. Add frozen raspberries; stir until thawed.

3. Stir in undrained pineapple.

4. Pour about ½ of the gelatin mixture (2-½ cups) into 8-inch square pan; refrigerate 30-45 minutes or until set.

5. Carefully spread sour cream over gelatin; spoon remaining gelatin mixture over sour cream.

6. Refrigerate at least 2 hours or until firm.

7. Cut into squares and serve attractively on lettuce leaves.

Pineapple-Rhubarb Beauty

Serves 8-10

Please don't overlook the possibility of including rhubarb in gelatin salads. All the rhubarb needs is a pleasing partner like pineapple. Bind the two flavors together with cherry gelatin for a lovely salad experience.

2   cups (1-inch slices) fresh or frozen rhubarb
½   cup water
⅓   cup sugar
1   (20 ounce) can pineapple tidbits packed in juice
2   (3 ounce) packages cherry flavored gelatin
1   cup water
1   tablespoon lemon juice
½   cup broken pecans

1. In medium saucepan, combine rhubarb, water and sugar. Cover and cook just till tender, about 5 minutes, drain thoroughly, reserving syrup.

2. Drain pineapple, reserving juice.

3. Measure combined rhubarb syrup and pineapple juice. Add water to make 2-½ cups liquid.

(Continued)

Pineapple-Rhubarb Beauty (continued)

4. Bring liquid to boiling; add gelatin and stir to dissolve. Add 1 cup water and lemon juice. Cool. Chill until partially set.

5. Fold in rhubarb, pineapple and pecans; pour into oiled 6-cup mold or attractive serving dish.

6. Garnish with salad greens. Serve with mayonnaise, if desired

Microwave

In step **1,** combine rhubarb, water and sugar in 2-quart microwave-safe measurer. Microwave on 100% power 4-6 minutes until tender, stirring twice.
In step **4,** microwave liquid in 2-quart microwave-safe measurer for 3-4 minute at 100% power.

Hawaiian Slaw

Serves 6-8

It's easy to forget that we can create a molded salad using unflavored gelatin as well as commercial flavored gelatins. It really works well as you can see in this delicious orange flavored salad. The benefit is a fresh-additive free combination packed with good nutrition.

2	**envelopes unflavored gelatin**
3	**cups unsweetened orange juice, divided**
1	**tablespoon lemon juice**
1	**(8 ounce) can crushed pineapple, undrained**
½	**cup grated carrot (about 1 carrot)**
1	**cup finely shredded cabbage**

1. In small saucepan, soften gelatin in 1 cup orange juice for a few minutes.

2. Heat over low heat until gelatin dissolves, stirring constantly.

3. Pour into large mixing bowl. Add remaining 2 cups orange juice and lemon juice.

4. Chill until slightly thickened.

5. Fold in undrained pineapple, carrot and cabbage. Blend thoroughly.

6. Pour into pretty serving dish or 8 cup oiled mold. Chill until firm.

7. Garnish with carrot curls before serving, if desired.

Microwave

In step **1,** soften gelatin in 1 cup orange juice in microwave-safe 2-quart measurer.
In step **2,** microwave on 100% power 2-3 minutes, stirring halfway through cooking time.
In step **3,** add remaining 2 cups orange juice and lemon juice to gelatin mixture.

124

Orange Almond Salad

Serves 6

Thanks to just one tablespoon of ketchup and vinegar, this everyday gelatin is changed into a first class molded salad. It would be a delicious and pretty addition to any menu.

2	(11 ounce) cans mandarin oranges
1	(3 ounce) package lemon flavored gelatin
1	tablespoon vinegar
1	tablespoon ketchup
½	cup slivered blanched almonds

1. Drain oranges, reserving liquid.

2. Add enough water to orange liquid to make 2 cups.

3. Heat half of the orange water to boiling.

4. Dissolve gelatin in hot liquid. Add remaining liquid.

5. Stir in vinegar and ketchup until evenly combined.

6. Chill until mixture is partially thickened.

7. Fold orange segments and almonds into gelatin mixture.

8. Pour into an oiled 1 quart mold or an 8x8x2 inch pan.

9. Chill until firm. Unmold or cut into squares.

Microwave

In step **3,** put half of the orange water in 1-quart microwave-safe measurer. Microwave on 100% power 2-3 minutes until boiling.

Lime-Applesauce Mold

Serves 4-6

There are times when the simplest is best and this gelatin is a perfect example. There is no chopping, very little measuring and no waiting until the mixture thickens to add ingredients. However, let me warn you this salad will disappear very quickly.

1	(15 or 16 ounce) can or jar applesauce
1	(3-ounce) package lime flavored gelatin
1	cup lemon-lime carbonated beverage

(Continued)

Lime-Applesauce Mold (continued)

1. In small saucepan, combine applesauce and gelatin.

2. Cook and stir until gelatin dissolves.

3. Cool to room temperature.

4. Gently stir in carbonated beverage.

5. Pour into oiled 3-cup mold or pretty serving dish.

6. Chill until firm.

7. Unmold on crisp lettuce leaves, if desired.

Microwave

In step **1,** combine applesauce and gelatin in 1-quart microwave-safe measurer.
In step **2,** microwave on 100% power 2-3 minutes until gelatin dissolves, stirring
every minute.

Grapefruit Sherbet Salad

Serves 8-10

This emerald beauty would be equally at home gracing a Christmas buffet
table or the center of attraction for a St. Patrick's day dinner. It's the perfect
blending of flavors and so easy to create.

2   **(16 ounce) cans grapefruit sections**
2   **(3 ounce) packages lime flavored gelatin**
1   **pint lime sherbet**
½   **cup chopped pecans**

1. Drain and dice grapefruit, reserving syrup.

2. Add enough water to grapefruit syrup to make 2 cups.

3. Heat liquid to boiling. Add gelatin and stir to dissolve.

4. Add sherbet and stir until dissolved.

5. Chill till partially set. If the sherbet separates from the gelatin beat until
smooth with wire whisk.

6. Fold in grapefruit sections and pecans.

7. Pour into oiled 6-cup mold or pretty serving dish.

8. Chill until set.

Microwave

In step **3,** put liquid in 2-quart microwave-safe measurer. Microwave on 100%
power 4-5 minutes until boiling.

126

Pear Royale Salad

Serves 8-10

When menus need a splash of color, a bright red salad can come to the rescue. This pleasing combination of raspberry, cranberry, and pear flavors goes well with many entrees.

2   **(3 ounce) packages raspberry flavored gelatin**
1   **cup boiling water**
2   **cups cold water**
1   **tablespoon lemon juice**
1   **(16 ounce) can whole cranberry sauce**
1   **(29 ounce) can pear halves, drained and chopped**
½   **cup chopped pecans**

1. Dissolve gelatin in boiling water; stir in cold water, lemon juice and cranberry sauce.

2. Chill until consistency of unbeaten egg white.

3. Fold in pears and pecans. Pour into lightly oiled 7-8 cup mold or pretty serving dish.

4. Chill until firm and then unmold, if molded, and garnish with fresh greens.

Pineapple Cheese Salad

Serves 8-10

I'm certain my Wisconsin roots and fondness for natural cheese contribute to my enjoyment of this interesting salad. The clear cool flavors in this gelatin would be delicious served with ham.

2   **(20 ounce) cans crushed pineapple, undrained**
2   **(3 ounce) packages lemon flavored gelatin**
    Enough water to make 2 cups liquid with drained pineapple juice
1   **cup mayonnaise**
3   **cups (12 ounces) shredded sharp cheddar cheese**

1. Drain pineapple, reserving juice. Set aside 1-½ cups pineapple juice.

2. Add water to remaining pineapple juice to make 2 cups liquid. Bring to a boil.

3. Dissolve gelatin in boiling liquid.

4. Stir in reserved 1-½ cups pineapple liquid.

5. Beat in mayonnaise with wire whisk, stirring until smooth. Chill until slightly thickened.

(Continued)

Pineapple Cheese Salad (continued)

6. Fold in drained pineapple and cheese; pour into oiled 8-cup mold or 9x13-inch baking pan. Chill.

7. Unmold on pretty plate and garnish with fresh salad greens.

Microwave

In step **2,** put 2 cups liquid in 2-quart microwave-safe measurer. Microwave on 100% power 4-6 minutes until boiling.

Raspberry Cream Salad

Serves 8-10

This colorful creamy creation may soon become one of your favorite gelatin salads. The subtle lemon flavor originates in frozen lemonade concentrate and vanilla ice cream adds smoothness to the texture. Frozen strawberries or peaches can be substituted with their companion flavored gelatins.

2   **(10 ounce) packages frozen raspberries, thawed**
2   **(3 ounce) packages red raspberry gelatin**
1   **pint vanilla ice cream**
1   **(6 ounce) can frozen lemonade concentrate**
½   **cup chopped pecans**

1. Drain thawed raspberries. Add water to make 2-⅓ cups liquid.

2. In medium saucepan, heat liquid to boiling.

3. Pour boiling liquid over gelatin into large mixing bowl. Add ice cream. Stir until melted.

4. Stir in lemonade. Chill until partially set.

5. Fold in drained raspberries and pecans.

6. Pour into oiled 6 cup mold or attractive serving dish.

7. Just before serving, garnish with fresh salad greens and fresh fruit, if desired.

Microwave

In step **2,** put liquid in 2-quart microwave-safe measurer. Microwave on 100% power 4-6 minutes until boiling.

Grape Delight

Serves 5

When lovely bunches of red and green grapes grace the produce counter, it's time to make this quick and easy sugar-free gelatin salad. It's an ideal recipe to double for a large group. I think a combination of both colors of grapes is appealing.

1   **envelope unflavored gelatin**
2   **cups unsweetened white grape juice, divided**
1-½ **cups red and/or green seedless grapes, halved**

1. Soften gelatin in 1 cup grape juice; let stand 10 minutes.

2. Bring remaining grape juice to a boil; add softened gelatin, stirring until dissolved.

3. Chill until consistency of unbeaten egg white.

4. Stir in grapes.

5. Pour into pretty serving dish. Chill until firm.

6. Garnish with additional grapes.

Grandmother's Cranberry Pineapple Salad

Serves 8-10

My mother, Lois Howell, who lives on our family farm near Janesville, Wisconsin, usually has this salad waiting in the refrigerator when we arrive for a visit from Michigan. That's because it's the favorite salad of her grandchildren, Sara and Paul House. Originally this cranberry gelatin was served at Thanksgiving, but we've found it's just as delicious on the Fourth of July.

2   **(3 ounce) packages strawberry or strawberry-banana flavored gelatin**
1-½ **cups boiling water**
1   **(10 ounce) package frozen cranberry relish**
1   **cup cold water**
1   **(20 ounce) can juice packed crushed pineapple, undrained**
2   **cups chopped unpeeled red eating apple**
1-½ **cups miniature marshmallows**
½   **cup chopped pecans, or walnuts if desired**

1. In large mixing bowl, dissolve gelatin in boiling water.

2. Stir in frozen cranberry relish until thawed.

3. Stir in cold water and undrained crushed pineapple.

(Continued)

Grandmother's Cranberry Pineapple Salad (continued)

4. Chill until partially thickened.

5. Fold in chopped apple, marshmallows and pecans.

6. Pour into attractive serving bowl. Chill until firm.

7. Serve the grandchildren first.

Blueberry Cream Mold

Serves 8

The lovely cream top layer of this gelatin salad is as delicious as it is beautiful. Supported by a blueberry filled layer, the contrast of color and flavors could easily earn the blue ribbon award.

1-½ teaspoons unflavored gelatin
¼ cup cold water
½ cup half and half coffee cream
½ cup sugar
1 cup cultured sour cream
1 (3 ounce) package raspberry flavored gelatin
1 cup boiling water
½ cup cold water
2 cups frozen blueberries, thawed, including juice

1. In 1 cup glass measurer, sprinkle gelatin over cold water to soften.

2. In small saucepan, combine coffee cream and sugar. Heat until sugar dissolves.

3. Add gelatin to coffee cream mixture and stir until dissolved. Cool.

4. Stir sour cream into cooled gelatin mixture.

5. Pour into oiled 6-cup gelatin mold to set.

6. In medium mixing bowl, dissolve raspberry gelatin in boiling water.

7. Stir in cold water and thawed blueberries, including liquid.

8. Cool until partially set.

9. Pour over sour cream layer and chill until firm.

10. Unmold on pretty serving plate; garnish with crisp green lettuce leaves, if desired.

Microwave

In step **2,** combine coffee cream and sugar in 1-quart microwave-safe measurer. Microwave on 100% power 2-4 minutes until sugar is dissolved, stirring once.

Fruit Salad Extraordinaire

Serves 6-8

When I served this wonderful fruit granola mixture to a special group of friends, it received rave reviews. Actually Linda Hull gets the credit for finding this interesting recipe of Mexican origin and then thoughtfully sharing it with me. It's a recipe that can be prepared as individual servings or created on a platter ready to please a crowd. Although it was designed as a breakfast fruit, this combination would be delicious at any meal.

1	papaya, peeled, seeded and cut into chunks
1	red eating apple, cored, unpeeled and diced
1	medium banana, sliced
1	fresh pineapple, cored, peeled and cut into chunks
1	cup shredded coconut
1	cup plain yogurt
1	to 1-½ cups granola
½	cup chopped walnuts
½	cup honey

1. Layer papaya, apple, banana, pineapple, and coconut on desired size plate or platter.

2. Pour yogurt over fruit.

3. Top with generous layer of granola.

4. Sprinkle with walnuts.

5. Drizzle with honey.

6. Cover and refrigerate an hour or two to develop flavors.

7. Serve. Enjoy the rave reviews.

Note: When selecting fresh papaya, look for greenish yellow to full yellow skins that yield slightly when fruit is pressed. Small spots on the ripe papaya skin are signs of ripeness and full flavor, not spoilage. Ripen green papayas at room temperature, out of direct sunlight, don't refrigerate until the papaya is fully ripe.

Rhubarb Mandarin Delight

Serves 6

Just one can of mandarin oranges puts a wonderful new depth of flavor into traditional rhubarb sauce. Start with either fresh or frozen rhubarb depending on the time of year. Serve at breakfast or as the salad course or for a light dessert.

1	(11 ounce) can mandarin orange sections
1	cup sugar
3	cups cut-up rhubarb, (¾ pound)

(Continued)

Rhubarb Mandarin Delight (continued)

1. Drain mandarin orange sections, reserving syrup.

2. In medium saucepan, combine reserved syrup, sugar and rhubarb.

3. Bring to boiling; cover and cook over low heat till rhubarb is tender, about 5 minutes.

4. Remove from heat.

5. Stir in mandarin orange sections. Chill.

6. Serve in sherbet cups or small sauce dishes. Enjoy.

Microwave

In step **2,** combine reserved syrup, sugar and rhubarb in 2-quart microwave-safe measurer.

In step **3,** microwave on 100% power 5-8 minutes until rhubarb is tender, stirring twice. (Frozen rhubarb requires longer cooking time.)

Fruit Medley

Serves 12

Calorie conscious cooks know that fruit without added dressing is really the best for waistline watchers. This colorful array of chilled fruit keeps this requirement in mind by using just a small amount of low calorie orange marmalade to glaze the top layer.

1   **(16 ounce) can juice packed pitted dark sweet cherries, drained**
1   **pint fresh strawberries**
1   **medium cantaloupe, cut into chunks**
1   **(20 ounce) can juice packed pineapple tidbits or chunks, drained**
2   **kiwi, peeled and sliced**
½   **cup low-calorie orange marmalade**
¼   **cup hot water**
1   **teaspoon finely chopped candied ginger**
1   **medium-large banana, sliced**
     Fresh mint, if available

1. Chill fruits. In your prettiest glass bowl, layer cherries, strawberries, cantaloupe, pineapple and kiwi in that order.

2. In small bowl, combine marmalade, hot water and candied ginger, drizzle over fruit. Chill.

3. Arrange banana slices atop layers of fruit. To keep banana from darkening, dip in ascorbic acid color keeper or pineapple juice.

4. Garnish with fresh mint, if available. Serve.

132

Honey Fruit Delight

Serves 6-8

This pleasing combination of fruit can be prepared ahead of time not only to avoid last minute rush, but to give flavors a chance to mellow and develop. The lovely green color of sliced kiwi highlights this delicious mixture.

1   **(20 ounce) can pineapple chunks or tidbits, juice pack**
2   **(11 ounce) cans mandarin orange sections, drained**
1-½ **cups seedless red grapes**
3   **kiwis, peeled, halved lengthwise, and sliced**
½   **cup orange juice**
¼   **cup honey**
1   **tablespoon lemon juice**

1. Drain pineapple, reserving juice.

2. In a large bowl, combine pineapple, mandarin oranges, grapes and kiwi slices.

3. Combine pineapple liquid, orange juice, honey and lemon juice. Pour over fruit.

4. Cover. Chill until ready to serve.

Light Fresh Fruit Compote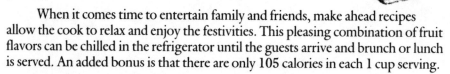

Serves 12

When it comes time to entertain family and friends, make ahead recipes allow the cook to relax and enjoy the festivities. This pleasing combination of fruit flavors can be chilled in the refrigerator until the guests arrive and brunch or lunch is served. An added bonus is that there are only 105 calories in each 1 cup serving.

1   **(20 ounce) can pineapple tidbits or chunks in unsweetened juice, undrained**
3   **tablespoons cornstarch**
2   **teaspoons sugar**
½   **teaspoon ground nutmeg**
1   **cup water**
3   **tablespoons lemon juice**
2   **medium-size oranges, peeled, seeded and sectioned**
2   **medium-size red apples, unpeeled and chopped**
1   **medium-size yellow apple, unpeeled and chopped**
2   **medium bananas, sliced**
1   **medium pear, unpeeled and chopped**
1   **cup seedless green grapes**
1   **cup seedless red grapes**

(Continued)

Light Fresh Fruit Compote (continued)

1. Drain pineapple, reserving juice; set aside.

2. Combine cornstarch, sugar and nutmeg in a medium saucepan; gradually add 1 cup water, stirring until smooth. Cook over medium heat, stirring until mixture comes to a boil; boil 1 minute.

3. Remove from heat, and stir in reserved pineapple juice and lemon juice; cool.

4. Combine reserved pineapple, oranges, apples, bananas, pear and grapes; pour dressing over top, tossing gently to coat.

5. Cover and chill thoroughly.

Microwave

In step **2,** combine cornstarch, sugar and nutmeg in 1-quart microwave-safe measurer. Stir in 1 cup water. Microwave on 100% power for 3-5 minutes stirring every minute or two.

Gingered Fruit

Serves 6

This lovely trio of fruit is one of my favorite sugar free recipes that has flair. You'll usually find fresh ginger in the produce section of the grocery store. Just peel off the skin and grate before adding to the other ingredients.

2   **medium red eating apples, cored and sliced or cubed**
2   **medium oranges, peeled and sectioned**
2   **medium bananas, sliced**
½   **cup unsweetened orange juice**
1   **tablespoon grated fresh ginger**

1. In medium mixing bowl, combine apples, oranges and bananas.

2. Add orange juice and grated ginger.

3. Cover and chill approximately two hours.

Frozen Apple Salad

Serves 9-12

A delicious frozen salad in the freezer is a comfort to any cook who experiences impromptu guests. In this salad, apples and celery join crushed pineapple for a very pleasing combination. I use the food processor to speed up the apple chopping.

1   **(8 ounce) can crushed pineapple**
2   **eggs**
½   **cup sugar**
⅛   **teaspoon salt**
3   **tablespoons lemon juice**
2   **cups unpeeled, chopped red eating apples (2 large apples)**
½   **cup chopped celery**
1   **cup heavy cream, whipped**

1. Drain pineapple; save juice. Add water to juice to make ½ cup liquid.

2. In small saucepan, beat two eggs with a fork. Add pineapple liquid, sugar, salt and lemon juice.

3. Cook over medium heat, stirring constantly until mixture thickens, about 5 minutes. Cool.

4. Fold drained pineapple, apples and celery into cooled dressing.

5. Gently fold in whipped cream.

6. Spoon into 8x8x2-inch dish or pan; cover; freeze firm.

7. Cut into squares and serve on lettuce leaves. Garnish with fresh apple slices, if desired.

Microwave

In step **2,** beat eggs with wire whisk in 1-quart microwave-safe measurer. Stir in pineapple liquid, sugar, salt and lemon juice.
In step **3,** microwave mixture on 100% power for 4-5 minutes, until thickened, stirring every minute. Cool.

Cranberry Freeze

Serves 10-12

When it comes to simplicity, this recipe definitely is a winner. The use of a muffin tin guarantees even individual servings at a minute's notice. Place the frozen salads on drained pineapple rings with curly lettuce leaves for a festive flair.

1   **(16 ounce) can whole cranberry sauce**
1   **(8 ounce) can crushed pineapple, drained**
1   **cup cultured sour cream**
¼   **cup confectioners' sugar**

(Continued)

Cranberry Freeze (continued)

1. In medium mixing bowl, combine cranberry sauce and crushed drained pineapple.

2. In small bowl, stir together sour cream and confectioners' sugar. Add these ingredients to the fruit and blend completely.

3. Pour mixture in 10-12 paper cup lined muffin pan.

4. Freeze until firm. Remove frozen salads from muffin tins and store in airtight plastic bags in freezer until needed.

Frozen Raspberry Salad

Serves 8-10

This creamy raspberry frozen delight could actually double as a dessert in many menus. It's a delicious cool recipe to keep in the freezer for spur of the moment needs.

1-½   **cups miniature marshmallows**
⅓   **cup orange juice**
½   **cup whipping cream**
1   **(3 ounce) package cream cheese, softened**
¼   **cup mayonnaise or salad dressing**
1   **(10 ounce) package frozen raspberries, thawed and undrained**
½   **cup chopped pecans**

1. In top of a double boiler, combine marshmallows and orange juice.

2. Cook over boiling water, stirring frequently, until marshmallows are melted. Let cool.

3. Beat whipping cream until soft peaks are formed.

4. Use unwashed beaters to beat cream cheese and mayonnaise into cooled marshmallow mixture. Beat mixture until smooth.

5. Stir in undrained raspberries and pecans.

6. Fold in whipped cream.

7. Pour mixture into paper cup lined muffin pans or 8x8-inch square pan.

8. Freeze firm. Store well covered in freezer.

9. Serve on lettuce lined plates, if desired.

Microwave

In step **1,** combine marshmallows and orange juice in 2 quart microwave-safe measurer.
In step **2** microwave on 100% power 2-4 minutes, stirring every minute. Let cool.

Frozen Banana Salad

Serves 9-12

When your supply of ripe bananas is abundant and you don't feel like baking, this delicious frozen salad is the perfect solution. Dotted with red maraschino cherries it will be an attractive addition to any menu.

4	bananas, mashed (use food processor)
1	(8 ounce) can crushed pineapple, undrained
1	tablespoon lemon juice
¾	cup maraschino cherries, well drained and cut into quarters
½	cup chopped pecans
¾	cup sugar
¼	teaspoon salt
2	cups (16 ounces) cultured sour cream
	Lettuce leaves

1. In large mixing bowl, combine mashed bananas, undrained pineapple, lemon juice, cherries, pecans, sugar, salt and sour cream. Stir gently to combine.

2. Pour into 8x8-inch baking pan. Freeze firm.

3. Store well covered in freezer until serving time.

4. Cut into squares and serve on lettuce leaves garnished with whole maraschino cherries.

Frozen Island Salad

Serves 6 to 8

If there is empty space in your freezer, then you could easily tuck away some frozen salads ready to use at a minute's notice. This recipe is so quick and easy it would be ideal for those who really don't enjoy cooking.

1	(3 ounce) package cream cheese, softened
2	(6 ounce) cartons pineapple yogurt
¼	cup sugar
1	(8 ounce) can crushed pineapple, drained

1. In medium mixing bowl, beat together cream cheese and yogurt with wire whisk or electric beater.

2. Stir in sugar and drained pineapple. Blend well.

3. Line 6 to 8 muffin cups with paper baking cups. Spoon mixture into cups. Freeze firm.

4. Remove salads from muffin pans. Store in airtight plastic bags.

5. At serving time, remove paper cups from salad and garnish with greens and fresh fruit such as strawberries, oranges, etc.

Michigan Coleslaw

Serves 4

The cabbage, celery and apples in this coleslaw recipe are grown abundantly here in Michigan. The bright red color of the apple skin adds just the right visual highlight.

1   cup shredded cabbage
1   cup chopped celery
1   large or 2 medium unpeeled red apples, cored and diced
½   cup raisins
⅓   cup salad dressing or mayonnaise
¼   teaspoon salt, if desired

1. In medium mixing bowl, gently combine cabbage, celery, apples and raisins.

2. Add salad dressing and salt. Toss lightly.

3. Put into pretty serving dish and garnish with apple slices, if desired.

Broccoli/Cauliflower Salad

Serves 6-8

When our family gathers with the Harley Behm family for a festive meal, all of us like to have Mary Ellen bring this great vegetable salad. It's a delicious colorful combination that's popular with all ages, especially the family members with membership in the black olive fan club.

1   head cauliflower, cut into small flowerettes
1   bunch broccoli, cut into flowerettes
1   (6 ounce) can ripe pitted olives, drained
2   carrots, peeled and sliced
1   pint cherry tomatoes
1   (8 ounce) bottle reduced calorie Italian salad dressing

1. In large mixing bowl, alternate layers of cauliflower and broccoli flowerettes.

2. Add black olives, carrots and tomatoes.

3. Pour dressing over vegetables and toss to thoroughly coat vegetables.

4. Cover and marinate at least 4 hours or overnight.

5. Serve in pretty serving dish.

Note: Mary Ellen sometimes adds fresh mushrooms, sliced green peppers and/or onions, depending on individual tastes.

Marinated Asparagus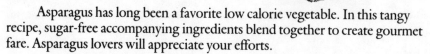

Serves 8

Asparagus has long been a favorite low calorie vegetable. In this tangy recipe, sugar-free accompanying ingredients blend together to create gourmet fare. Asparagus lovers will appreciate your efforts.

2   pounds fresh asparagus, cut in 1-inch lengths or
    2 (10 ounce) packages frozen asparagus cuts or 1 quart
    home frozen asparagus cuts
1   medium green pepper, coarsely chopped
5   green onions with tops, sliced
1   stalk celery, finely chopped
¾   cup unsweetened apple cider
½   cup red wine vinegar
    Dash of garlic powder
¼   teaspoon paprika
    Lettuce and/or pimiento strips, if desired

1. Cook asparagus, covered, in boiling water 6 to 8 minutes or until crisp-tender, drain. Frozen asparagus doesn't need to be cooked, just run cold water over it to remove ice crystals, drain well.

2. Put asparagus in shallow dish.

3. In small mixing bowl, combine green pepper, green onions, celery, apple cider, vinegar, garlic powder and paprika. Thoroughly combine. Pour over asparagus.

4. Cover and chill four hours or overnight.

5. Drain and serve on lettuce lined plates. Garnish with pimiento.

Tomato-Cheese Accordions

Serves 6

Cool seasoned cottage cheese looks so pretty and tastes so delicious when it's sandwiched between crisp red slices of tomatoes. Serve this light luncheon idea several times when tomatoes are in season.

1   (12 ounce) carton cottage cheese (1-½ cups.)
    Salt and pepper, if desired
¼   cup chopped green pepper
¼   cup shredded carrot
1   tablespoon green onion including top, sliced
6   medium tomatoes
6   leaf lettuce leaves

(Continued)

Tomato-Cheese Accordions (continued)

1. Drain cottage cheese well if creamed style is used.

2. In medium mixing bowl, combine drained cottage cheese, green pepper, carrot, onion and salt and pepper to taste.

3. Core each tomato.

4. Turn each tomato upside down.

5. Cut each tomato in ½ inch slices about ¾ way through.

6. Spread slices apart and spoon cottage cheese mixture between slices.

7. Serve on lettuce leaves.

Baked German Potato Salad

Serves 10-12

When you need hot potato salad for a crowd, this recipe is the perfect suggestion. The delicately seasoned mixture is easy to prepare and bakes effortlessly in the oven while other tasks are accomplished. Stir in radish slices just before serving for added color and crunch.

8	slices bacon, diced
1	cup chopped celery
1	cup chopped onion
3	tablespoons flour
1-⅓	cups water
1	cup cider vinegar
⅔	cup sugar
1	teaspoon salt
¼	teaspoon ground pepper
8	cups cooked potatoes cubed, (8 medium potatoes)
1	cup sliced radishes, if desired

1. Fry bacon in medium size skillet until crisp. Remove bacon and drain on paper towels. Put bacon aside, drain off grease. Measure and reserve ¼ cup grease.

2. Return the ¼ cup grease to skillet. Add celery and onion; cook 1 minute.

3. Blend in flour. Then stir in water and vinegar; cook, stirring constantly, until mixture is thick and bubbly.

4. Stir in sugar, salt and pepper.

5. Put potatoes and bacon in greased 3-quart casserole.

6. Pour thickened sauce over potatoes and bacon. Mix lightly. Cover.

7. Bake in preheated 350 degree oven for 30 minutes, until hot and bubbly.

8. Remove from oven. Stir in radishes, if desired. Serve at once.

Fruit-Jar Tomato Relish

Serves 6-8

Here is a clever way to marinate vegetables in a quart jar. For a very casual affair, the relishes could be carried in the jar in a cooler right to the picnic. The colorful layers would even add class to burgers and hot dogs.

2	medium tomatoes, peeled and chopped
1	cucumber, peeled and chopped
1	green pepper, chopped
¼	cup chopped onion
¼	cup olive or vegetable oil
2	tablespoons wine vinegar
1	tablespoon snipped fresh parsley
1	small clove garlic, minced or ⅛ teaspoon garlic powder
½	teaspoon salt
	Dash of pepper

1. In a 1-quart jar, alternate layers of tomatoes, cucumber, green pepper, and onion to make stripes when viewed from the side.

2. In small glass jar, combine oil, vinegar, parsley, garlic, salt and pepper. Cover jar tightly and shake well.

3. Pour dressing mixture over vegetables; cover and chill overnight.

4. Turn jar upside down during part of the chilling to marinate vegetables evenly.

Refrigerated Cole Slaw

Serves 8-10

Even if you shred cabbage in a food processor, you'll appreciate the convenience of a cabbage salad that stores almost indefinitely in the refrigerator. My friend, Mary Lindell, from Darlington, Wisconsin, shared this delicious crisp recipe with me. Make up a batch or two the next time cabbage is priced attractively.

8	cups shredded cabbage
1	large onion, thinly sliced
1	to 1-½ cups sugar
1	cup cider vinegar
¾	cup vegetable oil
1	teaspoon dry mustard
1	teaspoon celery seed
½	teaspoon salt, if desired

(Continued)

Refrigerated Cole Slaw (continued)

1. In large bowl, alternate layers of cabbage, onion and sugar.

2. In medium saucepan, combine vinegar, vegetable oil, mustard, celery seed and salt, if desired.

3. Simmer over low heat until well blended and just to boiling point.

4. Pour boiling liquid over cabbage mixture.

5. Let stand for 3 hours at room temperature. Stir.

6. Let stand for another 2-3 hours at room temperature. Stir.

7. Cover tightly and refrigerate.

8. Can be stored in the refrigerator for 5-6 weeks, if no one knows it's there.

Microwave

In step **2,** combine vinegar, vegetable oil, mustard, celery seed and salt in 1-quart microwave-safe measurer.
In step **3,** microwave on 100% power 3-5 minutes until boiling, stirring once or twice.

Picnic Macaroni Salad

Serves 6

Summertime is picnic time and macaroni salad time. Here is a basic recipe that is both easy and tasty. Remember it's important to carry cold food in coolers to the picnic spot. Happy picnicking.

1   **cup uncooked macaroni**
1   **cup chopped celery**
¼   **cup chopped onion**
⅓   **cup chopped sweet pickle**
⅓   **cup chopped green pepper**
1   **cup sharp cheddar cheese, cubed**
½   **cup frozen green peas, thawed**
½   **cup salad dressing or mayonnaise**

1. Cook macaroni according to package directions.

2. Drain macaroni and chill for approximately 2 hours.

3. In large mixing bowl, combine cooked macaroni, celery, onion, sweet pickle, green pepper, cheese and peas. Toss gently.

4. Add salad dressing tossing lightly to coat ingredients.

5. Chill.

6. Serve garnished with green pepper rings, if desired.

Food Processor Cucumbers Vinaigrette

Serves 4-6

These classy cucumbers are created very quickly in a food processor. The delicious dressing is easily made using the steel blade. This dressing is left in the work bowl to welcome the sliced cucumbers. It's a great one bowl recipe.

2   **or 3 sprigs fresh parsley**
1   **small clove garlic**
¼   **teaspoon salt**
    Dash of pepper
1   **tablespoon wine vinegar**
3   **tablespoons olive or vegetable oil**
⅛   **teaspoon dill weed**
1   **large or 2 small cucumbers**
1   **teaspoon fresh snipped or freeze dried chives**

1. Put steel blade in food processor work bowl.

2. Wash parsley and dry by squeezing it in paper towel. Cut garlic in two or three pieces.

3. With steel blade running, drop parsley and garlic through feed tube. Process until finely chopped, using pulsing motion, if necessary.

4. Add salt, pepper, vinegar, olive oil and dill weed. Pulse once or twice to combine.

5. Remove steel blade. Leave dressing in work bowl. Put slicing disc in place.

6. Peel cucumbers. If too large to fit in feed tube, split in half lengthwise and remove seeds with a teaspoon, if desired.

7. Stand cucumbers vertically in feed tube close together, but not too tight.

8. Push cucumbers through slicing disc.

9. Remove slicing disc.

10. Stir cucumbers to coat with dressing.

11. Put in serving dish; chill if desired.

12. Garnish with chives. Serve.

Vegetable Pasta Salad

Serves 6-8

Have you ever noticed the various sizes, shapes and flavors of pasta available at the grocery store? If you're looking for a recipe to use with some of these varieties, look no further for here is a colorful and flavorful suggestion. I especially like the green spinach and red tomato pasta cork screws or shells when I make this recipe.

2	cups attractive pasta
1	cup broccoli flowerettes
1	cup cauliflower flowerettes
½	cup chopped green pepper
½	cup sliced green onions
1	cup shredded carrots
1	cup Italian salad dressing

1. Cook pasta according to directions; drain and rinse with cold water.

2. In large mixing bowl, combine cooked pasta, broccoli, cauliflower, green pepper, green onions and carrots. Gently toss together.

3. Add Italian dressing and gently mix together.

4. Chill at least an hour or overnight.

Vegetable Rice Salad

Serves 6

Summertime is salad time. When the weather is warm this cool tasting salad is ready to take away hot weather blues. It's a delightful combination of selected vegetables and rice bound together with an easy dressing.

3	cups cooked regular rice, cooled
1	cup broccoli flowerettes
1	cup sliced yellow squash
1	cup chopped tomato
½	cup vegetable oil
3	tablespoons lemon juice
⅛	teaspoon garlic powder
½	teaspoon salt, if desired
¼	teaspoon freshly ground pepper

1. In a large mixing bowl, combine rice, broccoli, squash and tomato. Toss gently.

2. In a small jar, combine oil, lemon juice, garlic powder, salt and pepper. Cover tightly and shake vigorously.

3. Pour dressing over rice mixture. Toss gently.

4. Cover and chill thoroughly. Enjoy the picnic.

Zesty Spinach Salad

Serves 6-8

Every time I prepare a quick "made from scratch" salad dressing I remind myself how easy it is to be in complete control of the ingredients that go into a recipe. This way there are no additives and/or preservatives that would cause dietary restrictions. I think you'll like this spinach salad when it is tossed with this marvelous dressing. Probably you have all of the dressing ingredients on hand.

1	egg
¼	cup vegetable oil
1	tablespoon grated Parmesan cheese
2	tablespoons lemon juice
2	tablespoons Dijon mustard
1	teaspoon sugar
1	teaspoon Worcestershire sauce
½	teaspoon salt
	Dash of ground pepper
1	(10 ounce) bag fresh spinach, washed, drained and torn
¼	pound fresh mushrooms, sliced
6	slices bacon, cooked and crumbled
2	hard-cooked eggs, chopped

1. Put egg in wide mouth jar and beat with a fork; add oil, Parmesan, lemon juice, mustard, sugar, Worcestershire sauce, salt and pepper. Shake very well until blended. Chill thoroughly.

2. Put torn spinach leaves into salad bowl. Add mushrooms. Cover and chill, if desired.

3. Toss spinach mixture with chilled dressing until well coated.

4. Garnish with bacon and hard-cooked eggs.

Caesar Salad

Serves 6-8

I feel fortunate that my husband, George, likes to make a Caesar Salad at the table, because this is a recipe that is created just before eating. For ease in preparation, arrange pre-measured ingredients on a tray. The torn romaine leaves can wait patiently in an ice bucket. Just follow these easy directions, and you'll have a Caesar salad worthy of the fanfare it deserves.

1	clove garlic, halved
⅓	cup olive oil
8	anchovy fillets, cut up (optional)
1	teaspoon Worcestershire sauce

(Continued)

Caesar Salad (continued)

½ teaspoon salt
¼ teaspoon dry mustard
Freshly ground pepper
12 cups freshly torn romaine leaves, chilled (1 large bunch)
Coddled Egg (directions follow)
1 lemon
Garlic croutons (directions on page 146)
⅓ cup grated Parmesan cheese

1. Pre-measure all ingredients and prepare coddled egg and garlic croutons. Arrange on attractive tray all ready for salad making.

2. Just before serving, rub large salad bowl with cut clove of garlic.

3. Combine oil, anchovies, Worcestershire sauce, salt, mustard and pepper in bottom of salad bowl. Mix thoroughly.

4. Add romaine leaves and toss until leaves glisten.

5. Break egg onto romaine; squeeze juice from lemon over romaine.

6. Toss until leaves are well coated.

7. Sprinkle croutons and cheese over salad. Toss.

8. Serve to deserving discriminating guests and family members.

Coddled Egg

A "coddled" egg is gently cooked for a few seconds in water just below the boiling point. It is used in a Caesar salad as an agent to bind together all of the ingredients.

1. Place 1 cold egg in a small bowl of warm water.

2. In a small saucepan, heat enough water to completely cover egg.

3. With a spoon, immerse egg in boiling water. Remove pan from heat.

4. Cover and let stand 30 seconds.

5. Immediately cool egg in cold water.

6. Put in egg cup or other attractive small dish on tray with Caesar salad ingredients.

Garlic Croutons

For Caesar salad

These delicious croutons are the crispy garnish for the marvelous Caesar salad. If made ahead of time, store in covered container.

4   slices white bread
2   tablespoons butter or margarine, softened
¼   teaspoon garlic powder

1. Trim crusts from bread, saving crusts for another use.

2. Generously butter both sides of the bread slices.

3. Sprinkle both sides with garlic powder.

4. Cut into ½-inch bread cubes; place on 10x15-inch baking pan.

5. Bake in preheated 400 degree oven 10-15 minutes, stirring occasionally, until golden brown and crisp.

6. Store in airtight container.

7. Place in attractive soup bowl or basket on tray with other Caesar salad ingredients.

Strawberry/Orange/Spinach Salad

Serves 6 to 8

When fresh strawberry time arrives, I like to serve them in many different ways. One unique and wonderful suggestion is to combine these luscious berries with spinach for an unforgettable salad experience. You'll know spring has come.

1   (10 ounce) package fresh spinach
3   cups fresh strawberries, washed and hulled
1   (11 ounce) can mandarin oranges, chilled and drained
¾   cup walnut pieces
     Poppy Seed dressing on page 147

1. Wash the spinach; spin dry in greens spinner or pat dry with towel.

2. Tear spinach into bite-size pieces and place in salad bowl.

3. Reserve 6 to 8 whole strawberries for garnish. Cut the remaining berries in half and add to spinach.

4. Add drained mandarin orange segments to spinach.

5. Toss gently; cover with plastic wrap; refrigerate until serving time.

6. When ready to serve, pour desired amount of poppy seed dressing or any other favorite fruit salad dressing over salad and toss.

7. Garnish with reserved whole strawberries and walnuts. Enjoy.

Poppy Seed Dressing

Makes approximately 1 cup

This delicious homemade salad dressing is wonderful with the Strawberry/Orange/Spinach salad on page 146 or, for that matter, any other fruit salad. It's so quick and easy to make, that it may take longer to locate and measure the ingredients than to make the dressing.

6	tablespoons sugar
½	teaspoon dry mustard
¼	teaspoon salt
3	tablespoons cider vinegar
1	cup salad oil
2	tablespoons poppy seed

1. Combine sugar, mustard, salt and vinegar in blender container or food processor bowl. Process until blended.

2. With motor running, add the oil slowly, pouring it in a very thin stream, and continue beating until mixture thickens.

3. Add poppy seed and process a few seconds.

4. Store in tightly covered container and refrigerate until ready to use.

Apple-Spinach Salad

Serves 6

Fresh spinach is such a popular and wonderful salad green. Just add a touch of apple, bacon, almonds and onion to capture a spinach salad to remember. I think you'll like the quick and easy dressing that goes on this tasty salad.

1	(10 ounce) package fresh spinach, washed and dried
1	large red delicious apple, diced
5	slices bacon, cooked, drained, and crumbled
⅓	cup sliced almonds
2	green onions, sliced
	Dressing:
¼	cup salad oil
3	tablespoons tarragon vinegar
1	teaspoon sugar
½	teaspoon dry mustard
⅛	teaspoon salt, if desired
	Dash of ground pepper

1. In large salad bowl, tear spinach into bite size pieces. Add apple, bacon, almonds and onions.

2. In small glass jar, combine oil, vinegar, sugar, mustard, salt and pepper. Shake well.

3. Toss spinach mixture with dressing just before serving.

Romaine and Walnut Toss

Serves 8

Although we often think of romaine strictly for Caesar salad, it is an easy salad green to involve in lots of recipes. Here is an extremely easy, yet creative, salad that will please even the most discriminating salad lover. Part of the secret is the delicious honey flavored dressing.

½   cup salad oil
½   cup honey
2   tablespoons vinegar
½   teaspoon dry mustard
8   cups torn romaine lettuce leaves
1   cup coarsely broken walnuts

1. In jar, combine oil, honey, vinegar and mustard. Shake very well.

2. In pretty salad bowl, combine romaine and walnuts.

3. Just before serving, drizzle dressing over greens and toss to coat.

Oriental Spinach Salad

Serves 8

This grand spinach salad is short on calories and long on flavor. The dressing ingredients can probably be found in the cupboard. To toast sesame seeds, place seeds on flat baking pan in a preheated 300 degree oven for a few minutes. Stir occasionally to avoid burning. The toasty flavor is outstanding.

1   (10 ounce) package spinach, washed, drained, and torn into bite-size pieces
2   cups shredded or sliced Chinese cabbage
½   pound fresh mushrooms, sliced
3   green onions, sliced
2   tablespoons toasted sesame seeds
2   tablespoons vinegar
2   tablespoons vegetable oil
1   tablespoon soy sauce
¼   teaspoon ground ginger

1. In large salad bowl, combine spinach, cabbage, mushrooms, green onions and sesame seeds. Toss together.

2. In small jar, combine vinegar, oil, soy sauce and ginger. Cover tightly and shake vigorously.

3. Just before serving, pour over salad and toss.

Asparagus AuGratin

Serves 4

Asparagus is my sister-in-law's, Betsey House, favorite vegetable, so it's not surprising that this lovely creation came from her collection of treasured recipes. She prefers fresh asparagus, but frozen spears or cuts can be used.

1-¼   pounds fresh asparagus or 1 (10 ounce) package frozen asparagus
2   tablespoons butter or margarine
2   tablespoons chopped onion
2   tablespoons flour
½   teaspoon salt
⅛   teaspoon ground white pepper
       Dash of ground nutmeg
⅔   cup chicken broth
⅓   cup half and half coffee cream
½   cup (2 ounces) shredded cheddar cheese

1. Clean and cook asparagus in a small amount of boiling water. Drain. Arrange asparagus on oven proof platter. Set aside.

2. In medium saucepan, melt butter. Stir in onion and cook until transparent.

3. Stir in flour, salt, pepper and nutmeg over low heat until smooth.

4. Stir in broth and cream. Cook until thickened, stirring constantly.

5. Pour sauce over asparagus. Sprinkle with cheese.

6. Bake in preheated 400 degree oven for 8-10 minutes until cheese melts.

7. Serve with toast points.

Microwave

In step **1,** cook asparagus in covered microwave-safe casserole on 100% power 6-8 minutes, until crisp-tender, stirring once. Drain.
In step **2,** melt butter in 1 quart microwave-safe measurer on 100% power 20-30 seconds. Add onion and cook on 100% power 45-60 seconds.
In step **3,** stir in flour, salt, pepper and nutmeg.
In step **4,** add broth and cream. Cook on 100% power 2-3 minutes until thick, stirring every minute.
In step **6,** make certain asparagus is arranged on microwave-safe platter. Microwave on 80% power 1-3 minutes until cheese melts, rotating platter once.

Fresh Asparagus Oriental

Serves 6

When fresh asparagus is at its prime, this is a wonderful way to enjoy every mouth-watering stalk. This stir-fry procedure is just as easy as the short ingredient list indicates.

1   **tablespoon salad oil**
3   **cups fresh asparagus, cut in bias-cut pieces**
½   **teaspoon salt**
½   **teaspoon monosodium glutamate**
    Dash of pepper

1. Heat salad oil in wok or large skillet.

2. Add the pieces of asparagus. Sprinkle with salt, monosodium glutamate and pepper.

3. Stir-fry or cover skillet and shake constantly.

4. Cook asparagus only till tender, 4 to 5 minutes.

5. Reduce heat to medium, if necessary, during last minute of cooking. Don't over cook.

Asparagus Scallop

Serves 12

If you've been invited to a potluck dinner and asked to bring a vegetable dish, this asparagus/rice casserole will bring requests for the recipe. On another occasion, divide the ingredients in half and use this recipe for a casual family dinner.

3   **cups cooked rice**
2   **(10 ounce) packages asparagus cuts or 1 quart home frozen asparagus cuts**
2   **(10-¾ ounce) cans condensed cream of asparagus soup**
⅔   **cup milk**
4   **hard-cooked eggs, sliced**
½   **teaspoon salt, if desired**
    Freshly ground pepper
½   **cup dry bread crumbs**
2   **tablespoons melted butter or margarine**

1. Place half the rice in bottom of greased 2-quart casserole.

2. Thaw frozen asparagus under cold running water, drain well. Top rice with half the asparagus.

3. Blend together soup and milk. Spread half of soup mixture over asparagus.

(Continued)

Asparagus Scallop (continued)

4. Arrange sliced eggs over top; sprinkle with salt and pepper.

5. Add a second layer of remaining rice, asparagus and soup mixture.

6. Toss together bread crumbs and melted butter; sprinkle over top of casserole.

7. Bake in preheated 350 degree oven 30-45 minutes until hot and bubbly.

Raisin Sauced Beets

Serves 4

I've never really considered beets a glamorous vegetable, but this classy raisin-lemon sauce brings the humble red root vegetable to new heights. These beets are so delicious and easy to make it may be a good idea to double the recipe.

1   **(16 ounce) can beets, julienne cut, diced, or sliced (2 cups)**
⅓   **cup raisins**
¼   **cup sugar**
1   **teaspoon cornstarch**
3   **tablespoons lemon juice**
1   **tablespoon butter or margarine**

1. Drain beets, reserving ⅓ cup liquid.

2. In medium saucepan, combine reserved beet liquid and raisins.

3. Cover; simmer till raisins are plumped, about 5 minutes.

4. In small dish, combine sugar and cornstarch; stir into raisins in pan.

5. Add lemon juice and butter; cook and stir over medium heat till slightly thickened.

6. Stir in beets and simmer till mixture is heated through, about 5 minutes.

7. Put in an attractive serving dish. Garnish with a twist of lemon, if desired.

Microwave

In step **2,** combine reserved beet liquid and raisins in 1 quart microwave-safe measurer.
In step **3,** microwave on 100% power, uncovered, 4-5 minutes.
In step **5,** microwave on 100% power 2-3 minutes until thickened, stirring every minute.
In step **6,** stir in beets and microwave on 100% power 3-5 minutes until hot, stirring once.

Broccoli Bake

Serves 6

The fluffy topping on these broccoli cuts may remind you of a vegetable souffle. The only difference is that this is an easier plan. Bubbling hot from the oven, this casserole looks pretty when garnished with fresh parsley.

1   (10 ounce) package frozen broccoli cuts
1   egg
1   (10-¾ ounce) can cream of mushroom soup
½   cup shredded cheddar cheese (2 ounces)
¼   cup milk
¼   cup mayonnaise or salad dressing
1   tablespoon butter or margarine, melted
¼   cup fine dry bread crumbs

1. Cook frozen broccoli according to package directions, omitting salt that's called for; drain thoroughly.

2. Place drained broccoli cuts in 10x6x1 and ½ inch baking dish.

3. In medium mixing bowl, beat egg with a rotary beater or fork.

4. Stir mushroom soup, cheese, milk and mayonnaise gently into beaten egg.

5. Spread soup mixture over broccoli cuts.

6. In small bowl, combine melted butter and bread crumbs.

7. Sprinkle evenly over soup mixture.

8. Bake in preheated 350 degree oven for 45 minutes, until crumbs are lightly browned.

Microwave

In step 1, remove foil from broccoli package; puncture box 2 or 3 times with fork tines to allow a place for steam to escape. Place package on paper plate. Microwave on 100% power 5-6 minutes, turning package over halfway through cooking time. Drain thoroughly.

Broccoli-Onion Casserole

Serves 6

As I searched my files, I found this recipe thoughtfully written for me by my mother, Lois Howell, with the notation that our family was first introduced to this combination on Christmas 1973. Of course, it isn't necessary to wait until Christmas to enjoy broccoli and onions.

(Continued)

Broccoli-Onion Casserole (continued)

1   (16 ounce) package frozen broccoli cuts
1   (16 ounce) jar small cooked onions, drained
2   tablespoons butter or margarine
2   tablespoons flour
½   teaspoon salt
     Dash of pepper
1   cup milk
1   (3 ounce) package cream cheese, cubed
½   cup shredded cheddar cheese (2 ounces)
2   tablespoons butter or margarine, melted
1   cup soft bread crumbs

1. In medium saucepan, cook broccoli according to package directions. Drain thoroughly.

2. Place broccoli and drained onions in 1-½ quart casserole.

3. In small saucepan, melt 2 tablespoons butter; blend in flour, salt and pepper.

4. Add milk. Cook and stir until bubbly and thick. Remove from heat and blend in cream cheese.

5. Pour sauce over broccoli and onions in casserole.

6. Top with cheddar cheese.

7. In small bowl, toss together 2 tablespoons melted butter with soft bread crumbs.

8. Sprinkle bread crumbs around edge of casserole.

9. Bake, uncovered, in preheated 350 degree oven for 30 minutes until bubbly.

10. Serve.

Microwave

In step 1, put broccoli in 1-½ quart microwave-safe casserole. Microwave, covered with lid or vented plastic wrap, on 100% power 5-7 minutes until tender, stirring once. Drain thoroughly.

In step 3, place 2 tablespoons butter in 1-quart microwave-safe measurer. Microwave on 100% power 20-30 seconds until melted. Blend in flour, salt and pepper.

In step 4, add milk. Microwave on 100% power 3-4 minutes until thickened, stirring every minute with wire whisk.

In step 8, use whole wheat soft bread crumbs.

In step 9, microwave on 80% power 12-15 minutes until bubbly hot, rotating dish once.

Snowcapped Broccoli

Serves 6

This dynamic green and white vegetable idea is dedicated to my friends who have heart strings attached to Michigan State University. For you see, the green and white school colors have never looked prettier in a home cooked creation.

2   (10 ounce) packages frozen broccoli spears
2   egg whites
¼   teaspoon salt
⅓   cup mayonnaise or salad dressing
1   tablespoon butter or margarine melted
    Grated Parmesan cheese

1. Cook frozen broccoli spears according to package directions; drain well.

2. Beat egg whites and salt with rotary beater or electric mixer until stiff peaks form. Gently fold in mayonnaise or salad dressing; set aside.

3. Arrange cooked broccoli with stem ends toward center on an oven-proof platter or 9-inch pie plate; drizzle with melted butter.

4. Spoon the mayonnaise mixture over the broccoli stems to form a circle in the center of the plate. Sprinkle with parmesan cheese.

5. Bake in a preheated 350 degree oven for 12-15 minutes or until topping is golden.

Microwave

In step **1**, put broccoli spears in covered 2 quart microwave-safe casserole. Microwave on 100% power 8-10 minutes, rearranging spears once. Drain well.

Baked Escalloped Corn

Serves 6

It doesn't take long for this vegetable casserole to disappear when hungry family members gather together. It's chuck full of good basic ingredients topped off with a light dusting of Parmesan cheese for added interest and flavor.

2   eggs
1   (17 ounce) can whole kernel corn, drained
1   (17 ounce) can cream style corn
¼   cup crushed round buttery crackers
¼   cup chopped onion
¼   cup milk
1   (2 ounce) jar chopped pimientos, drained
¼   teaspoon salt
⅛   teaspoon ground pepper
2   tablespoons grated Parmesan cheese

(Continued)

Baked Escalloped Corn (continued)

1. In large mixing bowl, beat eggs with rotary beater or fork.

2. Stir into beaten eggs, drained whole kernel corn, cream-style corn, cracker crumbs, onion, milk, pimientos, salt and pepper. Combine thoroughly.

3. Pour into greased 1-½ quart casserole.

4. Sprinkle top with grated Parmesan cheese.

5. Bake, uncovered, in preheated 350 degree oven for 40-50 minutes, or until center is almost set.

6. Let stand 5 minutes before serving.

Microwave

In step **3,** use microwave-safe 1-½ quart casserole.
In step **5,** microwave on 100% power 14-18 minutes, rotating dish twice.

Carrot 'N Cauliflower Casserole

Serves 6-8

This winning vegetable combination is pleasing to both the palate and the eye. It would be an excellent choice to serve at a buffet dinner or carry to a potluck supper. You may have requests for the recipe.

5   **large carrots, peeled and cut into ¼ inch slices (1 pound)**
1   **medium head cauliflower, broken into flowerettes**
1   **(10-¾ ounce) can cream of chicken soup**
¾   **cup milk**
1   **cup soda cracker crumbs**
2   **tablespoons butter or margarine, melted**

1. Cook carrots and cauliflower in boiling water 10 minutes; drain.

2. Place vegetables in a lightly greased 2-quart casserole.

3. In small bowl, combine soup and milk, stirring well. Pour over vegetables.

4. In small bowl toss together cracker crumbs and melted butter.

5. Sprinkle over vegetables.

6. Bake in preheated 350 degree oven for 30 minutes.

Microwave

In step **1,** cook vegetables in covered microwave-safe casserole with ¼ cup water.
    Microwave on 100% power 14-16 minutes until crisp tender. Drain.
In step **2,** use microwave-safe 2 quart casserole.
In step **6,** microwave on 80% power 15-20 minutes, rotating dish once.

Candied Carrots

Serves 6

The secret ingredient that glazes these delicious carrots is a small amount of jellied cranberry sauce. It's a great idea for the menu that needs a special vegetable without lots of extra work or expense.

4   cups (½ inch) sliced carrots
2   tablespoons butter or margarine
¼   cup canned jellied cranberry sauce
2   tablespoons brown sugar
½   teaspoon salt

1. Cook carrots in boiling water till just tender 8-10 minutes. Drain.

2. In a skillet combine butter, cranberry sauce, brown sugar and salt. Heat slowly and stir till cranberry sauce melts.

3. Add drained carrots; heat stirring occasionally, till nicely glazed on all sides, about 5 minutes.

4. Garnish with fresh parsley and serve.

Microwave

In step **1,** put carrots in microwave-safe 1-½ quart casserole. Add 2 tablespoons water. Cover with lid or vented plastic wrap. Microwave on 100% power 7-10 minutes, stirring once. Drain.
In step **2,** add butter, cranberry sauce, brown sugar, and salt to carrots.
In step **3,** microwave on 100% power 3-5 minutes, stirring two or three times.

Minted Peas

Serves 6

Here is a tasty vegetable that has a hidden bonus flavor. The mint jelly melts as it's heated, leaving a wonderful mellow mint message for all to enjoy. These peas would be delicious with lots of entrees, but outstanding when served with roast leg of lamb or lamb chops.

1   (16 ounce) package frozen peas
¼   cup mint flavored apple jelly
1   tablespoon butter or margarine
½   teaspoon salt
     Dash of pepper

1. Cook peas in medium saucepan according to package directions, omitting salt.

2. Drain peas.

3. In medium saucepan, combine drained peas, mint jelly, butter, salt and pepper. Toss mixture together.

(Continued)

Minted Peas (continued)

4. Heat over very low heat until jelly and butter melts, stirring frequently.

5. Serve in a white serving dish, if available, for color contrast.

Microwave

In step **1,** put peas in 1 quart microwave-safe casserole. Cover with lid or vented plastic wrap. Microwave on 100% power 6-8 minutes, stirring once.
In step **3,** put peas in microwave-safe casserole or serving dish with mint jelly, butter, salt and pepper. Toss mixture together.
In step **4,** microwave 1-3 minutes until jelly and butter melt, stirring once.

Wonderful Snow Peas and Cucumbers

Serves 4

Have you ever thought of serving a vegetable surprise? This exciting green vegetable combination will certainly stimulate table conversation. I'll bet second servings will be requested.

2   **(6 ounce) packages frozen pea pods, thawed, drained or 1 lb fresh snow peas**
1   **medium cucumber**
¼   **cup chopped onion**
2   **teaspoons sugar**
½   **teaspoon salt**
⅛   **teaspoon ground ginger**
1   **tablespoon vinegar**
1   **teaspoon chopped pimiento**
    Dash or two of hot pepper sauce
    Vegetable spray coating

1. Peel cucumber; cut in half lengthwise and remove seeds. Cut crosswise into ¼ inch slices. Set aside.

2. In small bowl, combine sugar, salt, ginger, vinegar, pimiento and hot pepper sauce; set aside.

3. Heat large skillet or wok over medium heat. Spray with vegetable coating.

4. Add pea pods, cucumber and onion; stir-fry until crisp-tender, about 2-4 minutes. Stir in vinegar mixture. Serve piping hot.

5. Surprise your family and friends.

Microwave

In step **3,** use 1-½ quart microwave-safe casserole.
In step **4,** microwave on 100% power 4-6 minutes, stirring every 2 minutes.

Cider-Spiced Sweet Potatoes

Serves 8

The full bodied flavor of apple cider seems to be a natural companion when teamed with sweet potatoes and spices. This is one of those wonderful make ahead and/or "toteable" vegetable casseroles that fits so well into busy schedules.

4 fresh sweet potatoes
2 teaspoons cornstarch
¼ teaspoon salt
¼ teaspoon ground cinnamon
¼ teaspoon ground ginger
⅛ teaspoon ground nutmeg
1 cup apple cider
2 tablespoons light brown sugar
1 tablespoon butter or margarine, melted
¼ cup chopped pecans or walnuts

1. Cook potatoes until slightly tender in boiling water. Drain and cool.

2. Peel and slice into 1-inch slices. Arrange slices of sweet potato in buttered 1-½ quart casserole.

3. In small saucepan, combine cornstarch, salt, cinnamon, ginger, and nutmeg. Stir in cider and brown sugar. Cook over medium heat, stirring constantly until sauce has thickened. Pour sauce over potatoes. Cover casserole. (Potatoes can be refrigerated for later heating, if desired.)

4. Bake in preheated 350 degree oven for 20-30 minutes until potatoes are hot and bubbly.

5. Before serving, prepare garnish by stirring together melted butter and pecans. Sprinkle garnish over potatoes and serve.

Microwave

In step 1, cook pierced sweet potatoes 6-7 minutes per pound on 100% power, turning potatoes over when half done. Wrap in clean terry cloth towel and let rest 10-15 minutes before peeling.
In step 2, use 1-½ quart microwave-safe casserole.
In step 3, put cornstarch, salt, cinnamon, ginger, and nutmeg in 1 quart microwave-safe measurer. Stir in cider and brown sugar. Microwave on 100% power 3-4 minutes stirring every minute.
In step 4, microwave at 80% power 10-15 minutes until hot, rotating dish once.

Low-Calorie Escalloped Potatoes

Serves 8

No one will ever guess you have decalorized these wonderful escalloped potatoes. For you see, chicken bouillon and skim milk have replaced whole milk and butter in this recipe.

2	**pounds potatoes, pared and thinly sliced (about 5 cups)**
1	**cup thinly sliced onion**
2	**tablespoons flour**
1	**teaspoon salt**
⅛	**teaspoon ground pepper**
1	**cup skim milk**
1	**cup water**
1	**teaspoon chicken bouillon or 1 chicken bouillon cube, crushed**
	Paprika

1. Spray a 2 quart casserole with vegetable cooking spray.

2. Arrange one third of the potatoes in the casserole.

3. Arrange one third of the onion on top of the potatoes.

4. In small dish, combine flour, salt and pepper.

5. Sprinkle one third of the flour mixture over potatoes and onions.

6. Repeat layers twice.

7. In small saucepan, bring milk, water and chicken bouillon to a boil over medium heat.

8. Pour hot milk mixture over potatoes and onions.

9. Sprinkle with paprika. Cover casserole.

10. Bake in preheated 375 degree oven for 1 and ¼ hours.

11. Uncover and bake 30 minutes more or until potatoes are tender.

Microwave

In step **1,** use 3 quart microwave-safe casserole.
In step **7,** combine milk, water, and chicken bouillon in 1 quart microwave-safe measurer. Microwave on 100% power 3-4 minutes.
In step **10,** microwave on 100% power 30-40 minutes, rotating dish once.

Twice Baked Potato Casserole

Serves 8-10

When you try this delicious plan for mashed potatoes, you'll be glad that Bernie Rutgers shared the recipe with me. Actually, this casserole idea was introduced to their family by daughter, Nancy Piper, and soon became the requested potatoes at most family gatherings.

8-12 servings of instant mashed potatoes
1   cup cultured sour cream
1   cup shredded cheddar cheese
6   slices bacon, cooked and crumbled
¼   cup sliced green onions

1. Prepare the number of servings of potatoes needed according to package directions.

2. Spread prepared mashed potatoes in greased shallow 2-quart casserole.

3. Top with sour cream, cheese, then bacon and finally green onions.

4. Potatoes may be covered and refrigerated up to 24 hours, if desired.

5. Bake uncovered in preheated 350 degree oven until hot, about 30 minutes.

Microwave

In step **1,** remember to prepare potatoes in 3-quart microwave-safe casserole using the microwave to heat the liquid.
In step **5,** use the microwave probe set to 150 degrees at 70% power.

Cheesy Hash Browns

Serves 4-6

It doesn't take long to put these delicious potatoes in the oven. After all what could be more convenient than potatoes that are peeled and precooked. Just toss the hash browns and cheese together with supporting ingredients for a winning idea.

4   cups frozen hash brown potatoes, thawed (southern style)
1   cup shredded sharp cheddar cheese
¼   cup sliced green onion
1   teaspoon instant chicken bouillon or 1 chicken bouillon cube, crushed
½   cup boiling water
1   tablespoon butter or margarine

1. In a buttered 1-½ quart casserole, combine hash brown potatoes, shredded cheese and sliced green onion.

2. Dissolve chicken bouillon in boiling water.

3. Pour water over potato mixture. Dot with butter.

(Continued)

Cheesy Hash Browns (continued)

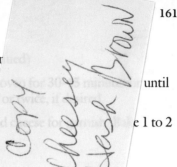

4. Bake, covered, in preheated 375 degree oven for 30-35 minutes until potatoes are tender, stirring gently once or twice, if desired.

5. If desired, top with triangles of processed cheese for a minute or so 1 to 2 minutes or until cheese melts.

Ratatouille

Serves 8

Although ratatouille originated in Provence, France, it contains all those summer vegetables that grow abundantly here in the Midwest. If you think family members might hesitate at the thought of eggplant, don't worry, this flavorful vegetable stew will win their tastebuds. Make several batches when gardens are producing and freeze for those frosty winter months.

2	**medium onions, sliced**
2	**cloves garlic, chopped or ¼ teaspoon garlic powder**
¼	**cup vegetable or olive oil**
2	**small zucchini, cut in ½ inch slices**
1	**small eggplant, peeled and cut in 1 inch cubes**
1	**large green pepper, seeded, cut in strips**
3	**medium tomatoes, diced**
2	**tablespoons chopped fresh parsley**
2	**teaspoons salt**
½	**teaspoon basil leaves**
⅛	**teaspoon ground pepper**

1. In large heavy skillet or dutch oven, saute onions and garlic in hot oil until tender (do not brown).

2. Add zucchini, eggplant, green pepper, tomatoes, parsley, salt, basil leaves and pepper. Cover and cook 15 minutes.

3. Uncover and continue cooking 30-40 minutes or until vegetables are tender and juice is thickened. Stir occasionally.

Microwave

In step **1,** reduce oil to 1 tablespoon. Saute onions and garlic in 3 quart covered microwave-safe casserole on 100% power 3-4 minutes, stirring once.

In step **2,** add zucchini, eggplant, and green pepper. Microwave on 100% power 6-8 minutes, stirring once. Add tomatoes, parsley, salt, basil leaves and pepper. Microwave on 100% power 8-12 minutes, stirring two or three times.

Squash and Apple Bake

Serves 6-8

When the supply of fresh squash and apples is plentiful, try this pleasing combination of flavors. It's an easy way to serve two fall favorites from the good earth.

2   **pounds butternut or buttercup squash**
2   **baking apples, cored and cut into ½ inch slices**
¼   **cup butter or margarine, melted**
½   **cup brown sugar**
1   **tablespoon flour**
1   **teaspoon salt**
½   **teaspoon ground mace**

1. Cut squash in half. Remove seeds and fibers; pare squash. Cut squash into ½ inch slices.

2. Arrange squash slices in ungreased 8x12-inch baking dish.

3. Top squash with apple slices.

4. In small mixing bowl, combine melted butter, brown sugar, flour, salt and mace.

5. Sprinkle sugar mixture over apples and squash.

6. Cover with foil.

7. Bake in preheated 350 degree oven for 50-60 minutes.

8. Garnish with bright red apple wedge.

Microwave

In step **2,** use microwave-safe 8x12-inch baking dish.
In step **6,** cover with vented plastic wrap.
In step **7,** microwave on 100% power 14-18 minutes or until squash is tender, rotating dish once.

Super Spinach Souffle

Serves 6-8

If you like rice and an interesting vegetable all wrapped up in one neat casserole, then this spinach souffle is for you. Actually the word souffle may be deceiving because this light mixture is stable enough to be carried to a pot luck supper.

½	cup chopped onion
1	(10 ounce) package frozen chopped spinach
4	eggs, separated
1	(10-¾ ounce) can cream of mushroom soup
½	cup cultured sour cream
½	teaspoon salt
¼	teaspoon seasoned pepper
	Dash of ground nutmeg
2	cups cooked rice
1	cup (4 ounces) shredded sharp cheddar cheese

1. Cook onion with spinach, following package directions. Drain thoroughly.

2. In large mixing bowl, beat egg yolks. Add soup, sour cream, salt, seasoned pepper and nutmeg. Mix well.

3. Stir in rice, spinach and cheese.

4. Beat egg whites until stiff, but not dry. Gently fold egg whites into rice mixture.

5. Turn into buttered shallow 2 quart baking dish.

6. Bake in preheated 325 degree oven for 45 minutes, or until knife inserted just off center comes out clean.

Microwave

In step **1,** put onion and spinach in 1 quart microwave-safe casserole. Cover with lid or vented plastic wrap. Microwave on 100% power 5-7 minutes, stirring twice. Drain thoroughly.

In step **5,** microwave on 80% power 15-20 minutes, rotating dish once. Let stand 5 minutes.

Escalloped Tomatoes
Serves 6-8

It's easy to overlook tomatoes when planning the hot vegetable course. No longer will that be true when you try this tomato casserole. You'll find it's quick to fix, looks wonderful, and carries well to the next cooperative dinner.

¼   cup chopped onion
¼   cup butter or margarine
2   (16 ounce) cans tomatoes, cut up or 2 pints home canned tomatoes
2   eggs, beaten
1   cup soda cracker crumbs
1   cup grated sharp cheddar cheese
½   teaspoon salt
    Paprika

1. In small saucepan or skillet, saute onion in butter just until tender.

2. In large mixing bowl, combine sauteed onions, tomatoes, eggs, cracker crumbs, cheese and salt. Mix well.

3. Pour mixture into lightly buttered shallow 2 quart baking dish. Sprinkle top with paprika.

4. Bake in preheated 350 degree oven for 30-40 minutes until set.

Microwave

In step **1,** put onion and butter in 2 quart microwave-safe measurer. Microwave on 100% power 1-3 minutes until onion is tender, stirring once.
In step **2,** add tomatoes, eggs, cracker crumbs, cheese and salt to onions. Mix well.
In step **3,** use microwave-safe shallow 2 quart baking dish.
In step **4,** microwave on 100% power 14-18 minutes, rotating dish twice.

Wild Rice and Mushrooms
Serves 4-6

Here is one grand way I like to use some of the coveted wild rice we receive at Christmas time from my Aunt Jessie and Uncle Bill Howell in Minnesota. The mushrooms add their own special class to this gourmet fare.

2   cups water
2   teaspoons chicken bouillon or 2 chicken bouillon cubes, crushed
½   cup chopped onion
¼   cup wild rice, rinsed
½   cup natural long grain rice
1   (4 ounce) can mushroom stems and pieces, undrained
1   tablespoon chopped fresh parsley

(Continued)

Wild Rice and Mushrooms (continued)

1. In medium saucepan, combine water, chicken bouillon and onion. Bring to a boil.

2. Add wild rice. Reduce heat, cover and simmer 20 minutes.

3. Add long grain rice and undrained mushrooms; bring to a boil.

4. Reduce heat, cover and simmer 15-20 minutes or until the liquid is absorbed.

5. Put in attractive serving dish. Garnish with snipped parsley.

Summer Squash Stir-Fry

Serves 6-8

Summer squash, like yellow crooked neck and zucchini, adapt well to the stir-fry method because their tender skins and flesh cook quickly. Add tomatoes for a dash of color and cheese for extended flavor to create this quick vegetable dish.

2	tablespoons vegetable oil
1	clove garlic, minced or ⅛ teaspoon garlic powder
1	large onion, sliced and separated into rings
4	cups thinly sliced zucchini
4	cups thinly sliced yellow squash
2	tomatoes, cut into wedges
¾	teaspoon salt
¼	teaspoon ground pepper
1	cup (4 ounces) shredded cheddar cheese

1. Pour oil into skillet or wok. Add garlic and stir fry briefly.

2. Add onion; stir-fry 1 or 2 minutes.

3. Stir in zucchini and yellow squash; cook several minutes until crisp-tender.

4. Add tomatoes, salt and pepper; stir well. Heat briefly.

5. Sprinkle cheese over vegetables, stirring just until cheese melts.

6. Serve immediately.

Zucchini Julienne

Serves 4

Just cut narrow strips of zucchini the size of matchsticks for this interesting quick summertime vegetable recipe. This clever combination of flavors came from the recipe file of my friend, Ann Paulson. It's a great way to keep your family interested in zucchini.

2   **tablespoons vegetable oil**
1   **medium onion, thinly sliced**
1   **pound zucchini, cut in julienne strips (4 cups)**
1   **tablespoon sesame seeds**
1   **tablespoon soy sauce**
    Salt and pepper to taste, if desired

1. In large skillet, heat oil.

2. Quickly saute onion and zucchini until lightly browned and crisply done.

3. Stir in sesame seeds and soy sauce.

4. Salt and pepper, if desired.

5. Serve immediately.

Calico Citrus Brussels Sprouts

Serves 4

Low sodium and low calorie characteristics come naturally to members of the citrus fruit family. This recipe has capitalized on the clear clean flavor of oranges to bind together a nice combination of brussels sprouts and carrots.

1   **pound fresh brussels sprouts**
1   **cup chicken broth**
1   **medium carrot, peeled and coarsely grated**
1-½ **teaspoons cornstarch**
½   **cup unsweetened orange juice**
⅛   **teaspoon orange rind**
⅛   **teaspoon ground nutmeg**

1. Wash brussels sprouts thoroughly, and remove discolored leaves. Cut off stem ends, and slash bottom of each sprout with a shallow X.

2. Combine brussels sprouts and broth in a medium saucepan; bring to a boil.

3. Cover, reduce heat and simmer 8 minutes.

4. Add carrots, and cook an additional 2-3 minutes or until tender. Drain well, and place in a serving dish.

(Continued)

Calico Citrus Brussels Sprouts (continued)

5. In small saucepan, combine cornstarch and orange juice, stirring well.

6. Heat mixture to boiling; cook 1 minute, stirring constantly.

7. Stir in orange rind and nutmeg; pour over vegetables, and toss gently.

8. Serve and enjoy.

Microwave

In step **2,** combine brussels sprouts and broth in 1-½-quart microwave-safe casserole.
In step **3,** microwave, covered with lid or vented plastic wrap, on **100%** power 6-8 minutes, stirring once.
In step **4,** add carrots and microwave on **100%** power 1-2 minutes until tender.
In step **5,** put cornstarch and orange juice in 2-cup microwave-safe measurer. Microwave on **100%** power 1-2 minutes until thickened, stirring every 30 seconds with a wire whisk.

Green Beans With Tomatoes

Serves 6-8

Here is an example of how well it works to use the herb basil in place of salt when cooking fresh vegetables. A small amount of onion, celery and green pepper cooked with the green beans gives an additional flavor boost.

1	**pound fresh green beans**
¼	**cup chopped onion**
½	**cup chopped celery**
¼	**cup chopped green pepper**
½	**teaspoon dried basil leaves, crushed**
¼	**teaspoon ground pepper**
2	**cups coarsely chopped peeled tomatoes**

1. Wash beans; trim ends, and remove strings. Cut beans into 1 and ½-inch pieces.

2. In medium saucepan, cook beans, onion, celery, green pepper, basil and pepper in a small amount of boiling water 10-12 minutes or until tender. Drain.

3. Add tomatoes, and cook until thoroughly heated.

Microwave

In step **2,** combine beans, onion, celery, green pepper, basil and pepper in 1-½ quart-microwave-safe casserole. Microwave, covered with lid or vented plastic wrap, on **100%** power 7-9 minutes until tender, stirring twice.
In step **3,** add tomatoes and microwave on **100%** power 1-3 minutes until thoroughly heated.

Teriyaki Bean Special

Serves 6

This vegetable combination will give an interesting Oriental flair to a menu with very little extra effort. It's a delicious way to serve green beans to family and friends. Pass extra soy sauce for those who are partial to its pungent flavor.

¼ **cup butter or margarine**
½ **cup chopped onion**
4 **cups cut fresh green beans or frozen loose pack green beans, cooked and drained**
1 **(16 ounce) can bean sprouts, drained (2 cups)**
1 **(4 ounce) can sliced mushrooms, drained**
3 **tablespoons soy sauce**

1. In medium skillet, melt butter and saute onion till tender.

2. Add green beans, bean sprouts, mushrooms and soy sauce; mix lightly.

3. Simmer, uncovered, for 15 minutes, stirring occasionally.

4. Serve with additional soy sauce.

Microwave

In step **1,** put butter and onion in 2 quart microwave-safe casserole. Microwave on 100% power 2-4 minutes until onion is tender, stirring once.
In step **3,** microwave on 100% power 8-10 minutes until hot, stirring 2 or 3 times.

Finale

Delicious desserts are described in this chapter. Whether your mouth waters for Russian Torte, Honeyed Rhubarb Pie or Kiwi Ice, here are detailed instructions designed to help you create a memorable finale.

Keep calorie conscious persons in mind by cutting small servings of desserts like Michigan Apple Pie or reduce sugar during the preparation process as exhibited in Slim Line Pumpkin Pie. Frozen desserts such as the Pineapple/Orange Freeze can add the perfect light ending to a marvelous menu.

Most of the recipes in this grouping feature make ahead qualities. The freezer works equally well for storing a carefully wrapped pan of Crowd Pleasing Tin Roof or a tightly covered hidden container of Candy and Peanut Jumbles.

Contents

Cinnamon Apple Cake

Serves 12

This treasured apple recipe was mailed to me by my friend Jean Hartman from Evansville, Indiana, whose sister, Marge, had sent it to her. Believe me it is a cake recipe worthy of sharing pieces of the cake as well as copies of the recipe.

1	cup vegetable shortening (use half margarine if desired)
1	cup sugar
½	cup brown sugar
2	eggs
2	cups flour (or use 1-½ cups flour and ½ cup whole wheat flour, if you wish)
1	teaspoon baking soda
1	teaspoon salt
1-½	teaspoons ground cinnamon
1	cup buttermilk
2	cups chopped peeled apples (use food processor)
⅓	cup sugar
½	teaspoon ground cinnamon

1. In large mixing bowl, cream together shortening, 1 cup sugar, and brown sugar until light and fluffy.

2. Add eggs, 1 at a time, beating well after each addition.

3. Mix together flour, whole wheat flour if used, soda, salt and 1-½ teaspoons cinnamon.

4. Add dry ingredients alternately with buttermilk, beginning and ending with dry ingredients. Beat well after each addition.

5. Stir in chopped apples.

6. Spread in greased 9x13-inch baking pan.

7. In small mixing bowl, combine ⅓ cup sugar and ½ teaspoon ground cinnamon.

8. Sprinkle cinnamon sugar on top of batter.

9. Bake in preheated 350 degree oven for 45-50 minutes until inserted wooden pick comes out clean.

10. Cool on wire rack.

Food Processor Carrot Cake

Serves 12

If your food processor has standard capacity, you can create this incredibly easy carrot cake by chopping the carrots while the batter is being mixed. The finished product is a moist flavorful cake that would be welcome at many occasions.

4	**eggs**
1	**cup vegetable oil**
2	**cups sugar**
1	**pound carrots, peeled and cut into 1-inch long chunks**
2	**cups flour**
3	**teaspoons baking powder**
1	**teaspoon baking soda**
1	**teaspoon salt**
2	**teaspoons ground cinnamon**

1. With the steel blade in place put eggs, vegetable oil, and sugar in food processor work bowl.

2. Process until smooth pulsing machine on and off.

3. With the machine running, slowly add the carrot chunks through the feed tube.

4. After all carrots have been added, pulse until large pieces of carrot disappear.

5. When the carrots appear fully grated, remove the lid and add flour, baking powder, soda, salt and cinnamon.

6. Replace the lid and process by pulsing until the dry ingredients are thoroughly blended.

7. Holding steel blade in place with index finger, pour batter into a well greased and floured 10-inch bundt baking pan.

8. Bake in preheated 400 degree oven 50-60 minutes until wooden pick inserted near the center comes out clean.

9. Let cake stand 5-10 minutes. Remove to cooling rack.

German Sweet Chocolate Cake

Serves 20

At our house this is the cake that is requested for birthdays and special occasions. Just one bite of this beautiful chocolate creation and there is no doubt that this cake is in a class by itself. For convenience, I use dry buttermilk powder in place of 1 cup buttermilk.

1	(4 ounce) package German sweet chocolate
½	cup boiling water
4	eggs, separated
1	cup butter or margarine, softened
2	cups sugar
1	teaspoon vanilla
2-¼	cups flour
¼	cup dry buttermilk powder
1	teaspoon baking soda
½	teaspoon salt
1	cup water

1. In small saucepan, melt chocolate in boiling water. Set aside to cool.

2. With electric beaters, beat egg whites until stiff.

3. In large mixing bowl, use unwashed beaters to cream softened butter with sugar until fluffy.

4. Add egg yolks, one at a time, beating well after each addition.

5. Blend in vanilla and cooled chocolate.

6. Sift flour with buttermilk powder, soda and salt.

7. Add alternately with 1 cup water to chocolate mixture, beating after each addition until smooth.

8. Gently fold in beaten egg whites.

9. Pour into three 9-inch greased and parchment or waxed paper lined pans.

10. Bake in preheated 350 degree oven for 30-35 minutes.

11. Turn out on wire racks to cool.

12. Frost tops only with Coconut-Pecan Frosting. Refrigerate and enjoy.

Coconut-Pecan Frosting

Frosts 1 cake

This is the traditional coconut-pecan topping used to assemble a German Sweet Chocolate Cake. If you use a microwave, I think you'll like the easy method that's suggested. Cooked either way, it's worth the time it takes.

(Continued)

Coconut-Pecan Frosting (continued)

3   egg yolks
1   cup evaporated milk
1   cup sugar
½   cup butter or margarine
1   teaspoon vanilla
1-⅓ cups flaked coconut
1   cup chopped pecans

1. In medium saucepan, slightly beat egg yolks. Stir in evaporated milk, sugar, butter and vanilla.

2. Cook and stir over medium heat until thickened, about 12 minutes.

3. Stir in coconut and pecans.

4. Cool until thick enough to spread, beating occasionally.

Microwave

In step **1,** slightly beat egg yolks in 2 quart microwave-safe measurer. Stir in evaporated milk, sugar, butter and vanilla.
In step **2,** microwave on 100% power 5-8 minutes, until thickened, stirring every 2 minutes.

Pecan Frosting

Frosts 1 cake

This is the companion frosting for the Coconut Pecan Cake on page 174. It's an easy frosting to make even for those cooks that usually avoid such experiences. On the very first attempt you can produce a glorious cake.

½   cup butter or margarine, softened
1   (8 ounce) package cream cheese, softened
1   pound of confectioners' sugar (4-½ cups)
1   teaspoon vanilla
1   cup chopped pecans

1. In medium mixing bowl, beat together butter and cream cheese with electric beater.

2. Add confectioners' sugar and beat well.

3. Beat in vanilla.

4. Stir in pecans.

5. Put together the three layers of the Coconut Pecan Cake using part of this frosting as filling.

6. Complete cake by frosting the sides and top.

7. Refrigerate. Admire. Serve.

Coconut Pecan Cake

Serves 20

Ever since the first time our son, Paul, baked this very special cake, it has been one of the family favorites. Although it does take time to make, one time-saving technique is to beat egg whites with clean beaters and then proceed with the unwashed beaters. It's a very stable cake that carries well so can easily be taken to the next family reunion.

5	eggs, separated
½	cup butter or margarine, softened
½	cup vegetable shortening
2	cups sugar
2	cups flour
¼	cup dry buttermilk powder
1	teaspoon baking soda
½	teaspoon salt
1	cup water
2	teaspoons vanilla
2	cups flaked coconut
1	cup chopped pecans

1. In medium mixing bowl, beat separated egg whites until very stiff. Set aside.

2. In large mixing bowl, use unwashed beaters to cream together butter, shortening and sugar until light and fluffy.

3. Add egg yolks, one at a time, beating well after each addition.

4. Sift together flour, buttermilk powder, soda and salt.

5. Add flour mixture alternately with water, beginning and ending with the flour mixture.

6. Stir in vanilla, coconut and pecans.

7. Gently fold in stiffly beaten egg whites.

8. Pour batter equally into 3 greased and parchment lined or floured 9-inch cake pans.

9. Bake in preheated 350 degree oven about 35-40 minutes until wooden pick inserted in center comes out clean. Turn out on wire racks to cool.

10. Frost layers and sides with Pecan Frosting on page 173.

Yogurt Shortcake

Serves 6

When my friend, Florence Thacher, from Janesville, Wisconsin, shared this wonderful recipe with me, she mentioned that this version brought back childhood memories of the shortcakes her mother baked. It's equally delicious with any fruit, but the Thacher family prefers strawberries.

2   **cups flour**
2   **tablespoons sugar**
3-½ **teaspoons baking powder**
¼   **teaspoon salt**
½   **cup butter or margarine, chilled**
¼   **cup plain yogurt**
¼-½ **cup milk**
2   **tablespoons butter or margarine, softened**
     Sweetened berries of your choice
     Whipped cream or light cream

1. In medium mixing bowl, sift together flour, sugar, baking powder and salt.

2. Cut in chilled butter with pastry blender, or fork.

3. Mix in yogurt with fork.

4. Add just enough milk to make a soft dough.

5. Scrape dough out of bowl onto a floured pastry cloth or surface. Knead for a few seconds to form a soft ball of dough.

6. Divide dough in half. Pat or roll one half of the dough into an 8-inch circle about ¾ inch thick.

7. Place this half of the dough in well-greased 8-inch round baking pan.

8. Spread softened butter on dough that is in pan.

9. Pat or roll the other half of the dough into an 8-inch circle about ¾ inch thick.

10. Put second half of dough on buttered dough.

11. Bake in preheated 400 degree oven 20-25 minutes until lightly browned.

12. Remove from pan; split layers; serve with sweetened berries and cream.

Russian Torte

Serves 12-16

This lovely torte deserves the honor of being served at the table after guests have had ample time to admire its beauty. Adults especially appreciate the pleasing subtle mocha flavor. What a wonderful make ahead dessert.

1   **envelope unflavored gelatin**
¼   **cup cold water**
2   **tablespoons instant coffee powder**
1   **cup sifted confectioners' sugar**
⅛   **teaspoon salt**
2   **cups whipping cream**
8   **egg yolks**
1   **teaspoon vanilla**
1   **(10-inch) baked angel food cake**
    Sliced unblanched or toasted almonds

1. In small saucepan, soften gelatin in cold water.

2. Cook over low heat until gelatin dissolves. Remove from heat.

3. Stir in coffee powder until dissolved. Add confectioners' sugar and salt. Mix well. Set aside.

4. In large mixing bowl, beat whipping cream until soft peaks form.

5. Use unwashed beaters to beat egg yolks in medium mixing bowl until thick and lemony.

6. Beat gelatin mixture into egg yolks.

7. Fold yolk mixture and vanilla into whipped cream.

8. Cut angel food cake into 3 horizontal layers.

9. Frost between layers with cream mixture.

10. Then frost sides and top of cake.

11. Decorate top edge of cake with almonds.

12. Refrigerate until serving.

13. Serve to admiring family and friends.

Chocolate Zucchini Cake

Serves 12-16

My friend, Jan Mora, says this is one of her son's, Bill, favorite cakes. Who would suspect that zucchini would end up in the middle of a moist delicious cake? The chocolate chips on top double the chocolate flavor and act as icing.

½   cup butter or margarine, softened
½   cup vegetable oil
1-¾ cups sugar
2   eggs
1   teaspoon vanilla
½   cup cultured sour cream
2-½ cups flour
1   teaspoon baking soda
½   teaspoon salt
¼   cup unsweetened cocoa
2   cups shredded zucchini
1   cup semi-sweet chocolate chips

1. In large mixing bowl, cream together butter, oil and sugar.

2. Beat in eggs and vanilla.

3. Stir in sour cream

4. Sift together flour, soda, salt and cocoa. Stir into creamed mixture. Add zucchini and blend completely.

5. Pour into greased and floured 9x13-inch baking pan.

6. Sprinkle with chocolate chips.

7. Bake in preheated 325 degree oven 45-50 minutes or until toothpick comes out clean.

8. Cool, cut into squares and serve with icy cold glasses of milk.

Candy and Peanut Jumbles

Makes 3-4 dozen

This popular drop cookie is a favorite with lots of cookie monsters. Chopped peanuts as well as candy pieces can be found hidden inside these tasty jumbles. Wrap pairs of cookies back to back with plastic wrap before placing in cookie tins for mailing to your favorite college student.

1   **cup margarine or butter, softened**
1   **cup sugar**
1   **cup brown sugar**
2   **eggs**
1   **teaspoon vanilla**
2   **cups flour**
1   **teaspoon baking soda**
½   **teaspoon salt**
1-½ **cups quick cooking oats**
2   **cups candy coated milk chocolate pieces**
1   **cup coarsely chopped peanuts**

1. In large mixing bowl, cream together margarine, sugar and brown sugar. Add eggs, one at a time, beating well after each addition. Stir in vanilla.

2. Sift together flour, baking soda and salt. Add to creamed mixture and mix well. Stir in oats.

3. Add chocolate pieces and peanuts. Mix thoroughly.

4. Drop by ejector spoon or teaspoon on parchment lined or lightly greased baking sheet.

5. Bake in preheated 350 degree oven 12-15 minutes or until light golden brown. Put on cooling rack to cool.

Sugar Topped Lemonade Cookies

Makes 3-4 dozen

These light lemony butter cookies have a delicate flavor that will please the palate. They would be a lovely companion for the Sherbet Bouquet recipe on page 198. Store conveniently in airtight container with waxed paper between layers.

1   **cup butter or margarine, softened**
1   **cup sugar**
2   **eggs**
3   **cups flour**
1   **teaspoon soda**
1   **(6 ounce) can frozen lemonade concentrate, thawed**
     Sugar

(Continued)

Sugar Topped Lemonade Cookies (continued)

1. In large mixing bowl, cream together butter and the 1 cup sugar.

2. Add eggs, one at a time, beating well after each addition.

3. Sift together flour and soda; add alternately to the creamed mixture with ½ cup lemonade concentrate.

4. Drop dough by teaspoon or ejector spoon on ungreased or parchment lined cookie sheet about 2 inches apart.

5. Bake cookies in preheated 400 degree oven about 8-10 minutes until lightly browned around the edges.

6. Brush hot cookies lightly with remaining lemonade concentrate; sprinkle with sugar.

7. Remove cookies to cooling rack.

Chocolate Lassies

3-4 dozen cookies

Whether you need a cookie for an after-school snack or to send in a college "care" package here is a wonderful suggestion. This treasured family recipe was graciously given to me by Mary Reineke and our family agrees that the molasses and chocolate flavors team together to create a real winner.

¾ **cup vegetable shortening**
¾ **cup sugar**
2 **eggs**
½ **cup molasses**
2-½ **cups flour**
1-½ **teaspoons baking soda**
½ **teaspoon salt**
½ **teaspoon ground cinnamon**
½ **teaspoon ground ginger**
1 **(6 ounce) package semi-sweet chocolate chips**

1. In medium mixing bowl, cream shortening and sugar together.

2. Add eggs, one at a time, beating well after each addition. Stir in molasses.

3. Sift together flour, soda, salt, cinnamon and ginger. Add to creamed mixture and stir until flour disappears.

4. Stir in chocolate chips.

5. Drop by ejector spoon or teaspoon on parchment lined or lightly greased baking sheet.

6. Bake in preheated 375 degree oven for 8-10 minutes. Be careful not to over bake. Remove from oven. Cool on rack.

One Cup Of Everything Cookies

6 dozen

This clever cookie recipe has recently been traveling through the House family from state to state. It started when Irene House in Illinois shared the recipe with Gladys House in Wisconsin who in turn gave a sampling of the cookies complete with recipe to Betsey House in Minnesota and to me, Deanna House, in Michigan.

1　cup butter or margarine, softened
1　cup vegetable oil
1　cup sugar
1　cup brown sugar
1　egg
3-½ cups flour
1　teaspoon baking soda
1　teaspoon cream of tartar
1　teaspoon vanilla
1　cup quick cooking oats, uncooked
1　cup crisp rice cereal
1　cup shredded coconut
1　cup semi-sweet chocolate chips
1　cup chopped walnuts or pecans

1. In large mixing bowl, cream together butter, oil, sugar and brown sugar until light and fluffy.

2. Add egg and beat well.

3. Sift together flour, soda and cream of tartar. Stir dry ingredients into creamed mixture.

4. Stir in vanilla, oatmeal, cereal, coconut, chocolate chips and walnuts.

5. Roll into 1-inch balls and place on ungreased or parchment lined baking sheet. Flatten with fork.

6. Bake in preheated 350 degree oven for 10-15 minutes. Cool on wire rack.

Miracle Cookies

2-3 dozen

The miracle of these cookies is that there is no flour and/or leavening agent and yet they look and taste like a great peanut butter cookie. So for those on special diets or those who have run out of flour, here's a recipe for you.

1　cup peanut butter
1　cup sugar
1　egg, beaten
1　teaspoon vanilla

(Continued)

Miracle Cookies (continued)

1. In medium mixing bowl, combine peanut butter and sugar; mix well.

2. Stir in egg and vanilla.

3. Roll dough into ¾-inch balls.

4. Place balls on ungreased or parchment lined cookie sheets.

5. Flatten with a floured fork.

6. Bake cookies in preheated 350 degree oven for approximately 10 minutes.

7. Allow to cool before removing from cookie sheets.

Refrigerator Caramel Nut Slices

Makes 8 dozen

I remember calling this type of cookie an ice box cookie, so you know they are an old fashioned idea. However, how neatly these crisp cookie slices fit into today's busy world. Mix, refrigerate, and bake at your convenience.

½   cup margarine or butter, softened
½   cup vegetable shortening
2   cups brown sugar
2   eggs
3-½ cups flour
1   teaspoon baking soda
½   teaspoon salt
1   cup chopped walnuts or pecans

1. In large mixing bowl, cream together margarine, shortening and brown sugar until light and fluffy with an electric mixer.

2. Add eggs, one at a time, beating well after each addition.

3. Sift together flour, baking soda and salt. Add to creamed mixture and thoroughly mix together. Stir in walnuts.

4. Divide dough in half and shape each half into 12-inch roll. Wrap in waxed paper and then aluminum foil. Refrigerate overnight.

5. Cut each roll into 48 slices, about ¼ inch thick.

6. Place slices, about 2 inches apart, on greased or parchment lined baking sheets.

7. Bake in preheated 400 degree oven 5-7 minutes or until golden brown. Remove from baking sheets; cool on racks.

182

Honey-Oatmeal Cookies

Makes 6 dozen

Oatmeal cookies have been favorites with the homebaked cookie set for years and years. This variation boasts honey and sour cream for added flavor and moistness. Wrap back to back with plastic wrap before packing in covered containers for mailing to family members away from home.

1	cup butter or margarine, softened
1	cup sugar
¼	cup honey
2	eggs
½	cup cultured sour cream
2	cups flour
1	teaspoon baking soda
1	teaspoon salt
1	teaspoon ground cinnamon
1	teaspoon ground ginger
3	cups quick cooking oats
1	cup chopped dates

1. In large mixing bowl, cream together butter, sugar and honey until light and fluffy.

2. Add eggs, one at a time, beating well after each addition.

3. Stir in sour cream and mix well.

4. Sift together flour, soda, salt, cinnamon and ginger; add to creamed mixture. Combine thoroughly.

5. Stir in oats and dates, mixing well.

6. Drop dough by ejector spoon or teaspoon onto parchment lined or lightly greased baking sheet.

7. Bake in preheated 375 degree oven 10-12 minutes until lightly browned.

8. Cool a few minutes before removing to cooling rack.

9. Store in airtight container.

Crisp Sugar Cookies

Makes 4-5 dozen cookies

This delightful sugar cookie recipe comes from my mother, Lois Howell. Family members who return to her Wisconsin farm home during the holidays can often find these cookies topped with muscat raisins stored in cookie tins on the back porch table.

(Continued)

Crisp Sugar Cookies (continued)

1 cup margarine or butter, softened
1-½ cups sugar
1 teaspoon vanilla
3 egg yolks
2 cups flour
1 teaspoon baking soda
1 teaspoon cream of tartar
⅛ teaspoon salt

1. In large mixing bowl, cream together margarine, sugar and vanilla until light and fluffy.

2. Add egg yolks, one at a time, beating well after each addition.

3. Sift together flour, soda, cream of tartar and salt. Stir dry ingredients into creamed mixture.

4. Chill dough thoroughly.

5. Shape dough into small round balls and place on parchment lined or ungreased baking sheet. Press flat with fork dipped in milk.

6. Bake in preheated 350 degree oven 10-12 minutes. Cool on rack.

Pecan Petites

Makes 3 dozen

These sugar-coated party cookies are often called Mexican Wedding Cakes or Russian Teacakes. I like this particular version of the recipe because it is quick, easy and the dough doesn't require chilling before shaping. If you need to furnish a dozen cookies for the next church or school function, these will be appreciated.

1 cup butter or margarine, softened
¼ cup sugar
1 teaspoon vanilla
2 cups flour
1 cup chopped pecans
  Confectioners' sugar

1. In medium mixing bowl, cream together butter and sugar until light and fluffy. Blend in vanilla.

2. Add flour; mix well. Stir in nuts.

3. Shape rounded teaspoonfuls of dough into balls; place on parchment lined or ungreased cookie sheet.

4. Bake in preheated 325 degree oven about 20 minutes.

5. Cool slightly; shake in plastic bag with confectioners' sugar. Cool completely. Again shake in plastic bag with confectioners' sugar.

Iced Ginger Creams

Makes 4 dozen cookies

My brother, Rich Howell from Dallas Texas, always liked these ginger cake-like gems when we were growing up on the family farm in southern Wisconsin. Iced with a little vanilla frosting, they are just as tasty today.

⅓   cup shortening
½   cup sugar
1   egg
½   cup molasses
½   cup water
2   cups flour
1   teaspoon ground ginger
½   teaspoon salt
½   teaspoon baking soda
½   teaspoon ground nutmeg
½   teaspoon ground cloves
½   teaspoon ground cinnamon
      Vanilla Butter Frosting

1. In large mixing bowl, cream together shortening and sugar. Beat in egg.

2. Stir in molasses and water.

3. Sift together flour, ginger, salt, soda, nutmeg, cloves and cinnamon.

4. Stir dry ingredients into creamed mixture.

5. Cover and chill thoroughly.

6. Drop dough by teaspoonfuls onto ungreased or parchment lined baking sheet.

7. Bake in preheated 400 degree oven 8-10 minutes or until almost no imprint remains when touched with finger.

8. Immediately remove from baking sheet; cool on wire rack.

9. Ice with Vanilla Butter Frosting.

10. For Vanilla Butter Frosting, blend together 3 tablespoons softened butter or margarine with 1-½ cups confectioners' sugar. Stir in ¾ teaspoon vanilla and about 1 tablespoon milk; beat until frosting is smooth and of spreading consistency.

Old-Fashioned Chocolate Drops

4-5 dozen cookies

This recipe reminds me of my growing-up years on our family farm in southern Wisconsin. All of us liked chocolate, especially my Dad. These cake-like hearty cookies were one of his favorites, especially when iced with creamy chocolate frosting.

½	cup butter or margarine, softened
½	cup vegetable shortening
2	cups brown sugar
4	squares unsweetened chocolate, melted and cooled
2	eggs
4	cups flour
1	teaspoon baking soda
¾	teaspoon baking powder
1	teaspoon salt
1-½	cups milk
1	teaspoon vanilla
1	cup chopped walnuts or pecans
½	cup raisins
½	cup shredded coconut

1. In large mixing bowl, cream together butter, shortening, and brown sugar.

2. Add eggs, one at a time, beating well after each addition. Stir in melted chocolate.

3. Sift together flour, soda, baking powder and salt. Add dry ingredients alternately with milk, beginning and ending with the flour mixture.

4. Stir in vanilla, nuts, raisins and coconut.

5. Drop by ejector spoon or teaspoon on parchment lined or lightly greased baking sheet.

6. Bake in preheated 350 degree oven for 12-15 minutes.

7. Cool. Frost with chocolate frosting, if desired.

186

Sara's Chocolate Chip Bars

3 dozen bars

Our daughter Sara can whip up a batch of these chocolate chip favorites in a matter of minutes. Bar cookies bake so quickly that even on a warm summer day, the oven doesn't need to heat very long. Remember, these cookies mail easily and are great for college "care packages."

1	cup butter or margarine, softened
¾	cup sugar
¾	cup brown sugar
2	eggs
1	teaspoon vanilla
2-¼	cups flour
1	teaspoon baking soda
1	teaspoon salt
1	cup semi-sweet chocolate chips
½	cup chopped pecans or walnuts, if desired

1. In large mixing bowl, cream together butter, sugar and brown sugar.

2. Add eggs, one at a time, beating well after each addition. Stir in vanilla.

3. Sift together flour, soda and salt. Stir into creamed mixture until all flour disappears.

4. Stir in chocolate chips and pecans.

5. Spread into greased 10x15x1 inch baking pan.

6. Bake in preheated 375 degree oven for 20 minutes. Cool and cut into squares.

No-Bake Chocolate Cookies

3-4 dozen cookies

It doesn't take long to stir up these chocolate treats. Encourage young family members to get in the action by helping to measure the ingredients and by dropping the cookies onto waxed paper.

2	cups sugar
½	cup milk
½	cup butter or margarine (1 stick)
3	tablespoons unsweetened cocoa
1	teaspoon salt
3	cups uncooked quick-cooking oats
1	teaspoon vanilla
½	cup chopped walnuts or pecans
1	cup shredded coconut

(Continued)

No-Bake Chocolate Cookies (continued)

1. In large saucepan, combine sugar, milk, butter, cocoa, and salt. Bring to a boil, stirring constantly.

2. Remove from the heat and stir in the oats, vanilla, walnuts, and coconut.

3. Drop from teaspoon or ejector spoon onto waxed paper.

4. Chill until set.

5. Store covered and hidden in the refrigerator.

Microwave

In step 1, put sugar, milk, butter, cocoa and salt in 2 quart microwave-safe measurer. Microwave on 100% power 7-10 minutes, stirring every 2 minutes.

Butterscotch Bars

16 bars

If you need a lightning quick cookie recipe that uses common everyday ingredients, then here is an excellent suggestion. These tasty golden butterscotch bars are the perfect companion for ice cold glasses of milk.

¼	cup butter or margarine
1	cup brown sugar
1	egg
¾	cup flour
1	teaspoon baking powder
¼	teaspoon salt
½	teaspoon vanilla
½	cup chopped walnuts or pecans

1. Melt butter in medium saucepan.

2. Stir in brown sugar. Add egg and beat well.

3. Stir in flour, baking powder and salt until flour disappears.

4. Stir in vanilla and walnuts.

5. Pour into greased 8x8-inch square baking pan.

6. Bake in preheated 350 degree oven for 25 minutes. Do NOT overbake.

7. Cool on wire rack and cut into bars.

Microwave

In step 1, melt butter in microwave safe 2-quart measurer on 100% power 20-30 seconds until melted.

Mary's Marvelous Applesauce Brownies

3-4 dozen brownies

No cookbook would be complete without at least one brownie recipe. Here is a delicious version using applesauce for added moistness and flavor. How appreciative I am that my friend, Mary Reineke, shared this recipe with me.

½   cup butter or margarine, softened
1-½   cups sugar
2   eggs
2   cups flour
2   tablespoons unsweetened cocoa
1-½   teaspoons baking soda
½   teaspoon salt
½   teaspoon ground cinnamon
2   cups applesauce, unsweetened or sweetened
1   cup semi-sweet chocolate chips
½   cup chopped walnuts or pecans

1. In large mixing bowl, cream together the butter and sugar. Add eggs, 1 at a time, beating well after each addition.

2. Sift together flour, cocoa, soda, salt and cinnamon.

3. Add dry ingredients alternately with applesauce. Mix completely.

4. Pour into lightly greased 9x13 inch baking pan.

5. Sprinkle with chocolate chips and walnuts or pecans.

6. Bake in preheated 350 degree oven for 30-35 minutes.

Michigan Apple Pie

Serves 8

If you live in apple country, treat yourself to a U-pick trip and select your favorite pie apples right off the tree. Then home to the kitchen to create the best of home baking experiences; a freshly baked apple pie. Have vanilla ice cream ready for the a la mode fans.

Pastry for 2-crust pie

¾   cup sugar
2   tablespoons flour
¾   teaspoon ground cinnamon
⅛   teaspoon nutmeg
¼   teaspoon salt
6   to 7 cups sliced peeled apples (about 2 to 2-½ lbs.)
2   tablespoons butter or margarine

(Continued)

Michigan Apple Pie (continued)

1. In large mixing bowl, combine sugar, flour, cinnamon, nutmeg, and salt.

2. Add sliced apples to sugar mixture and lightly mix together.

3. Heap in pastry-lined 9-inch pie pan. Dot with butter. Adjust top crust and flute edges; cut vents.

4. Bake in preheated 425 degree oven 50-60 minutes, or until crust is browned and apples are tender.

Microwave

In step **3,** use microwave-safe pie plate.
In step **4,** elevate pie on microwave roasting rack. Microwave on 100% power 8-12 minutes, rotating after 5 minutes. Place pie in preheated 425 degree oven for 15-20 minutes or until juice bubbles up appearing thick.

Slim Line Pumpkin Pie

Serves 8

Here is a low sugar variation of the ever-popular pumpkin pie. My friend, Ann Paulson, developed this recipe and I think you'll agree she can be proud of her efforts. Remember this recipe the next time pumpkin pie comes to mind.

3	**eggs**
1/3	**cup brown sugar**
1	**(16 ounce) can pumpkin (2 cups)**
1	**cup fat free evaporated milk**
1	**teaspoon ground cinnamon**
1/4	**teaspoon ground nutmeg**
1/4	**teaspoon ground cloves**
1/4	**teaspoon ground ginger**
1/2	**teaspoon salt**
1	**unbaked 9-inch pie shell**

1. In large mixing bowl, beat eggs and sugar with rotary beater.

2. Stir in pumpkin and milk. Add cinnamon, nutmeg, cloves, ginger and salt. Mix well.

3. Pour into unbaked pie shell.

4. Sprinkle with additional nutmeg.

5. Bake in preheated 425 degree oven for 15 minutes.

6. Reduce temperature to 350 degrees and continue baking 45 minutes or until a knife inserted in the center comes out clean.

White Christmas Chiffon Pie

Serves 8

Many years ago when students shared favorite recipes in a Holiday Foods course which I taught, Janet Mick contributed this outstanding recipe. Few holiday desserts are as lovely as this feathery light chiffon pie. Treat yourself to this luscious finale this Christmas.

1	envelope unflavored gelatin
¼	cup cold water
½	cup sugar
¼	cup flour
½	teaspoon salt
1-½	cups milk
3	large egg whites
¼	teaspoon cream of tartar
½	cup sugar
¾	teaspoon vanilla extract
¼	teaspoon almond extract
1	cup whipping cream, whipped
⅔	cup shredded coconut
1	(9-inch) baked pie shell with high fluted edge

1. In 1 cup glass measurer, soften gelatin in cold water. Set aside.

2. In medium saucepan, mix sugar, flour and salt. Gradually stir in milk.

3. Cook mixture slowly, stirring constantly, until it boils. Boil 1 minute.

4. Add softened gelatin and cool thoroughly.

5. In medium mixing bowl, beat egg whites with cream of tartar, till frothy. Gradually add sugar. Beat till thick and glossy.

6. When milk mixture is cool and partially set, beat with unwashed beaters until smooth.

7. Add extracts to milk mixture.

8. Fold in whipped cream and coconut.

9. Carefully fold in beaten egg whites.

10. Pile in pie shell, sprinkle with a little coconut on top of pie. Chill several hours or overnight.

11. Garnish with red and green cherries for the holidays, if desired.

Microwave

In step **2,** mix sugar, flour and salt in 2 quart microwave-safe measurer. Gradually stir in milk.

In step **3,** microwave on 100% power 4-6 minutes, until thickened, stirring every minute with wire wisk.

Berries and Cream Pie

Serves 6-8

This delicious rich creation is best when served as the star attraction rather than following a full meal. Guests may be so impressed with your culinary skills you'll get a standing ovation.

1-½ cups crushed vanilla wafer crumbs
⅓ cup butter or margarine, melted
½ cup butter or margarine, softened
1-½ cups confectioners' sugar
2 eggs
1 (8 ounce) can crushed pineapple, very well drained
1 cup whipping cream
1-½ cups sweetened strawberries or raspberries, drained

1. Reserve 2 tablespoons of the crushed vanilla wafers for topping.

2. In small mixing bowl, combine remaining crushed vanilla wafers and ⅓ cup melted butter. Press into buttered 9-inch pie plate. Chill until firm (about 45 minutes).

3. In medium mixing bowl, combine ½ cup softened butter, confectioners' sugar and eggs. Beat until light and fluffy with electric mixer.

4. Spoon into chilled crust, smooth the top.

5. Put very well drained crushed pineapple over egg mixture.

6. Whip whipping cream until soft peaks form. Gently fold in well drained sweetened berries.

7. Spread the whipped cream mixture over the pineapple layer. Sprinkle reserved crumbs over pie.

8. Chill 6 to 8 hours to develop flavor.

9. Serve and enjoy.

Honeyed Rhubarb Pie

Makes 1 pie

My husband, George, knows that spring has officially arrived when he bites into a slice of this absolutely wonderful rhubarb pie. Honey and grated lemon peel enhance the pie filling flavor in a gracious and subtle way.

Pastry for 2-crust pie

4   cups (½ inch pieces) rhubarb
1-¼ cups sugar
¼   cup plus 2 tablespoons flour
½   teaspoon salt
2   teaspoons grated lemon peel
⅓   cup honey
4   to 5 drops red food coloring, if desired
2   tablespoons butter or margarine

1. In large mixing bowl, combine rhubarb, sugar, flour, salt, and lemon peel; mix well.

2. Blend in honey and food coloring. Let stand several minutes.

3. Spoon rhubarb mixture into pastry-lined 9-inch pie pan; dot with butter.

4. Adjust top crust and flute edges; cut vents. (For sparkling top, brush with milk and sprinkle with sugar.)

5. Bake in preheated 400 degree oven 50-60 minutes.

Microwave

In step **3,** use microwave-safe pie plate.

In step **5,** elevate pie on microwave roasting rack. Microwave on 100% power 8-12 minutes, rotating after 5 minutes. Place pie in preheated 400 degree oven for 15-20 minutes or until juice bubbles up appearing thick.

Strawberry Angel Pie

Serves 8-10

There is no last minute preparation for the cook who has a filled meringue shell stored in the refrigerator. Show off this picture pretty dessert and save time, too, by slicing and serving it at the table.

1   (10 ounce) package frozen sliced strawberries, thawed and
**   drained or 1 pint home frozen strawberries, thawed and drained**
1   (3 ounce) package strawberry flavored gelatin
1   cup whipping cream
1   Lovely Meringue Shell (recipe on page 193)

(Continued)

Strawberry Angel Pie (continued)

1. Drain thawed strawberries into 2 cup glass measurer. Add water to make 1-¼ cups liquid.

2. In small saucepan, heat liquid until boiling.

3. Dissolve gelatin in hot liquid. Chill until gelatin mixture is partially set.

4. Whip cream till soft peaks form; fold cream and strawberries into gelatin mixture.

5. Chill until mixture mounds slightly.

6. Pile into Lovely Meringue Shell. Chill 4 to 6 hours or overnight.

7. Garnish with additional whipped cream, if desired.

Microwave

In step **1,** drain thawed strawberries into 1-quart microwave-safe measurer. Add water to make 1-¼ cups liquid.
In step **2,** microwave on 100% power 2 to 3 minutes until boiling.

Lovely Meringue Shell

Serves 8-10

Here is the perfect way to transform three egg whites into a very special dessert. This marvelous crackly angel-white shell is ready to be filled with ice cream or fruit or custard.

3   **egg whites, at room temperature (⅓ to ½ cup)**
¼   **teaspoon cream of tartar**
¾   **cup sugar**

1. In medium mixing bowl, beat egg whites and cream of tartar until foamy with electric mixer.

2. Beat in sugar, 1 tablespoon at a time; continue to beat until stiff and glossy. Do not underbeat.

3. Cover baking sheet with parchment paper or brown paper.

4. Draw a 9 inch circle on paper. (I trace around a 9-inch cake pan.)

5. Shape meringue on paper in 9-inch shape, building up sides.

6. Bake in preheated 275 degree oven 1-½ hours. Turn off oven; leave meringue in oven with door closed 1 hour or longer.

7. Remove from oven; finish cooling meringue on rack.

8. Fill with ice cream and top with fresh berries, cut up fruit, chocolate or butterscotch sauce.

194

Pecan Pie

Serves 6-8

Save this rich mouth watering pie for a very special occasion. I like to serve slices of pecan pie separate from a meal so that each mouth watering bite can be thoroughly savored.

3	eggs
1	cup dark corn syrup
⅔	cup sugar
	Dash of salt
⅓	cup butter or margarine, melted
1	cup pecan halves
1	9-inch unbaked pastry shell

1. In large mixing bowl, beat eggs thoroughly with rotary beater.

2. Add corn syrup, sugar, salt and melted butter. Beat again.

3. Stir in pecan halves.

4. Pour into unbaked pastry shell.

5. Bake in preheated 350 degree oven 50 minutes or until knife inserted halfway between outside and center of filling comes out clean.

6. Cool before serving.

7. This lovely pie freezes very well.

Chocolate Mousse

Serves 8-12

It's rich...It's creamy...It's wonderful... This chocolate mousse can even be made ahead and frozen for up to one month. Thaw in the refrigerator before serving.

¼	cup butter
8	ounces (8 squares) semi-sweet chocolate, broken in half
4	egg yolks
1	teaspoon vanilla
4	egg whites
¼	cup sugar
1	cup whipping cream, whipped

1. In medium saucepan, over low heat, melt butter and chocolate just until melted, stirring constantly. Remove from heat. Cool slightly.

2. In large mixing bowl, combine egg yolks and vanilla.

3. Using wire whisk, gradually add chocolate mixture to egg yolks, blending well.

(Continued)

Chocolate Mousse (continued)

4. In small mixing bowl, beat egg whites until soft peaks form.

5. Gradually add sugar, beating until stiff peaks form.

6. Fold egg whites into chocolate mixture.

7. Fold in whipped cream.

8. Gently pour into pretty serving dishes. Refrigerate at least 1 hour.

9. Garnish with additional whipped cream, if desired.

Microwave

In step **1,** put butter and chocolate in microwave-safe dish. Microwave at 50% power 2-4 minutes, stirring every minute until melted. Cool slightly.

Blueberry Crisp

Serves 6

Blueberries are known for being low in calories. However, sometimes we ruin this quality by adding sweet and rich ingredients. That's not true in this dessert recipe for each thoughtful addition helps to stretch flavor rather than add unwanted calories.

3	**cups frozen or fresh blueberries**
¼	**cup white grape juice**
½	**teaspoon allspice**
⅓	**cup quick-cooking rolled oats, uncooked**
¼	**cup whole wheat flour**
2	**tablespoons brown sugar**
½	**teaspoon baking powder**
⅛	**teaspoon ground nutmeg**
3	**tablespoons margarine, softened**

1. In medium saucepan, combine blueberries, grape juice and allspice. Bring to a boil; reduce heat and simmer 2 minutes, stirring occasionally.

2. Pour blueberry mixture into 8-inch square baking dish coated with cooking spray.

3. In small mixing bowl, combine oats, whole wheat flour, brown sugar, baking powder, nutmeg and softened margarine until crumbly.

4. Sprinkle crumb mixture on top of blueberries.

5. Bake in preheated 350 degree oven 25-30 minutes.

Microwave

In step **1,** use 2 quart microwave-safe casserole for blueberries, grape juice and allspice. Microwave on 100% power 5-10 minutes, stirring once or twice. (Frozen berries take longer).

Blueberry Cobbler

6 servings

A cobbler is one of the most creative ways I know of putting together those basic ingredients of flour, milk, shortening and leavening agents. In this recipe, thickened blueberries provide the perfect setting for the biscuit topping.

½ cup sugar
1 tablespoon cornstarch
4 cups fresh or frozen blueberries
1 teaspoon lemon juice
1 cup flour
1 tablespoon sugar
1-½ teaspoons baking powder
½ teaspoon salt
3 tablespoons margarine
½ cup milk

1. Preheat oven to 400 degrees.

2. Blend ½ cup sugar and the cornstarch in medium saucepan. Stir in blueberries and lemon juice. Cook, stirring constantly, until mixture thickens and boils. Boil and stir 1 minute.

3. Pour into ungreased 2-quart casserole. Keep fruit mixture hot in oven while preparing biscuit topping.

4. Measure flour, 1 tablespoon sugar, the baking powder and salt into bowl. Cut margarine into flour mixture with fork or pastry blender until mixture resembles coarse meal.

5. Add milk and stir until flour disappears.

6. Drop 6 medium spoonfuls onto hot fruit.

7. Bake 25-30 minutes or until biscuit topping is golden brown. Serve warm. Top with whipped cream or ice cream, if desired.

Fruit Pizza Wheel

Serves 8-12

If ever there was an eye catching dessert, this fruit pizza is it. What a great way to show off a beautiful selection of fruit. The added bonus is the ease with which you can make this treat. Remember you are the artist, so be creative.

½   **cup butter or margarine, softened**
¼   **cup brown sugar**
1   **cup flour**
¼   **cup quick-cooking oats**
¼   **cup finely chopped walnuts or pecans**
1   **(8 ounce) package cream cheese, softened**
⅓   **cup sugar**
½   **teaspoon vanilla**
     Assorted fruits like orange segments, strawberry halves, kiwi slices, banana slices, pineapple tidbits, blueberries, raspberries, or seedless grapes, halved
½   **cup orange marmalade, peach or apricot preserves**
2   **tablespoons water**

1. In small mixing bowl, cream together butter and brown sugar. Work in flour, oats and walnuts.

2. Press dough onto lightly oiled or parchment lined 12-inch pizza pan. Prick dough with fork.

3. Bake in preheated 375 degree oven 10-12 minutes or until golden brown. Cool; leave crust on pizza pan or move to round cake plate or cardboard.

4. In medium mixing bowl, combine cream cheese, sugar, and vanilla beating until well blended. Spread over crust.

5. Arrange fruit on cream cheese mixture.

6. In small bowl, combine marmalade and water. Brush over fruit to form a glaze. Chill.

7. Cut into wedges with pizza cutter.

Toasted Pecan Balls

Keep these pecan covered scoops of ice cream in the freezer for an impressive impromptu dessert. Make this wonderfully smooth and rich hot fudge sauce or use purchased toppings if time is at an essence.

Chopped pecans, plain or salted
Vanilla ice cream
1   **cup miniature marshmallows**
1   **cup semi-sweet chocolate chips**
1   **cup evaporated milk**

1. Toast desired amount of chopped pecans on a 10-½ by 15-½-inch jelly-roll pan in a preheated 325 degree oven 10-15 minutes. Stir at least once and watch carefully to avoid burning. Cool thoroughly.

2. Select size scoop desired for ice cream.

3. Scoop balls of ice cream and roll in cooled toasted pecans. Freeze firm on tray in freezer.

4. After they are frozen, store in well covered container.

5. For fudge sauce, combine miniature marshmallows, chocolate chips, and evaporated milk in top of double boiler over hot water.

6. Heat and stir mixture until melted and thickened.

7. Cool to room temperature.

8. At serving time, remove a toasted pecan ball from the freezer for each indulging person.

9. Place toasted pecan balls on individual dessert plates or dishes.

10. Generously top each one with fudge sauce.

11. Enjoy...Enjoy...Enjoy...

Microwave

In step **5,** make fudge sauce by combining marshmallows, chocolate chips and evaporated milk in microwave-safe 2-quart measurer.
In step **6,** microwave on 100% power 3-4 minutes until thickened, stirring every minute.

Sherbet Bouquet

This is a creative "no cook" idea, just plan and organize the serving of sherbet so there is no last minute dipping mess. The best part is that you can color coordinate the sherbet into your own custom designed bouquet.

Assorted fruit flavored sherbet (raspberry, lemon, lime, orange, pineapple, etc.).

(Continued)

Sherbet Bouquet (continued)

1. Select an ice cream scoop that will form the size sherbet servings you desire.

2. Form round balls of sherbet using the scoop.

3. Place on waxed paper lined tray, dip scoop in cold water in between each dip.

4. Freeze sherbet until serving time. Cover if it will be longer than 2 hours.

5. Pile firm frozen sherbet balls in pretty serving dish.

6. If the serving dish is freezer-safe, the sherbet bouquet could be created and kept in the freeze until serving time.

Lemon Frost

Serves 12

This budget pleasing dessert is light, lemony and luscious. It would be the perfect ending to a springtime luncheon or bridge playing session.

1	**cup crushed coconut bar cookies (12 or 13 cookies)**
2	**tablespoons butter or margarine, melted**
2	**egg yolks**
1	**teaspoon grated lemon peel**
⅓	**cup lemon juice**
⅔	**cup sugar**
	Dash of salt
2	**egg whites**
⅔	**cup nonfat dry milk powder**
⅔	**cup water**

1. Combine cookie crumbs and melted butter. Press ¾ cup of the crumbs in an 8x8x2-inch baking pan.

2. In small mixing bowl, stir together egg yolks, lemon peel and lemon juice. Add sugar and salt; mix well.

3. In large mixing bowl, combine egg whites, dry milk powder and water.

4. Beat at high speed of electric mixer until stiff peaks form, (about 5 minutes).

5. Add egg yolk mixture, beating at low speed just till blended.

6. Pour over crumbs in pan.

7. Top with remaining ¼ cup crumbs.

8. Cover tightly with plastic wrap and then aluminum foil. Freeze firm.

Peach Melba Ice Cream Pie

Serves 6-8

When I hear the word melba, wonderful thoughts of red raspberry sauce come to mind. Add this bright red sauce to an easy ice cream pie garnished with peaches and you have a dessert to remember. If you have difficulty finding peach ice cream at your grocery store, try an ice cream shop.

1-½ **cups flaked coconut**
½ **cup finely chopped walnuts**
2 **tablespoons butter or margarine, softened**
1 **quart peach ice cream or frozen yogurt, softened**
1 **pint vanilla ice cream or frozen yogurt, softened**
1 **(10 ounce) package frozen red raspberries, thawed**
½ **cup sugar**
1 **tablespoon cornstarch**
2 **cups sliced peaches, sweetened (frozen or canned may be used)**

1. In small mixing bowl, combine coconut, nuts and butter.

2. Press coconut mixture firmly and evenly against bottom and sides of 9-inch pie plate. Bake in preheated 325 degree oven for 10-15 minutes or until golden brown. Cool.

3. Spoon peach ice cream into crust, spreading to edges. Freeze until firm. Spoon vanilla ice cream over the peach ice cream. Freeze firm.

4. Drain raspberries, reserving syrup.

5. In small saucepan, combine sugar, cornstarch and reserved syrup.

6. Cook over medium heat, stirring constantly, until thickened. Remove from heat and add drained raspberries. Cool.

7. Just before serving, arrange peaches on pie. Cut frozen pie in wedges; garnish with peaches. Serve with raspberry sauce.

Microwave
In step **5,** combine sugar, cornstarch, and reserved raspberry syrup in 1 quart microwave-safe measurer.
In step **6,** microwave on 100% power 2-4 minutes, stirring every minute.

Cranberry Ice

Serves 8-10

This recipe has special meaning because it was given to me by my friend Kay Myers Harding when we spent hours together proofreading my first cookbook, House Specialties. It's with loving memories that I think of her as I now share one of her treasured family recipes with you. This delicious cranberry ice could be served not only for dessert, but as an appetizer or accompaniment depending on the menu.

(Continued)

Cranberry Ice (continued)

4   cups fresh or frozen cranberries, washed and sorted
6   cups water
1   (3 ounce) package lemon-flavored gelatin
2   cups boiling water
2   cups sugar
1-½ cups orange juice

1. In large saucepan or dutch oven, cook cranberries and water until the cranberry skins pop.

2. Put through sieve or food mill.

3. Dissolve lemon-flavored gelatin in boiling water.

4. Add sugar and stir to dissolve.

5. Combine cranberry juice, lemon syrup, and orange juice in the large saucepan. Stir to combine.

6. Pour into three 1-quart freezer containers. Freeze firm.

7. Let stand at room temperature 10 minutes before serving.

Pineapple/Orange Freeze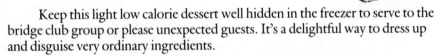

Serves 9

Keep this light low calorie dessert well hidden in the freezer to serve to the bridge club group or please unexpected guests. It's a delightful way to dress up and disguise very ordinary ingredients.

⅔   cup plus 2 tablespoons graham cracker crumbs, divided
2   tablespoons margarine, softened
½   cup instant nonfat dry milk powder
½   cup unsweetened orange juice, chilled
1   egg white
1   tablespoon lemon juice
¼   cup sugar
1   (8 ounce) can crushed pineapple in unsweetened juice, drained

1. Combine ⅔ cup graham cracker crumbs and margarine, mixing well. Press into an 8-inch square pan; set aside.

2. In large mixing bowl, combine milk powder, orange juice, egg white and lemon juice. Beat at high speed of electric mixer for 3 minutes.

3. Add sugar and beat an additional 3 minutes; fold in drained pineapple.

4. Pour into graham cracker lined pan.

5. Sprinkle with the remaining 2 tablespoons graham cracker crumbs on top.

6. Freeze firm. Cover and store frozen.

Pink Peppermint Ice Cream

Serves 6-8

A pretty sherbet glass filled with this lovely homemade peppermint ice cream would be the perfect ending to a delicious meal. At Christmas time, add miniature candy canes for a festive garnish.

1	**envelope unflavored gelatin**
½	**cup cold milk**
1-½	**cups milk, scalded**
1	**cup crushed hard peppermint-stick candy (use food processor)**
¼	**teaspoon salt**
2	**cups heavy cream, whipped**
	Few drops red food coloring, if desired

1. In 1 cup glass measurer, soften gelatin in ½ cup cold milk.

2. Stir softened gelatin into hot milk until it is dissolved. Add candy and salt; stir until candy dissolves.

3. Pour into refrigerator tray or 8x8-inch baking pan. Freeze until firm.

4. Whip cream with chilled beaters.

5. Break frozen peppermint mixture into chunks and place in large mixing bowl.

6. With unwashed beaters, beat frozen mixture with electric mixer until smooth.

7. Gently fold whipped cream into frozen mixture. Add food coloring to tint delicate pink, if desired. Return mixture to tray or pan.

8. Cover and freeze firm.

Kiwi Ice

Serves 8

Kiwi is the delicious egg-shaped fruit with fuzzy brown skin. It is an excellent source of vitamin C, high in potassium and low in sodium. No wonder this mouth-watering Ice is the grand champion of all light desserts…only 26 calories in each half cup serving.

4	**kiwi, peeled and cubed**
2	**cups unsweetened apple juice**
1	**tablespoon lemon juice**
½	**teaspoon grated orange rind**

1. Combine kiwi, apple juice and lemon juice in container of an electric blender or bowl of food processor.

2. Blend or process until smooth.

(Continued)

Kiwi Ice (continued)

3. Stir in orange rind.

4. Pour mixture into an 8-inch square baking pan, and freeze until almost firm.

5. Spoon frozen mixture into a mixing bowl; beat with an electric mixer until fluffy.

6. Return to pan, and freeze until firm.

7. Let stand at room temperature 10 minutes before serving.

8. Garnish with orange slices, if desired.

Orange Frost

Serves 6-8

It doesn't take long to whip up this cool and refreshing orange frost. Calorie counters will appreciate your thoughtfulness as they savor your new frozen creation. You could even add some mandarin orange slices for garnish, if you like the idea.

1	**envelope unflavored gelatin**
½	**cup cold water**
1-½	**cups orange juice**
¼	**cup sugar**

1. In small saucepan, sprinkle gelatin over cold water.

2. Cook and stir over low heat 3 minutes or until gelatin is dissolved.

3. Remove from heat. Stir in orange juice and sugar.

4. Pour into metal bowl.

5. Chill ½ hour or until very thick.

6. Beat with electric mixer until creamy and doubled in volume, about 5 minutes.

7. Pour into 8x4-inch loaf pan. Cover and freeze until firm.

8. Before serving, allow to stand at room temperature 5 minutes. Scoop into sherbet dishes.

9. If desired, garnish with mandarin orange sections.

10. Serve immediately or return to freezer until serving time, as dessert softens quickly.

Microwave

In step **1**, sprinkle gelatin in cold water in 1-quart microwave-safe measurer.
In step **2**, microwave on 100% power 30-45 seconds until gelatin is dissolved, stirring once.

Crowd Pleasing Tin Roof

Serves 24

Every recipe collection should include a sinfully delicious dessert that will feed a crowd or can be kept tucked in the freezer for unexpected needs. I think this ice cream creation is the perfect recipe to meet these qualifications. The ingredient list may look long, but each step is extremely easy. So get into action soon.

30	creme-filled chocolate sandwich cookies, finely crushed
¼	cup butter or margarine, melted
½	gallon brick-style vanilla ice cream, slightly softened
1	cup Spanish peanuts
2	cups confectioners' sugar
1	(6 ounce) package semi-sweet chocolate chips (1 cup)
1	(12 ounce) can evaporated milk
½	cup butter or margarine
1	teaspoon vanilla
1	cup whipping cream
2	tablespoons confectioners' sugar
½	teaspoon vanilla

1. Reserve ⅔ cup of the crumbs for sprinkling on top of the whipped cream.

2. Combine remaining crumbs with melted butter. Press lightly in bottom of 9x13-inch pan.

3. Cut ice cream into 1-inch thick slices; place over cookie crumb crust. Spread ice cream lightly with spatula to cover entire crumb base.

4. Sprinkle peanuts over ice cream. Cover. Freeze.

5. In medium saucepan, combine confectioners' sugar, chocolate chips, evaporated milk and margarine; bring to boil over medium low heat. Cook approximately 8 minutes, stirring constantly. Remove from heat. Add vanilla. Cool.

6. Pour cooled chocolate sauce over peanuts and ice cream. Cover and freeze firm.

7. Whip cream with confectioners' sugar and vanilla. Spread whipped cream over chocolate. Sprinkle with reserved cookie crumbs.

8. Cover. Store in the freezer until a special treat is needed.

Microwave

In step **5,** prepare chocolate sauce by putting confectioners' sugar, chocolate chips, evaporated milk and margarine in 2 quart microwave-safe measurer. Microwave on 100% power 6-8 minutes until thickened, stirring two or three times.

Microwave

As the use of microwave ovens increases in popularity so does the need for quick reliable recipes. Here is a sampling of microwave favorites with emphasis on enticing entrees.

For fast one dish meals cooked in their own serving casseroles try Jiffy Goulash, Quick Ham AuGratin, or Hurry Up Tuna. Clear concise directions will help even the novice cook understand the principles of cooking a less tender cut of beef or pork roast the microwave way.

Keep the microwave oven in constant use by preparing a variety of vegetables like the Glazed Carrots and Pea Pods, super salads such as Wilted Greens, and delicious desserts as described in Cran-Apple Crisp. Get into action now and make use of the marvelous microwave.

Contents

Meat Loaf Logs

Serves 4 or 5

Every time I make these easy logs, I am amazed that such simple ordinary ingredients could taste so great. Put scrubbed and pierced potatoes in the microwave to bake while you are preparing the meat mixture. Potatoes can then rest covered on the counter while the meat logs cook.

⅓   **cup catsup**
2   **tablespoons brown sugar**
1   **teaspoon Worcestershire sauce**
¼   **teaspoon garlic salt**
½   **teaspoon prepared mustard**
1   **pound ground beef**
1   **slice bread, crumbled**
¼   **cup milk**
1   **egg**
½   **teaspoon salt**
    Dash pepper

1. In small mixing bowl, combine catsup, brown sugar, Worcestershire sauce, garlic salt and mustard; set aside.

2. In medium mixing bowl, combine ground beef, bread, milk, egg, salt and pepper. Add 2 tablespoons of catsup mixture. Mix thoroughly.

3. Shape mixture into 4 or 5 log shaped loaves about 3 inches long. Arrange on microwave-safe meat rack. Cover with waxed paper.

4. Microwave on 100% power for 6 to 7 minutes, rotating dish once.

5. Spoon remaining sauce evenly on meat logs.

6. Microwave, uncovered, on 100% power 1 to 2 minutes or until meat is desired doneness.

Jiffy Goulash

Serves 4-5

Pasta that cooks right in the serving dish is a great microwave time saver. Team that feature with the convenience of dry onion soup mix and you have one quick dinner. I like to keep pound packages of browned ground beef in the freezer all ready for recipes like this one.

1   **pound ground beef**
3   **cups uncooked noodles**
2   **cups water**
1   **(8 ounce) can tomato sauce**
1   **envelope (ounce) dry onion soup mix**

(Continued)

Jiffy Goulash (continued)

1. Crumble ground beef into hard plastic colander or plastic hamburger cooker. Rest in microwave-safe container to catch grease.

2. Microwave on 100% power, uncovered, 5-7 minutes or until meat is set, stirring once, discard grease.

3. In 2-quart microwave-safe casserole, combine browned ground beef, uncooked noodles, water, tomato sauce and dry onion soup mix. Mix well. Cover tightly with casserole lid or vented plastic wrap.

4. Microwave on 100% power 14-17 minutes or until noodles are tender, stirring twice.

Sloppy Joes

Serves 8

Browning ground beef in the microwave is popular because it takes such a short time to produce fat-free cooked ground beef. Add just a few seasonings and you have created the favorite Sloppy Joe sandwich that's ready to be heated whenever a family member is hungry.

1-½ pounds hamburger
½ cup chopped onion
¾ cup catsup
2 tablespoons water
1 teaspoon salt
1-½ teaspoons sugar
½ teaspoon monosodium glutamate
¼ teaspoon dry mustard
1 teaspoon vinegar

1. Put ground beef and onion in hard plastic colander or 2-quart microwave-safe casserole.

2. Microwave on 100% power 8-10 minutes, breaking meat up with a fork once or twice as it cooks, drain well.

3. In 2 quart microwave-safe casserole, combine drained browned ground beef, catsup, water, salt, sugar, monosodium glutamate, dry mustard, and vinegar.

4. Microwave on 100% power 4-6 minutes or until hot, stirring once.

5. Fill hamburger buns and enjoy.

Spinach Lasagna

Serves 6-8

Who would expect to find spinach, sandwiched lasagna style, in the evening entree? Yes, here it is and the delicious nutritious flavor is worthy of your efforts soon.

1	(10 ounce) package frozen chopped spinach
1	pound ground beef
2	tablespoons instant minced onion
⅛	teaspoon garlic powder
1	(15-½ ounce) jar spaghetti sauce
4	tablespoons dry bread crumbs, divided
1	cup creamed cottage cheese
1	egg
⅛	teaspoon ground pepper
1	cup (4 ounces) shredded mozzarella cheese
2	tablespoons grated Parmesan cheese

1. Poke frozen spinach package 2 or 3 times with fork tine to allow steam to escape. Place on microwave-safe plate and microwave on 100% power 3-5 minutes, turning package over halfway through cooking time.

2. Drain spinach thoroughly and put in medium mixing bowl. Set aside.

3. Crumble ground beef into a hard plastic colander. Set colander in 9-inch glass pie plate to collect the grease. Add minced onion and garlic powder to ground beef.

4. Microwave on 100% power 5-7 minutes, or until meat is no longer pink, breaking up meat with a fork halfway through cooking time, discard grease.

5. Put drained ground beef in 2-quart microwave-safe casserole. Stir in spaghetti sauce. Microwave on 100% power 4-5 minutes, or until hot and bubbly, stirring once. Mix in 2 tablespoons bread crumbs.

6. Add cottage cheese, egg, pepper and remaining 2 tablespoons bread crumbs to drained spinach. Mix well.

7. Spread half of the meat mixture in an 8x8-inch square microwave-safe dish.

8. Cover with spinach mixture. Sprinkle with mozzarella cheese.

9. Top with remaining meat; sprinkle with Parmesan cheese.

10. Microwave on 100% power 3-4 minutes.

11. Reduce power to 50% and microwave 7-10 minutes or until thoroughly heated, rotating dish halfway through cooking time.

12. Let stand 5 minutes. Cut into squares and serve.

Meatball Stew

Serves 6

The star attractions of this hearty healthy stew are tasty miniature meatballs. Cooked together with an interesting variety of vegetables, this one dish meal is a real winner. Complete the menu with ice cold glasses of milk, hot crusty bread and fragrant fresh fruit.

4-5   **medium potatoes, peeled and cut into one-inch cubes**
3-4   **large carrots, peeled and thinly sliced**
1   **small onion, sliced**
2   **tablespoons instant beef bouillon**
1-½ **cups water**
1   **pound ground beef**
1   **egg**
⅓   **cup dry bread crumbs**
⅓   **cup milk**
½   **teaspoon salt**
1   **teaspoon Worcestershire sauce**
1   **(10 ounce) package frozen peas**
½   **cup water**
3   **tablespoons flour**
½   **teaspoon salt**
½   **teaspoon browning and seasoning sauce**

1. In 2-½ to 3 quart microwave-safe casserole, combine potatoes, carrots, onion, bouillon and water. Cover with lid or vented plastic wrap.

2. Microwave on 100% power 13 to 15 minutes or until vegetables are just about tender, stirring once. Set aside.

3. In medium mixing bowl, combine ground beef, egg, bread crumbs, milk, salt and Worcestershire sauce.

4. Form into meatballs about one inch in size. Place on microwave roasting rack or in 9-inch glass pie plate. Cover with waxed paper.

5. Microwave on 100% power 6-7 minutes or until meat is set, rotating dish once, drain. Add meatballs and frozen peas to vegetables.

6. In 1-cup glass measurer, combine water, flour, salt and browning sauce. Stir into meatball mixture. Cover with lid or vented plastic wrap.

7. Microwave on 100% power 8 to 10 minutes or until mixture boils and thickens, stirring twice.

Beef Strips with Snow Peas and Tomatoes

Serves 6

This flank steak show-off will entice not only the low calorie crowd, but anyone who enjoys delicious beef. The tempting flavor is extended with the colorful addition of pea pods and cherry tomatoes in this easy microwave stir-fried recipe.

1	small onion, sliced
1	tablespoon water
1	pound flank steak, thinly sliced across grain
1	pint (8 ounces) fresh mushrooms, sliced
⅛	teaspoon garlic powder
1	teaspoon sugar
½	teaspoon beef bouillon granules or ½ beef bouillon cube, crushed
1-½	tablespoons cornstarch
3	tablespoons soy sauce
1	(6 ounce) package frozen pea pods
1	pint (2 cups) cherry tomatoes, halved

1. In 2-quart microwave-safe casserole, combine onion and water. Cover with lid or vented plastic wrap. Microwave on 100% power for 3 minutes.

2. Add meat, mushrooms, garlic, sugar, bouillon, cornstarch and soy sauce; mix lightly.

3. Microwave, covered with paper towel, on 100% power 8 to 10 minutes or until meat is just about done, stirring twice. Add pea pods.

4. Microwave, covered with paper towel, on 100% power 2 minutes.

5. Add tomatoes, stir lightly to mix.

6. Microwave, uncovered, on 100% power 1-½ to 3 minutes until heated.

7. Serve on hot rice.

Beef Pot Roast in Gravy

Serves 6

Less tender cuts of beef can be cooked to perfection in the microwave oven if you use reduced power. The key to tender meat success is slow cooking in a moisture filled environment. Cook less tender cuts of beef on 50% power for 25-30 minutes per pound or at 30% power for 45-50 minutes per pound. Standing time is essential. It completes tenderizing and allows flavors to blend.

1   **(3 to 4 pound) boneless chuck roast**
1   **teaspoon browning and seasoning sauce for meat and gravy**
½   **teaspoon Worcestershire sauce**
1   **cup water**
1   **(¾ ounce) package mushroom gravy mix**
1   **(10-¾ ounce) can condensed cream of onion soup**

1. Combine ½ teaspoon browning sauce and Worcestershire sauce. Brush roast on all sides with mixture.

2. In 1-quart glass measurer, combine water, the remaining ½ teaspoon browning sauce, mushroom gravy mix and onion soup. Mix completely.

3. Cut a ½-inch strip from the open end of an oven cooking bag. Save this strip for a tie for the bag.

4. Pour one third of the gravy mixture into the bottom of the oven cooking bag. Place roast on top. Spread with remaining mixture.

5. Place meat-filled oven cooking bag in an 8x12x2-inch microwave-safe baking dish. Tie bag together loosely with the ½ inch plastic strip you have cut off bag in step # 3.

6. Use the cooking guideline of 25-30 minutes per pound at 50% power or 45-50 minutes per pound at 30% power. Multiply the weight of the roast by the minutes per pound that you selected.

7. Divide the total time into 4 segments. Microwave in the 4 time segments at either 50% power or 30% power, turning the roast over after each completed time segment.

8. When the cooking time is completed, turn meat over and let stand for 20-30 minutes in the cooking bag. (This is an excellent time to prepare the rest of the meal.)

9. Remove roast from cooking bag. Slice thinly and arrange on serving platter. Spoon some mushroom gravy over slices and pass remaining gravy.

Speedy Chop Suey

Serves 4

Whenever I have cooked meat in the refrigerator, one of the tastiest meals I can create is this quick and easy main dish idea. The brown gravy coloring that's made from bead molasses can be purchased in the Oriental food section of the grocery store. Chop Suey is delicious on a hot bed of rice or chow mein noodles.

1   (16 ounce) can chop suey vegetables, reserve liquid
4   teaspoons cornstarch
1   tablespoon brown gravy coloring sauce (bead molasses)
2   teaspoons soy sauce
2   cups cooked beef, pork or turkey cut in bite size pieces

1. Drain liquid from vegetables into microwave-safe 1-½-quart casserole. Stir in cornstarch.

2. Microwave on 100% power 2 minutes until thickened, stirring halfway through cooking time.

3. Stir in brown gravy coloring sauce, soy sauce, meat and drained vegetables.

4. Microwave on 100% power 3-5 minutes until hot, stirring once.

5. Serve on hot rice or chow mein noodles. Pass extra soy sauce.

Gingered Ham Kabobs

Serves 6-8

Wooden skewers make great microwave kabobs because, of course, they are free of metal. Just thread an interesting variety of quick cooking foods on a wooden skewer and presto dinner is ready. Look for the skewers wherever Oriental foods are available.

¼   cup pineapple juice
2   teaspoons lemon juice
¼   cup honey
¼   cup brown sugar
¾   teaspoon ground ginger
1   large green pepper, cut in 1-½-inch cubes
1   pound fully cooked ham, cut in 1-inch cubes
1   (8 ounce) can juice pack pineapple chunks, ¼ cup juice reserved
1   (16 ounce) can sweet potatoes, drained (cut in chunks, if necessary)
6   wooden skewers (9 or 12 inch length)

1. In 2-cup glass measurer or small microwave-safe bowl, combine pineapple juice, lemon juice, honey, brown sugar and ginger.

2. Microwave on 100% power for 1 to 1-½ minutes, or until mixture boils, stirring once. Set aside.

(Continued)

Gingered Ham Kabobs (continued)

3. Place green pepper in small microwave-safe bowl. Cover with vented plastic wrap and microwave on 100% power for 1-2 minutes, or until tender crisp.

4. Thread ham, pepper, pineapple and sweet potatoes on wooden skewers.

5. Place kabobs on microwave-safe roasting rack. Baste with half of the glaze.

6. Cover with waxed paper. Microwave on 100% power 6-7 minutes, or until hot, rotating dish after half the cooking time.

7. Serve with remaining glaze.

Pork Roast A La Microwave

Serves 6-8

Cooking pork roasts in the microwave oven has often been a topic of discussion. Researchers have identified the concern as "evaporative cooling", which means that the internal temperature of cooked meat is higher than the actual surface temperature of the meat. The simple remedy for this problem is to cook pork roasts in an oven cooking bag or other closed environment. Use this easy plan.

1   (3-4 pound) evenly shaped boneless pork roast
     Browning and Seasoning Sauce for Meat and Gravy
1   large oven cooking bag

1. Lightly brush roast with browning sauce.

2. Cut a ½ inch strip from open end of the oven cooking bag to use as a tie.

3. Place roast into the oven cooking bag and place in a microwave-safe baking dish.

4. Close bag loosely by tying plastic strip, leaving a space for steam to escape.

5. Microwave on 30% power (defrost setting) for approximately 22 minutes per pound of meat.

6. Invert or turn roast over halfway through cooking period and rotate dish ½ turn.

7. For the second half of the cooking time, insert microwave temperature probe or microwave meat thermometer right through the plastic bag into pork roast.

8. Cook meat to an internal temperature of 165 degrees.

9. When cooking is completed, remove roast from microwave. Cover roast (in bag) with foil and allow to stand at least 10 minutes.

10. Carve roast and arrange attractively on hot serving platter.

Parmesan Fish Fillets

Serves 3-4

It doesn't take long to prepare these delicious fish fillets for cooking. Just add 5-7 minutes in the microwave and presto and entree is ready to enjoy. I'm partial to orange roughy for this recipe, but any fish fillets work well.

1   **pound frozen fish fillets, thawed (orange roughy, sole, cod or haddock)**
1   **egg**
1   **tablespoon water**
½   **cup dry bread crumbs**
¼   **cup grated Parmesan cheese**
½   **teaspoon paprika**
3   **tablespoons flour**

1. Cut fish into serving size pieces.

2. In shallow dish, beat egg and water with rotary beater.

3. On a piece of waxed paper, mix together bread crumbs, Parmesan cheese, and paprika.

4. Put flour on another piece of waxed paper.

5. Coat fish with flour, dip into egg mixture and then coat with crumb mixture.

6. Place fish in attractive microwave-safe dish.

7. Microwave on 100% power, uncovered, 5-7 minutes, rotating dish once.

8. Garnish with fresh snipped parsley.

Tuna Rice Quiche

Serves 4

Rice forms a tasty crust in this slim-line quiche. Filled with nutrient packed tuna and broccoli, this quick entree is great reduced calorie fare. Select fresh fruit to complete the menu.

1   **(10 ounce) package frozen chopped broccoli**
1-½ **cups cooked rice**
¾   **cup shredded cheddar cheese**
3   **eggs**
1   **(6-½ ounce) can water-packed tuna, drained**
⅓   **cup skim milk**
¾   **teaspoon salt**

(Continued)

Tuna Rice Quiche (continued)

1. Pierce frozen broccoli package with fork tines three times so steam can escape. Place package on paper plate. Microwave on 100% power for 5 minutes, turning package over after half of the cooking time, drain.

2. In small bowl, combine rice, half the cheese and 1 egg. Press evenly over bottom and sides of 9-inch microwave-safe pie plate or quiche dish.

3. Top rice with drained broccoli and tuna.

4. In medium bowl, beat together remaining 2 eggs, milk and salt. Pour over tuna.

5. Microwave on 100% power, uncovered, 8-10 minutes, rotating dish once.

6. Sprinkle with remaining cheese.

7. Microwave 100% power, uncovered, 1-2 minutes, or until cheese is melted.

8. Let stand 5 minutes. To serve, cut in wedges.

Crumb Coated Fish Fillets

Serves 3-4

Create your own fish crumb coating mix by using this quick and easy recipe. If dietary needs call for low sodium intake, omit salt and use salt free bread crumbs. It's a great way to cook fish fillets in the microwave.

3	tablespoons yellow cornmeal
1	tablespoon unseasoned dry bread crumbs
1	teaspoon dried parsley flakes
½	teaspoon onion powder
½	teaspoon paprika
⅛	teaspoon salt, if desired
	Dash of cayenne pepper
1	pound frozen fish fillets, thawed (haddock, orange roughy, cod, or sole)

1. On a piece of waxed paper, combine cornmeal, bread crumbs, parsley flakes, onion powder, paprika, salt and cayenne. Mix well.

2. Dip fillets in coating, pressing lightly to coat.

3. Arrange on microwave-safe platter or roasting rack.

4. Microwave on 100% power 5-7 minutes or until fish flakes easily with a fork, rotating dish once.

5. Garnish with lemon slices and fresh parsley. Serve.

Hurry-Up Tuna

Serves 4-5

If time is limited, create a home cooked meal in a jiffy by serving this tuna casserole as the entree. Serve with crisp apple wedges, bread sticks and mugs of milk. Ice cream would be a perfect ending for this nifty menu.

1   (10-¾ ounce) can condensed cream of mushroom soup
1   (6-½ ounce) can water-packed tuna, drained
2   cups uncooked noodles
1-⅓ cups milk
1   cup frozen peas
⅛   teaspoon ground pepper

1. In 1-½-quart microwave-safe casserole, combine mushroom soup, tuna, noodles, milk, peas and pepper. Mix well.

2. Cover with casserole lid or vented plastic wrap.

3. Microwave on 100% power 12-15 minutes or until noodles are tender and sauce is creamy, stirring twice.

4. Let stand covered 5 minutes.

5. Garnish with parsley and serve.

Chipper Fish

Serves 4

If you'd like to lure family members into eating more fish, then this idea might just be the answer. Even small folk will see the crushed potato chip topping and decide it's an entree to try. The tasty seasoning comes from the salad dressing.

1   pound fish fillets (orange roughy, cod, perch, haddock, etc.)
⅓   cup Caesar salad dressing
1   cup crushed potato chips

1. Rinse fish fillets with cold water and pat dry with paper towel.

2. Coat fillets with salad dressing and dip into crushed potato chips.

3. Place coated fish fillets in a 9-inch microwave-safe pie plate.

4. Sprinkle remaining chips on top of fish.

5. Do not cover so that fish will stay as crisp as possible.

6. Microwave on 100% power 5-7 minutes, rotating dish midway through cooking. Let stand 3 minutes, until fish flakes easily.

7. Serve with lemon wedges.

Glazed Chicken Breasts

Serves 4-6

The phrase "finger lickin' good" aptly describes these yummy chicken breasts. While they are cooking in the microwave, toss together a garden salad and butter some French bread. Presto supper is ready.

3   **whole chicken breasts, split and skinned**
½   **cup apricot preserves**
¼   **cup Russian salad dressing**
2   **tablespoons dry onion soup mix**
1   **tablespoon mayonnaise**

1. Arrange chicken breasts on microwave roasting rack; place in 8x12-inch microwave-safe dish.

2. In small mixing bowl, combine apricot preserves, Russian dressing, onion soup mix and mayonnaise. Mix well.

3. Spread apricot mixture over chicken, covering well.

4. Cover chicken with waxed paper and microwave on 100% power 20-22 minutes, rotating dish once. (Use the guideline of 7 minutes per pound.)

5. Let stand for 5-10 minutes before serving. Enjoy.

Slim Pickin' Chicken

Serves 4

Calorie watchers on the lookout for chicken breast recipes will like this microwave idea. Rosemary, an herb member of the mint family, has a warm, mint-like flavor that adds character to this entree.

¾   **teaspoon rosemary leaves**
¾   **teaspoon paprika**
¾   **teaspoon garlic salt**
2   **whole chicken breasts, cut in half and skinned**

1. Crush rosemary leaves, to release flavor, with mortar and pestle or edge of rolling pin. Stir in paprika and garlic salt.

2. Rinse chicken and pat dry.

3. Sprinkle herb mixture over chicken pieces and rub into surface.

4. Arrange chicken on microwave roasting rack, putting meaty edges to the outside.

5. Cover with waxed paper.

6. Microwave on 100% power 14-16 minutes or until chicken is tender, rotating rack once. (Guideline is 7 minutes per pound of chicken.)

Quick Ham Au Gratin

Serves 6

Microwave cooks are always on the search for entree ideas like this recipe. It's almost a complete meal wrapped up in one tasty mixture. Ham, vegetables, and cheese need only a crusty roll and fresh fruit to polish off a well-balanced menu.

1   (16 ounce) package frozen vegetable combination (broccoli, carrots and cauliflower)
2   cups cubed cooked ham
1   (11 ounce) can condensed cheddar cheese soup
1   (8 ounce) can sliced water chestnuts, drained
1   (3-½ ounce) can French-fried onions

1. In 2-quart microwave-safe casserole, put frozen vegetables, ham, cheese soup and water chestnuts. Mix gently to combine.

2. Cover with lid or vented plastic wrap.

3. Microwave on 100% power 12-14 minutes or until heated and vegetables are tender, stirring once or twice.

4. Remove lid or plastic wrap and sprinkle casserole with French-fried onions.

5. Microwave, uncovered, on 100% power for 1-2 minutes until onions are hot.

Hot Dog Boats

Serves 6-8

Young folks will smile when these mashed potato filled hot dogs are on the menu. Somehow, it is tastier when the mashed potato is in the "boat", rather than just beside the hot dog. Add finger-size fresh fruit and milk to complete this quick and easy meal.

    Four servings of instant mashed potatoes
2   tablespoons parsley flakes
2   teaspoons instant minced onion
¼   teaspoon dry mustard
6-8 wieners
    Paprika
¼   cup grated sharp cheddar cheese

1. In a 2-quart microwave-safe measurer put the amount of liquid ingredients required by the instant mash potato package directions. Microwave on 100% power until boiling, about 3-4 minutes.

2. Stir in parsley flakes, minced onion and mustard into hot liquid with desired amount of instant potatoes, salt and butter. Fluff with a fork.

(Continued)

Hot Dog Boats (continued)

3. Cut weiners in half lengthwise, being careful not to cut completely through.

4. Place cut-side-up in 8x12-inch microwave-safe baking dish.

5. Spread about 3 tablespoons potato mixture on each wiener.

6. Sprinkle with paprika and cheese.

7. Cover with waxed paper and microwave on 70% power 7-9 minutes until hot, rotating dish once.

8. Call the kids for Hot Dog Boats.

Hot Polynesian Salad

Serves 5-6

Salads are not always served cold. Here is one excellent example of a delicious fresh-tasting hot salad. There is lots of flavor and crunch packed in these popular ingredients. What better way to heat this creation than the marvelous microwave.

¼	cup finely chopped onion
1	tablespoon butter or margarine
1	cup chopped celery
1	(8 ounce) can sliced water chestnuts, drained
1	(20 ounce) can pineapple chunks or tidbits, drained
¼	cup raisins
2	cups chopped cooked chicken or turkey
¾	cup mayonnaise
¼	cup apricot preserves
¼	teaspoon ground ginger

1. In 2-quart microwave-safe casserole, combine onion and butter.

2. Cover with lid or vented plastic wrap. Microwave on 100% power for 1-½ to 2-½ minutes.

3. Stir in celery, water chestnuts, pineapple, raisins and chicken.

4. In small mixing bowl combine mayonnaise, apricot preserves and ginger.

5. Pour over salad mixture and gently combine.

6. Cover and microwave on 70% power for 8 to 10 minutes until hot, stirring once or twice.

Open-Faced Crab Bunwiches

Serves 6

Open-faced sandwiches work well in the microwave when the meat mixture is spread on a conventionally toasted bread product. As with most bread products in the microwave, heating these bunwiches on 50% power ensures a nice hot entree without overcooked bread.

1   (6 ounce) can crab, drained and flaked
½   cup finely chopped celery
½   teaspoon Worcestershire sauce
¼   teaspoon salt
½   cup mayonnaise or salad dressing
3   hamburger buns, halved, buttered and toasted
1   cup shredded sharp cheddar cheese

1. In medium mixing bowl, combine crab, celery, Worcestershire sauce, salt and mayonnaise. Mix lightly.

2. Spread crab mixture on buns; sprinkle with shredded cheese.

3. Place filled buns on paper towel that is covering a microwave-safe roasting rack.

4. Microwave at 50% power 1 minute for each bunwich just until cheese melts; rotating rack once.

Vegetable Medley Soup

Serves 6

Making soup in the microwave is actually not time saving, but it is efficient if you can both cook and serve in the same microwave-safe soup tureen or large casserole. Here is a lovely light vegetable soup that can cook while you enjoy the evening paper.

½   cup thinly sliced celery
½   cup thinly sliced carrot
¾   cup cubed potato (1 large potato)
1   (16 ounce) can tomatoes, cut up or 1 pint home canned tomatoes
1   cup thinly sliced zucchini
½   cup broken spaghetti
3   cups hot water
2   teaspoons instant beef bouillon granules or 2 beef bouillon cubes
¼   teaspoon instant minced garlic
1   teaspoon basil leaves
1   tablespoon dried parsley flakes
1-½ cups loose pack frozen green beans
    Salt and pepper to taste

(Continued)

Vegetable Medley Soup (continued)

1. In microwave-safe soup tureen or 3-quart casserole, combine celery, carrots, potato, tomatoes, zucchini, spaghetti, water, bouillon, garlic, basil and parsley flakes. Mix well. Cover with lid or vented plastic wrap.

2. Microwave on 100% power 25-35 minutes or until vegetables are tender, stirring once or twice and adding frozen green beans about half way through cooking time.

Note: Fresh green beans may be used. Add them in the beginning with the other vegetables.

Crunchy Asparagus

Serves 6-8

I like recipes that have flair and character like this outstanding asparagus idea. From the toasted almonds to the water chestnut slices, this vegetable combination is filled with crunch. Asparagus fans will appreciate your efforts.

¼ **cup butter or margarine**
¼ **cup slivered blanched almonds**
2 **(10 ounce) packages frozen asparagus cuts or 1 quart home frozen asparagus**
1 **cup diced celery**
1-⅓ **cups sliced water chestnuts**
2 **tablespoons soy sauce**

1. In 2-quart microwave-safe serving dish or casserole, combine butter and almonds.

2. Microwave on 70% power 3-4 minutes. Stir and continue cooking on 70% power an additional 3-4 minutes or until golden brown. (If you do not have reduced power, use 100% power 4-5 minutes, stirring every minute.)

3. Remove almonds from casserole. Set aside for garnish.

4. Add asparagus, celery and water chestnuts to butter in casserole. Cover with lid or vented plastic wrap.

5. Microwave on 100% power for 7 minutes. Stir to break up frozen asparagus.

6. Continue cooking on 100% power 5-7 minutes, until crisp tender.

7. Stir in soy sauce.

8. Garnish with toasted almonds. Serve.

Wonderful Winter Squash

2 servings per pound of squash

Winter squash cooks beautifully right in its own skin in the microwave oven. The procedure is like baking a potato in that the outer skin is punctured to let steam escape and then cooked at 100% power for 6-7 minutes per pound of squash. Remember, cooked squash freezes well, so take advantage of this time saving technique during the crisp cool autumn months.

1. Wash and dry squash. Weigh the squash.

2. Puncture several holes with fork tines in the squash to allow steam to escape.

3. Place squash on microwave roasting rack.

4. Microwave on 100% power 6 to 7 minutes per pound, turning squash over halfway through cooking time.

5. Wrap in clean terry cloth dish towel and let stand at least 10 minutes.

6. Cut open squash. Clean out the seeds.

7. Put squash pulp in mixing bowl.

8. Mash squash with potato masher and season with butter or margarine and salt. (Calorie watchers can use very little butter and low sodium watchers can eliminate the salt.)

9. Put seasoned squash in microwave-safe serving dish.

10. Microwave, uncovered, at 80% power until hot. (Length of time will depend on starting temperature of squash.)

11. This cooked squash could easily be probed to 150 degrees at 80% power of the microwave.

Harvard Beets

Serves 4

Cooked beets in a sweet-sour sauce have been popular in New England for more than a century. Now we can make this traditional recipe quickly and easily the modern way in the microwave. Make these tasty beets for your family soon.

1	**(16 ounce) can diced beets, drained and reserve juice**
1	**tablespoon cornstarch**
2	**tablespoons sugar**
¼	**teaspoon salt**
½	**cup beet juice and water**
¼	**cup vinegar**

(Continued)

Harvard Beets (continued)

(continued)

1. In 1-quart microwave-safe casserole, blend cornstarch, sugar and salt.
2. Stir in beet juice and vinegar.
3. Microwave on 100% power for 2-4 minutes, stirring every minute until thickened.
4. Add beets and microwave on 100% power 3-4 minutes until hot, stirring once.

Sweet Potato Delight

Serves 8-10

Sweet potatoes show themselves off in fine style in this delicately seasoned casserole. The marshmallow topping melts beautifully in the microwave, however, don't overcook because if overheated marshmallows disappear.

¼   cup margarine or butter
2   (23 ounce) cans sweet potatoes, drained
¼   cup milk
½   teaspoon salt
½   teaspoon ground cinnamon
½   teaspoon ground nutmeg
¼   cup orange marmalade or honey
¼   cup raisins
1   cup miniature marshmallows

1. Place margarine in large microwave-safe bowl. Microwave on 100% power 20-30 seconds until melted.
2. Put drained sweet potatoes in bowl with melted margarine. Mash until smooth with potato masher or electric mixer.
3. Add milk, salt, cinnamon and nutmeg to sweet potatoes.
4. Stir marmalade and raisins into sweet potato mixture.
5. Put sweet potatoes into 1-½ quart microwave-safe casserole. (May be refrigerated at this point.)
6. Microwave on 100% power 12-14 minutes, rotating casserole once, until hot. (This mixture could be probed to 160 degrees at 80% power, if desired.)
7. Top with marshmallows. Cover lightly with waxed paper.
8. Microwave on 100% power 1 to 2 minutes until marshmallows begin to soften, and melt.

Candied Yams

Serves 6

Just like white potatoes, yams bake beautifully in the microwave oven. Follow the guideline of 6-7 minutes per pound on 100% power. In this recipe, cranberry sauce not only adds delicious flavor, but provides a wonderful color contrast.

7	medium yams or sweet potatoes
6	tablespoons butter or margarine
½	cup brown sugar
½	teaspoon salt
⅓	cup raisins
½	cup whole cranberry sauce

1. Arrange yams on a microwave roasting rack in a star-burst arrangement.

2. Microwave on 100% power 18-20 minutes (6-7 minutes per pound) turning yams over halfway through cooking time.

3. Wrap yams in clean terry towel and let rest 10-15 minutes.

4. In 1-quart microwave-safe measurer put butter, brown sugar and salt.

5. Microwave, uncovered, 2-½ to 3 minutes or until hot and bubbly, stirring once. Stir in raisins and cranberry sauce.

6. Peel yams; cut into 1-inch slices. Arrange in 2-quart microwave-safe flat casserole.

7. Pour cranberry sauce over the yams as evenly as possible.

8. Cover and refrigerate until ready to serve or heat immediately.

9. Microwave, covered with wax paper, on 80% power 8-12 minutes or until heated through, rotating dish once. (Remember that refrigerated yams will take longer to reheat.)

Green Beans 'N Bacon

Serves 6

I like the sweet and sour flavor in this tasty green bean-bacon duo. Cooking the bacon in the serving dish is a great time and energy saving technique, just add seasonings and cooked beans for a quick first-class vegetable idea.

4	slices bacon, cut into 1-inch pieces
4	green onions, sliced
2	tablespoons vinegar
2	teaspoons dill weed
1	teaspoon sugar
½	teaspoon salt
2	(10 ounce) packages frozen French style green beans

(Continued)

Green Beans 'N Bacon (continued)

1. In a 1-½-quart microwave-safe casserole, combine bacon and onions. Microwave on 100% power, uncovered, 5 to 6 minutes or until bacon is crisp, stirring once.

2. Add vinegar, dill weed, sugar and salt; set aside.

3. Remove foil wrapping from packages of green beans, if necessary; pierce packages with fork to let steam escape. Place on microwave-safe plate.

4. Microwave on 100% power 10-12 minutes, turning packages over halfway through cooking time, drain.

5. Add drained beans to bacon mixture; toss lightly to season evenly.

6. Microwave, uncovered, on 100% power 2-3 minutes or until thoroughly heated.

Glazed Carrots and Pea Pods

Serves 6

If a menu needs a bright green vegetable with a splash of orange, let me suggest this wonderful combination of frozen pea pods and fresh carrots. The flavors blend perfectly when subtly supported by green onions, butter and brown sugar.

3   cups thinly sliced carrots (a little over a pound)
2   tablespoons water
1   (6 ounce) package frozen pea pods
2   tablespoons sliced green onions
2   tablespoons butter or margarine
1-½ tablespoons packed brown sugar
½   teaspoon cornstarch
¼   teaspoon salt
        Dash of pepper

1. Combine carrots and water in 1-½-quart microwave-safe casserole.

2. Cover with lid or vented plastic wrap. Microwave on 100% power 7 to 8 minutes or until crisp tender, stirring once.

3. Add pea pods and green onions.

4. Microwave on 100% power 3 to 4 minutes until pea pods are hot.

5. Drain vegetables. Mix in butter, brown sugar, cornstarch, salt and pepper.

6. Microwave on 100% power, uncovered, 1 to 2 minutes or until hot, stirring once.

Parmesan Potatoes

Serves 6

These great tasting potatoes can cook in the microwave while steaks are on the grill. It's the type of recipe that's easy to increase or decrease depending on appetites. Just remember fresh potatoes take 6-7 minutes per pound to cook in the microwave on 100% power.

6   **baking potatoes**
¼   **cup butter or margarine, melted**
½   **cup grated Parmesan cheese**

1. Scrub baking potatoes, do not peel, unless desired. Cut in quarters lengthwise.

2. Dip potatoes in melted butter; then in grated Parmesan cheese.

3. Put potatoes in 1-½-quart microwave-safe casserole.

4. Cover with lid or vented plastic wrap.

5. Microwave on 100% power 12-14 minutes until potatoes are tender, stirring once.

Easy Creamed Peas

Serves 3-4

Surprise your family with these jiffy creamed peas. As with many microwave recipes, all cooking can be done right in the serving dish. Not only is that easy on the cook, but a blessing to those in charge of dish washing.

2   **tablespoons butter or margarine**
2   **tablespoons flour**
1-½ **tablespoons dry nondairy coffee creamer**
1   **(16 ounce) can peas, undrained**

1. In 1-quart microwave-safe casserole, melt butter on 100% power for 20-30 seconds.

2. Blend in flour and coffee creamer. Add undrained peas.

3. Microwave on 100% power 5-6 minutes, until hot and slightly thickened, stirring once or twice.

4. Season with salt and pepper, if desired.

Note: If using 1 (10 ounce) package frozen peas, add 1 cup water.

Tasty Filled Onions

Serves 6-8

One of the fun things to do in a microwave oven is to partially cook onions; then easily remove the centers leaving a shell to be filled. In this recipe a well flavored spinach mixture takes the center spotlight. Do try this idea soon.

3	or 4 medium onions
1	(10 ounce) package frozen chopped spinach
¼	cup milk
2	tablespoons flour
½	teaspoon salt
2	tablespoons butter or margarine
½	cup shredded cheddar cheese
1	tablespoon butter or margarine
3	tablespoons dry bread crumbs

1. Peel onions and halve each crosswise. Place cut side down in round microwave-safe baking dish. Cover with waxed paper.

2. Microwave on 100% power 7-9 minutes or until onions are tender-crisp. Remove centers from onions and set aside for use in other dishes.

3. Separate onion halves into one or two shells each, leaving 2 or 3 layers of onion in each. Place shells cut side up in microwave-safe 2-quart baking dish. Set aside.

4. Puncture frozen spinach package with fork tine 2 or 3 times. Microwave on 100% power 5 to 6 minutes or until thawed, turning package over halfway through cooking time, drain well.

5. Put drained spinach in 1-quart microwave-safe casserole. In 1 cup microwave-safe measurer, combine milk, flour and salt; stir into spinach. Add two tablespoons butter.

6. Microwave, uncovered, on 100% power 2-3 minutes, until thickened, stirring once. Stir in cheese.

7. Microwave on 100% power 1 tablespoon butter in small microwave-safe dish for 20-30 seconds or until melted. Stir in bread crumbs.

8. Spoon spinach mixture into onion shells; top with buttered crumbs.

9. Microwave, covered with waxed paper, on 80% power 5-8 minutes until heated through.

Wilted Greens

Serves 4-6

Sometimes salads are overlooked when we think of microwave cooking, but what a perfect way to prepare a hot dressing for fresh salad greens. Start by efficiently cooking bacon, and then add several simple ingredients to create a tasty dressing.

6   slices bacon
½   cup sliced green onion
¼   cup red wine vinegar
¼   cup water
1   tablespoon sugar
¾   teaspoon salt
6   cups torn fresh salad greens (leaf lettuce, spinach, etc.)
1   cup sliced red radishes

1. Place bacon on microwave roasting rack designed to save the bacon grease during cooking. Cover with paper towel.

2. Microwave on 100% power 4-6 minutes or until crisp, rotating rack once.

3. Remove bacon. Crumble and set aside.

4. Pour bacon grease in 1 quart microwave-safe measurer. Stir in onion. Cover with waxed paper. Microwave on 100% power 2-3 minutes, stirring once.

5. Add vinegar, water, sugar and salt.

6. Place torn greens in a large salad bowl.

7. Just before serving, microwave dressing mixture on 100% power 2 minutes or until boiling.

8. Pour hot dressing over the greens and toss lightly.

9. Garnish with crumbled bacon and sliced radishes.

10. Serve immediately.

Cabbage Waldorf Slaw

Serves 6-8

The thought of making a cooked dressing from scratch can sometimes seem overwhelming and not worth the effort. However, with the aid of a microwave oven, a dressing can be created in a matter of minutes. Take, for example, this delicious citrus dressing that puts a special homemade seal of approval on this cabbage slaw.

(Continued)

Cabbage Waldorf Slaw (continued)

¼   **cup sugar**
1   **tablespoon cornstarch**
1   **teaspoon salt**
¾   **cup orange juice**
2   **tablespoons lemon juice**
1   **egg**
1   **teaspoon grated lemon peel**
½   **cup cultured sour cream**
4   **cups shredded cabbage**
2   **fresh unpeeled red skinned eating apples, diced**
½   **cup coarsely chopped blanched peanuts**

1. In 1-quart microwave-safe measurer, combine sugar, cornstarch and salt. Use wire whisk to thoroughly combine.

2. Add orange juice, lemon juice, egg and lemon peel. Whisk to combine.

3. Microwave on 100% power 3-4 minutes, until thick, stirring every minute with wire whisk. Cool.

4. At serving time, blend sour cream into cooled cooked dressing.

5. In large mixing bowl, combine cabbage, apples and peanuts. Toss with dressing.

6. Put in pretty serving dish. Garnish with fresh apple slices.

Orange Cranberry Sauce

Serves 6

I can think of no easier way to make traditional cranberry sauce. It works equally well to use fresh or frozen cranberries. The only difference is the longer cooking time for frozen berries. Whether you're a cranberry sauce novice or pro, you'll like this method.

1   **(12 ounce) bag fresh or frozen cranberries, freshly washed**
¼   **cup plus 2 tablespoons orange juice**
1   **cup plus 2 tablespoons sugar**

1. In large 3-quart microwave-safe casserole, combine cranberries and orange juice.

2. Microwave, covered with lid or vented plastic wrap, on 100% power 6-8 minutes, stirring once or twice. (Add 4-6 extra minutes for frozen cranberries.)

3. Add sugar and mix well. Re-cover and allow to stand. Cool. Refrigerate.

Note: Add more or less sugar depending on personal preference.

Rosy Applesauce

Serves 4

Applesauce cooked in the microwave oven is one of those simple pleasures of life. It's easy, efficient and extra specially delicious. This festive version uses cinnamon red hots to add color and flavor.

8-10 medium cooking apples, peeled, cored and quartered
2   tablespoons water, if desired
¼   cup cinnamon red hots
2-4   tablespoons sugar, depending on tartness of apples

1. In large 3-quart microwave-safe casserole, combine apples and water. Cover.

2. Microwave on 100% power 10-12 minutes or until apples are tender, stirring 3 or 4 times.

3. Stir in red hots and sugar.

4. Microwave on 100% power 2 to 4 more minutes, or until red hots are completely dissolved, stirring every minute.

5. Cool. Chill. Enjoy.

Lambs Wool

Makes 12-½ cup servings

Melted marshmallows look just like fluffy lambs wool floating on top of this flavorful hot beverage. The next time guests arrive on a cold winter's night have this surprise heating in the microwave oven.

4   cups apple cider or juice
2   cups orange juice
¼   cup honey, if desired
3   tablespoons lemon juice
1   teaspoon grated lemon peel
12-16 large marshmallows

1. In 2 quart microwave-safe punch bowl or attractive casserole, combine apple cider, orange juice, honey, lemon juice and lemon peel.

2. Microwave on 100% power 12-15 minutes until piping hot, stirring once. (Probe to 160 degrees)

3. Top with marshmallows.

4. Microwave on 100% power 1-½ to 2-½ minutes until marshmallows melt.

Herbed Pretzels

Serves 6-8

It won't take long to transform everyday pretzels into herbed flavored treats, if you use this quick and easy recipe. Store in airtight containers ready for munching on a minute's notice.

¼   **cup butter or margarine**
½   **teaspoon dried dill weed**
1   **teaspoon dried parsley flakes**
¼   **teaspoon celery salt**
¼   **teaspoon onion salt**
1   **(10 ounce) package or box miniature pretzels**

1. Put butter in 2-quart microwave-safe casserole. Microwave on 100% power for 20-30 seconds to melt.

2. Stir dill weed, parsley flakes, celery salt and onion salt into melted butter.

3. Add pretzels. Toss to coat with butter mixture.

4. Microwave on 100% power 3 minutes, stirring every minute.

5. Cool. Store in airtight container.

Super Shrimp Dip

10-12 appetizer servings

If you need a super quick appetizer or snack, this idea may come to your rescue. It is designed to be served hot, however, I've known guests to enjoy it warm and/or cold.

1   **(8 ounce) package cream cheese**
1   **(10-¾ ounce) can cream of shrimp soup, undiluted**
4   **green onions, including 4 inches of green tops, finely sliced**

1. Place cream cheese in 2-quart microwave-safe measurer. Microwave on 100% power 45 seconds to soften cream cheese.

2. Stir soup and onions into softened cream cheese.

3. Microwave on 80% power 3-4 minutes until dip is hot, stirring once.

4. Serve with crisp crackers or assorted fresh vegetables.

Caramel Biscuit Ring

Serves 4

This quick sweet treat is often called "Monkey Bread" by the younger set. In just a matter of minutes, it's possible to have hot caramel rolls right out of the microwave to enjoy with ice cold glasses of milk.

⅓   **cup firmly packed brown sugar (use dark brown for better color)**
3   **tablespoons butter or margarine**
1   **tablespoon water**
⅓   **cup chopped pecans or walnuts**
1   **(7-½ ounce) can refrigerated biscuits**

   1. In a shallow 1-quart microwave-safe casserole or 8-inch round glass dish, combine the brown sugar, butter, and water.

   2. Microwave on 100% power, uncovered, for 1 minute.

   3. Stir to melt the butter and dissolve the sugar. Stir in the pecans.

   4. With kitchen scissors or knife, cut each biscuit into four pieces and add to the sugar mixture. Stir to coat each piece.

   5. Use a rubber scraper to push the mixture and biscuits evenly away from the center. Place a small empty custard cup or medium-sized drinking glass in the center with open side up to form a ring mold.

   6. Microwave, elevated on microwave roasting rack, for 2 minutes on 80% power.

   7. Rotate dish one half turn. Again, microwave on 80% power 2-3 minutes or until dough is no longer sticky when lightly touched.

   8. Let the mixture "carry-over-cook" for 1-2 minutes. Carefully remove the custard cup and invert on a serving plate.

   9. Serve immediately.

Note: If only 100% power is available, microwave on 100% power 1 minute in step 6 and 1-1-½ minutes in step 7.

Budget Hot Chocolate Sauce

Makes 1-¼ cups

There are times when I've wanted to make hot chocolate sauce but didn't have the exact ingredients I needed. With this economical recipe, all that's required is unsweetened cocoa plus some kitchen regulars. Believe me, it's a delicious topping for ice cream or cake.

(Continued)

Budget Hot Chocolate Sauce (continued)

1   cup water
1   cup sugar
⅓ cup unsweetened cocoa
2   tablespoons flour
¼ teaspoon salt
1   tablespoon butter or margarine
1   teaspoon vanilla

1. In 1 cup microwave-safe measurer, microwave water on 100% power 2-4 minutes until boiling.

2. Meanwhile in 1 quart microwave-safe measurer, blend together sugar, cocoa, flour and salt.

3. Add boiling water to sugar mixture. Stir well with wire whisk.

4. Microwave on 100% power 2-4 minutes until very thick, stirring each minute with a wire whisk.

5. Stir in butter and vanilla.

6. Serve hot or store in covered jar in refrigerator. Heat when needed.

Cherry Crunch Cobbler

Serves 8

Keep the supplies for this favorite dessert on the cupboard shelf, for it doesn't take long to create this hot bubbly sweet tooth delight. Top off each serving with a big scoop of ice cream if you feel like a splurge. Other flavors of prepared pie fillings work well too.

½ cup butter or margarine
1   (21 ounce) can prepared cherry pie filling
1   (8 ounce) can crushed pineapple, undrained
1   (9 ounce) package yellow cake mix (one layer size)
½ cup chopped pecans or walnuts

1. In small microwave-safe dish, microwave butter on 100% power for 30-60 seconds or until melted.

2. In 2 quart round microwave-safe dish, combine pie filling and undrained pineapple.

3. Sprinkle dry cake mix and nuts over fruit; drizzle with melted butter.

4. Microwave, uncovered, on 100% power 15-17 minutes or until bubbly and butter is absorbed.

5. Serve warm with vanilla ice cream, if desired.

234

Double Quick Gingerbread

Serves 12

Convenience cake mixes come in handy when preparing a quick dessert. In this recipe, a crunchy streusel topping adds the desired homemade appearance to a box of gingerbread mix.

1   (14.5 ounce) package gingerbread mix
⅓   cup brown sugar
¼   cup flour
½   teaspoon ground cinnamon
3   tablespoons butter or margarine
⅓   cup chopped walnuts or pecans

1. Prepare gingerbread following package directions.

2. Grease bottom only of an 8-inch square microwave-safe baking dish.

3. Pour gingerbread batter evenly in prepared dish.

4. Microwave on 50% power, uncovered, 10 minutes rotating dish once.

5. In small mixing bowl, combine brown sugar, flour and cinnamon. Cut in butter with pastry blender or fork until mixture is crumbly. Stir in walnuts.

6. Sprinkle topping evenly on top of cake.

7. Microwave on 50% power for 3-4 minutes.

8. Then, microwave on 100% power 3-5 minutes or until cake is done, rotating dish once.

9. Cool with dish set on smooth surface to encourage carry over cooking.

Cran-Apple Crisp

Serves 8

Bright red cranberries dot this quick apple crisp adding wonderful color and flavor. On almost a minute's notice, this dessert is ready for family and friends to enjoy. Top with vanilla ice cream for a la mode pleasure.

2   cups fresh or frozen cranberries
4   cups sliced, peeled apples (4 medium apples)
¾   cup sugar
½   cup margarine or butter, softened
½   cup packed dark brown sugar
½   cup flour
1   cup quick cooking or old-fashioned rolled oats
½   teaspoon ground cinnamon

(Continued)

Cran-Apple Crisp (continued)

1. In 8-inch microwave-safe baking dish, combine cranberries, apples and sugar. Mix lightly and spread evenly in dish. Set aside.

2. In small mixing bowl, cream together margarine and brown sugar; mix in flour, oats and cinnamon until crumbly.

3. Sprinkle over cranberries and apples.

4. Microwave on 100% power 10-12 minutes or until fruits are tender, rotating dish once. If frozen cranberries are used, cooking time may be longer.

5. Serve warm with ice cream, if desired.

Rhubarb Crisp

Serves 6-8

When a thoughtful friend brings me fresh stalks of rhubarb, I know it's spring. The quickest way to enjoy this taste of spring is to pop a crisp in the microwave oven. To extend this spring flavor all year long, frozen rhubarb can be used too.

4	cups sliced fresh or frozen rhubarb
1	cup sugar
2	tablespoons flour
1	egg, slightly beaten
	Few drops red food coloring, if desired
½	cup flour
½	cup quick oats
⅓	cup dark brown sugar
¼	teaspoon ground nutmeg
¼	cup margarine or butter, chilled

1. If you are using frozen rhubarb, microwave rhubarb on 100% power 3-4 minutes to thaw.

2. In 8-inch round microwave-safe dish, combine rhubarb, sugar, 2 tablespoons flour and egg. Mix until evenly combined. Add red food coloring, if desired.

3. In small mixing bowl, combine ½ cup flour, quick oats, brown sugar and nutmeg. Cut in margarine with pastry blender or fork until crumbly.

4. Sprinkle over rhubarb.

5. Microwave on 100% power, uncovered, 12-14 minutes or until rhubarb is tender, rotating dish once or twice.

Crunchy Treats

Makes 2 dozen squares

There are times when a quick sweet treat is needed and this recipe would be a great way to meet that need. It's a recipe that can easily be adapted to the ingredients found in your kitchen. Whether you start with butterscotch or chocolate chips, these squares will be devoured immediately.

1   **(12 ounce) package butterscotch or semi-sweet chocolate chips**
1   **cup crunchy peanut butter**
1   **cup quick-cooking oats**
1   **cup whole grain cereal flakes**
1   **cup raisins**
1   **cup coconut**

1. In 2-quart microwave-safe measurer, microwave butterscotch or chocolate chips on 50% power 4-5 minutes until melted, stirring once.

2. Stir in peanut butter. If needed, microwave on 100% power 30-45 seconds to melt peanut butter.

3. Add oats, cereal, raisins and coconut. Stir to coat well.

4. Spread mixture in a buttered or waxed paper-lined 8x12-inch baking dish.

5. Chill.

6. Cut into squares.

Chocolate Peppermint Fondue

Serves 6-8

Few desserts are quicker than this creamy fondue. The flavors of mint and chocolate are teamed together in a creation that will easily win the stamp of approval of family and friends.

1   **(5-½ or 6 ounce) box thin chocolate-covered mints**
1   **(6 ounce) package semi-sweet chocolate chips (1 cup)**
⅓   **cup half and half light cream**

1. Combine mints, chocolate chips and light cream in 1 quart microwave-safe measurer.

2. Microwave on 50% power for 3 to 4 minutes, stirring once or twice.

3. Put in small candle-warmed chocolate pot, if available.

4. Spear small pieces of angel food cake or pound cake or fruit and dip into the chocolate peppermint fondue.

Cheese Sauce

Makes 1-½ cups

Super sauces can be created in the microwave with minimal watching and stirring. This basic cheese sauce is an excellent example of how quickly a quality sauce can be made. It's a delicious way to show off your culinary skill.

2   tablespoons butter or margarine
2   tablespoons flour
½   teaspoon salt
1   cup milk
1   cup (4 ounces) shredded sharp cheddar cheese

1. Put butter in small microwave-safe dish. Microwave on 100% power until butter is melted, about 15 seconds.

2. Blend in flour and salt to make a smooth paste. Set aside.

3. In a one-quart microwave-safe measurer, measure milk. Microwave on 100% power 2-3 minutes, or until milk boils.

4. Beat flour paste into hot milk using a wire whisk.

5. Microwave on 100% power 1-2 minutes until thickened, stirring once.

6. Add cheese, stirring until cheese melts.

7. Serve over your favorite cooked vegetable or use as desired.

Gravy

Makes 2 cups

There is no need to strain out lumps of flour when the microwave oven is used for gravy making. Season first with bouillon for extra flavor and then use browning and seasoning sauce that adds both color and flavor.

¼   cup flour
1-½ cups water or milk
½   cup pan drippings
     Instant bouillon, if desired
     Salt and pepper, if desired
¾   teaspoon browning and seasoning sauce for gravy

1. Combine flour and water in 1-quart microwave-safe measurer.

2. Stir in pan drippings.

3. Microwave, uncovered, on 100% power 3-4 minutes until mixture boils, stirring once or twice.

4. Season with bouillon or salt and pepper.

5. For added color, add browning and seasoning sauce.

Cooked Chicken

3 cups cooked chicken

When cooked chicken is needed for a recipe, prepare it the easy way using the microwave oven. This is a real time-saving cooking technique, so try using this method soon. The guideline to remember is that chicken needs to be cooked on 100% power 7-8 minutes per pound.

3   pounds meaty chicken pieces (like breasts, thighs or legs)

1. Wash pieces of chicken in cold water. Do not dry.

2. Leave skin on chicken pieces as it will be removed when the cooked chicken is removed from the chicken bones.

3. Put chicken parts on microwave roasting rack with meaty parts facing toward the outside of the rack.

4. Cover with waxed paper.

5. Microwave on 100% power 21-24 minutes until meat is tender, rotating dish once.

6. Cool until easy to handle.

7. Discard skin, remove meat from bones and cut into desired size pieces.

Microwave Browned Ground Beef

1 pound browned ground beef

Just in case you have not tried this easy method to brown ground beef in the microwave oven. I'm including the directions for you to follow. Remember that this is a good way to have fat free browned ground beef to use in a variety of recipes. If the recipe calls for onions and green peppers to be browned, just put them in the colander with the ground beef.

1   pound hamburger or ground beef

1. Place ground beef in a hard plastic colander.

2. Rest colander over 1-quart microwave-safe measurer or bowl.

3. Microwave on 100% power 3 minutes. Break up meat with a fork or small hand chopper.

4. Microwave on 100% power 2-3 minutes more until meat looks cooked. Break up meat with fork again.

5. Use immediately or package and refrigerate for a short time or freeze for later use.

6. Pour off and discard fat after each pound of meat that is browned.

Food Gifts

Homemade food gifts are the perfect unspoken way to show care and concern, or appreciation and approval, or recognition and reward to those you know. This chapter includes a proven collection of gifts from your kitchen guaranteed to please both family and friends.

Length of preparation time can vary from the baked Gift Giving Danish Puff to the almost instant Fruit-Nut Mix. Made from scratch mixes are a thoughtful gift ideas that are non-perishable allowing the recipient to quickly finish the preparation when desired.

These gifts come from the heart. They are a sharing of time, talent, and energy that say in a very subtle way, "I care."

Contents

Gift Giving Danish Puff

2 coffee cakes

Two beautiful coffee cakes are the result of this thoughtful recipe. Your family will be happy to "taste test" one and the other can be placed on a rectangular bread board ready for gift giving. It's a tender mouth-watering pastry, so your baking efforts will be appreciated.

½   **cup butter or margarine, softened**
1   **cup flour**
2   **tablespoons water**
½   **cup butter or margarine**
1   **cup water**
1   **teaspoon almond extract**
1   **cup flour**
3   **eggs**
1-½   **cups confectioners' sugar**
2   **tablespoons butter or margarine, softened**
1-½   **teaspoons vanilla**
1-2   **tablespoons warm water**
½   **cup chopped walnuts or pecans**

1. In small mixing bowl, cut ½ cup butter into 1 cup flour until particles are the size of small peas.

2. Sprinkle 2 tablespoons water over flour mixture; mix with fork.

3. Gather pastry into a ball; divide into halves.

4. Pat each half into rectangle, 3x12-inches, on ungreased or parchment lined cookie sheet. Rectangles should be about 3 inches apart.

5. In medium saucepan, heat ½ cup butter and 1 cup water to a rolling boil; remove from heat.

6. Quickly stir in almond extract and 1 cup flour. Stir vigorously over low heat until mixture forms a ball, about 1 minute; remove from heat.

7. Add eggs; beat until smooth and glossy.

8. Spread half of the topping over each rectangle.

9. Bake in preheated 350 degree oven until topping is crisp and brown, about 1 hour; cool.

10. In small bowl, combine confectioners' sugar, 2 tablespoons softened butter and vanilla. Stir in warm water, 1 tablespoon at time, until smooth and of desired consistency.

11. Spread half of this frosting on each of the coffee cakes.

12. Sprinkle with chopped walnuts.

13. Give with pleasure.

Sour Cream Pound Cake

Serves 12-16

This lovely versatile cake would make a fantastic food gift because it is so easy to carry or mail. Attractive cake serving boards, available at cake decorating shops, work well as non-returnable cake plates. Over wrap cake with plastic bubble wrap for mailing.

1	cup butter or margarine, softened
6	eggs
2-⅔	cups sugar
3	cups flour
¼	teaspoon baking soda
½	teaspoon salt
1	cup cultured sour cream
½	teaspoon lemon extract
½	teaspoon orange extract
½	teaspoon vanilla extract

1. Bring the butter or margarine and the eggs to room temperature. Grease and flour the bottom and sides of a 10-inch bundt pan or tube pan; set aside.

2. In large mixing bowl, beat butter with electric mixer until creamy. Gradually add the sugar, beating at medium speed till light and fluffy.

3. Add eggs, one a time, beating about 1 minute after each; scrape bowl frequently, guiding mixture toward beaters. Beat 2 minutes more.

4. Sift together flour, soda and salt. Add to creamed mixture alternately with sour cream, beginning and ending with flour mixture. Beat well after each addition.

5. Add lemon, orange and vanilla extracts; beat just until thoroughly blended.

6. Pour batter into prepared 10-inch bundt or tube pan.

7. Bake in preheated 350 degree oven for 1-½ hours or until wooden pick inserted in center comes out clean and dry.

8. Cool cake in pan on wire rack for 15 minutes; remove from pan.

9. Cool completely.

10. Sprinkle with confectioners' sugar, if desired. Package in a festive way.

Lebkuchen Bars

4 dozen bars

Have you ever made German lebkuchen bars? They are a fragrant fruit-filled holiday spice cookie that's frosted with a complementary lemon glaze. Lots of cooks like to bake lebkuchen early in the season so that the bars can be stored in airtight containers to mellow and develop flavor. These delicious bars then make great impromptu gifts from your kitchen.

1	egg
1	cup firmly, packed brown sugar
½	cup molasses
½	cup honey
3-½	cups flour
½	teaspoon baking soda
⅛	teaspoon salt
1	teaspoon ground cinnamon
1	teaspoon ground nutmeg
1	teaspoon ground cloves
¾	cup chopped candied cherries
¾	cup slivered almonds, toasted
	Lemon Icing (recipe follows)

1. In large mixing bowl, beat together egg and brown sugar with electric mixer. Mix in molasses and honey.

2. Sift together flour, soda, salt, cinnamon, nutmeg and cloves.

3. In medium mixing bowl, combine 1 cup flour mixture with cherries and almonds tossing to coat; set aside.

4. Stir remaining flour into molasses mixture, stirring well; fold in cherries and almonds.

5. Pat dough into a greased 15x10x1-inch jelly-roll pan.

6. Bake in preheated 300 degree oven for 40 minutes.

7. Cool on wire rack, and frost with lemon icing; cut into bars as soon as icing is set.

8. Store in airtight container ready for gift giving.

Lemon Icing

Frosts 1 recipe of Lebkuchen Bars

This lemon icing forms a very thin glaze over lebkuchen bars. I think it is a good idea to cut the bars very soon after the icing sets, to prevent cracking of the glaze. The flavor combination of lemon and spice is wonderful.

(Continued)

Lemon Icing (continued)

1   egg white
2   cups sifted confectioners' sugar
½   teaspoon grated lemon peel
1   tablespoon lemon juice
⅛   teaspoon salt, if desired

1. In medium mixing bowl, beat egg white until soft peaks form with electric mixer.

2. Beat in sugar, lemon peel, lemon juice and, if desired, salt.

3. Spread lemon icing on cooled lebkuchen bars.

4. Cut into bars as soon as icing is set.

Cranberry-Pecan Tassies

Makes 2 dozen

Cranberries add a wonderful festive touch to these miniature pecan tasties. Slip into petite red paper liners and package in a decorated white foam egg carton for a creative gift from your kitchen. These tassies morsels store very well in the freezer, if kept hidden from family members.

1   (3 ounce) package cream cheese, softened
½   cup margarine or butter, softened
1   cup flour
1   egg
¾   cup packed brown sugar
1   teaspoon vanilla
    Dash of salt
⅓   cup finely chopped fresh or frozen cranberries (use food processor)
3   tablespoons chopped pecans

1. In medium mixing bowl, blend together cream cheese and margarine. Stir in flour. Cover and chill at least 1 hour.

2. Shape dough into 24, 1-inch balls; place in ungreased 1-¾-inch muffin pans.

3. Press dough evenly against bottom and sides of pan with fingertips or wooden "stamper", if available.

4. In 1 quart glass measurer, beat together egg, brown sugar, vanilla and dash of salt just until smooth.

5. Stir in cranberries and pecans.

6. Spoon into pastry-lined muffin cups.

7. Bake in preheated 325 degree oven 30-35 minutes. Cool in pans. Carefully run knife around outside to remove from pans.

Mincemeat-Nut Bread

1 loaf

I can picture a luscious loaf of this mincemeat bread gaily wrapped with pretty ribbons all ready for holiday gift giving. Be certain to add an attractive label, especially for those recipients that thought mincemeat only came in pies.

½	cup butter or margarine, softened
¾	cup sugar
2	eggs
2-½	cups flour
1-½	teaspoons baking powder
½	teaspoon baking soda
½	teaspoon salt
½	cup milk
1-⅓	cups prepared mincemeat, (½ of a 28 ounce jar)
½	cup chopped walnuts

1. In large mixing bowl, cream together butter and sugar until light and fluffy.

2. Add eggs, one at a time, beating well after each addition.

3. Sift together flour, baking powder, soda and salt.

4. Add dry ingredients alternately with milk, beginning and ending with the flour mixture.

5. Stir in mincemeat and walnuts.

6. Spread in greased and floured, or parchment lined, 9x5-inch baking pan.

7. Bake in preheated 350 degree oven 60-70 minutes until wooden pick inserted near center comes out clean.

8. Cool 10 minutes. Remove from pan to cooling rack.

9. Wrap attractively for gift giving.

Forgotten Kisses

Makes 4-5 dozen

Hidden in your oven overnight, these sweet-tooth delights will be ready first thing in the morning to be packed into airtight containers for quick and welcome gifts. No one ever needs to know the unbelievable ease of this baking experience.

2	egg whites, at room temperature
½	cup sugar
1	teaspoon almond extract
¼	teaspoon vanilla extract
1	cup miniature chocolate chips
1	cup chopped pecans

(Continued)

Forgotten Kisses (continued)

1. In medium mixing bowl, beat egg whites until foamy. Gradually add sugar, beating until stiff. Add almond extract and vanilla. Mix well.

2. Fold in chocolate chips and pecans.

3. Drop by ejector spoon or teaspoon on parchment lined or aluminum foil-lined cookie sheets. (The kisses do not spread)

4. Place in preheated 350 degree oven; immediately turn oven off.

5. Let stand 8 to 10 hours or overnight. DO NOT OPEN OVEN DOOR.

6. Store in airtight containers ready for gift giving.

Chocolate Applesauce Bread

Makes 1 loaf

It doesn't take long to mix up a loaf of this tasty quick bread for a special gift from your kitchen. The applesauce in this loaf adds a wonderful moist quality and chocolate contributes the full bodied flavor.

⅓   cup margarine or butter
2   (1-ounce) squares unsweetened chocolate
1-½ cups flour
1-¼ cups sugar
1   teaspoon baking soda
¼   teaspoon baking powder
¼   teaspoon salt
¼   teaspoon ground nutmeg
½   teaspoon ground cinnamon
2   eggs, beaten
½   cup unsweetened applesauce
½   cup chopped walnuts

1. In small saucepan or double boiler, melt margarine and chocolate over very low heat. Cool slightly.

2. In large mixing bowl, sift together flour, sugar, soda, baking powder, salt, nutmeg and cinnamon.

3. Add chocolate mixture, beaten eggs, applesauce and walnuts to flour mixture and mix well.

4. Pour into a greased and floured or parchment lined 9x5x3-inch loaf pan.

5. Bake in preheated 350 degree oven for 50-60 minutes or until a wooden pick inserted in the center comes out clean.

6. Cool bread in pan 10 minutes; remove from pan and cool completely on cooling rack.

7. Wrap cleverly for gift giving.

Aladdin Fruit Cake Bars

Makes 4 dozen

Fruit and nut filled baked products are especially popular during the Christmas holiday season. This wonderful bar cookie recipe will make enough for several gifts. Wrap bars individually in plastic wrap before packing in attractive tins for mailing.

¾ **cup butter or margarine, softened**
1-½ **cups brown sugar**
2 **eggs**
2 **tablespoons heavy cream**
2 **cups flour**
1 **teaspoon baking soda**
¼ **teaspoon salt**
½ **teaspoon ground cinnamon**
½ **teaspoon ground nutmeg**
1 **cup diced, mixed candied fruit**
1 **cup raisins**
1 **cup currants**
1 **cup chopped walnuts or pecans**

1. In large mixing bowl, cream together butter and brown sugar until light and fluffy.

2. Beat in eggs, one at a time, beating well after each addition. Beat in cream.

3. Sift together flour, soda, salt, cinnamon and nutmeg. Stir into creamed mixture.

4. Stir in candied fruit, raisins, currants and walnuts.

5. Spread mixture evenly in greased 15-½ by 10-½ inch jelly-roll pan.

6. Bake in preheated 300 degree oven 45-50 minutes.

7. Cool in pan on cooling rack.

8. Cut into bars, squares and/or diamonds. Dust with confectioners' sugar.

Gingerbread Girls and Boys

Makes 2-3 dozen

Children of all ages—the young and the young at heart will appreciate these wonderful gingerbread cut-outs. The chilled dough handles well and cuts into shapes easily. I like to roll the dough in confectioners' sugar instead of flour to keep the cookies tender.

½	cup vegetable shortening
½	cup sugar
½	cup molasses
1-½	teaspoons vinegar
1	beaten egg
3	cups flour
½	teaspoon baking soda
¼	teaspoon salt
½	teaspoon ground cinnamon
½	teaspoon ground ginger

1. In small saucepan, bring shortening, sugar, molasses and vinegar to a boil.

2. Cool; add egg.

3. Sift together flour, baking soda, salt, cinnamon and ginger.

4. Add dry ingredients to molasses mixture.

5. Chill thoroughly.

6. On confectioners' sugar dusted pastry cloth or surface, roll dough ¼-inch thick.

7. Cut into gingerbread girl or boy shapes. Trim with raisins or candied cherries, if desired.

8. Place on greased or parchment lined cookie sheet.

9. Bake in preheated 375 degree oven 8-12 minutes, until set.

10. Cool 5 minutes; remove from cookie sheet to cooling racks.

11. Decorate with frosting, if desired.

Microwave

In step **1,** combine shortening, sugar, molasses and vinegar. Microwave on 100% power 2-4 minutes until mixture boils, stirring once.

248

Peppy Cheese Spread

Makes 2 cups

When Joy Wickline gave me a copy of this zesty cheese spread, she said it was one of her husband's favorite snacks. That's testimony enough to convince me this quick and easy cheese combination would make a great gift. Attach a spreader and box of crackers to a crock of this cheese spread for a special gift from your kitchen.

1   (8 ounce) package cream cheese, softened
1   (8 ounce) container sharp cheddar cold pack cheese food, softened
1   (0.7 ounce) package dry Italian salad dressing mix

1. In medium mixing bowl, thoroughly combine cream cheese and cheese food.

2. Add dry Italian salad dressing mix. Stir to evenly blend.

3. Put in gift giving containers.

4. Label with directions to keep refrigerated.

Cranberry Chutney

Makes 1 quart

Gifts from your kitchen are not only fun to give, but wonderful to receive. This lovely cranberry mixture makes a wonderful gift at holiday time as it goes well with many entrees. Fill several small jars and give this very festive food gift.

1   (20 ounce) can pineapple tidbits or chunks
2   cups sugar
4   cups fresh or frozen cranberries
1   cup white raisins
½   teaspoon ground cinnamon
½   teaspoon ground ginger
¼   teaspoon ground allspice
¼   teaspoon salt
1   cup walnuts, broken

1. Drain juice from pineapple into saucepan. Set pineapple aside. Add sugar, cranberries, raisins, cinnamon, ginger, allspice and salt to pineapple juice.

2. Heat to boiling; lower heat and simmer for about 25 minutes, until thick, stirring occasionally.

3. Add reserved pineapple and walnuts. Remove from heat.

4. Put into pretty jars or containers for gift giving. Label with directions to keep refrigerated.

(Continued)

Cranberry Chutney (continued)

Microwave

In step **1,** drain pineapple juice into a 2-quart microwave-safe measurer. Set pineapple aside. Add sugar, cranberries, raisins, cinnamon, ginger, allspice and salt to pineapple juice.

In step **2,** microwave on 100% power 10-12 minutes until thick, stirring three or four times.

Carrot and Pepper Relish

Makes 10 cups

This marinated vegetable duo is an eye catching food gift when packed in attractive glass jars. Attach a label indicating that this delicious relish can be kept in the refrigerator for three weeks. Finish off your gift with color coordinated ribbons.

3   **pounds carrots, cut into ½ inch slices**
2   **green peppers, chopped**
2   **medium onions, sliced**
1   **(10-¾ ounce) can condensed tomato soup**
⅔   **cup sugar**
⅔   **cup vinegar**
½   **cup vegetable oil**
1   **teaspoon salt**
1   **teaspoon Worcestershire sauce**
½   **teaspoon ground pepper**
½   **teaspoon dry mustard**
½   **teaspoon dried dill weed**

1. Cook carrots in 1 inch of boiling salted water until crisp tender.

2. Drain carrots and add green peppers and onions.

3. In medium saucepan, heat together tomato soup, sugar, vinegar, oil, salt, Worcestershire sauce, pepper, dry mustard and dill weed until the mixture boils, stirring occasionally.

4. Remove from heat; cool 5 minutes.

5. Pour over vegetables. Put in jars or containers for gift giving, noting on the label to refrigerate no longer than three weeks.

Microwave

In step **1,** cook carrots in 3 quart microwave-safe casserole. Add 1 teaspoon salt dissolved in ½ cup water. Cover. Microwave on 100% 15-18 minutes, stirring 3 or 4 times. Drain.

In step **3,** heat ingredients in 2 quart microwave-safe measurer on 100% power for 3-5 minutes, stirring every minute.

Seasoned Coating Mix

Makes 2 cups

This nicely seasoned bread crumb mixture might seem like an unusual food gift, but just think how helpful it would be for the busy cook. In a matter of minutes the recipient can have chicken or fish in the oven or microwave for quick cooking. Package attractively in wicker basket with attached instructions.

2   cups fine dry bread crumbs
2   teaspoons paprika
1-½   teaspoons salt
1-½   teaspoons poultry seasoning
1   teaspoon onion salt
1   teaspoon garlic salt
½   teaspoon ground pepper

1. In medium mixing bowl, combine bread crumbs, paprika, salt, poultry seasoning, onion salt, garlic salt and pepper. Mix well.

2. Package entire mixture in tightly covered container or divide up in appropriate size attractive packages. (Enough for four 2 and ½ to 3 pound broiler-fryer chickens using ½ cup seasoned coating mix per chicken) or (Enough for 6 pounds of fish fillets using ⅓ cup per pound).

Attach the directions that are applicable:

Season Coated Chicken

1. Pour 2 tablespoons vegetable oil into foil lined broiler pan or 10x15x1-inch jelly-roll pan.

2. Shake chicken, 2 or 3 pieces at a time, with ½ cup coating mix in plastic or paper bag until coated.

3. Place skin side down in pan and bake uncovered in preheated 375 degree oven until done 45-60 minutes.

To Microwave Chicken

In step **1,** remove skin from chicken.
In step **3,** place chicken on microwave-safe roasting rack. Cover with waxed paper. Microwave on 100% power 7 minutes per pound, rotating dish once. Let stand 10 minutes before serving.

Seasoned Coated Fish

1. Pour 1 tablespoon of vegetable oil into baking pan, 8x12x2-inches.

2. Coat 1 pound fish fillets with ⅓ cup seasoned coating mix.

3. Put coated fish in oiled pan.

4. Bake uncovered in preheated 350 degree oven about 30 minutes, until fish flakes easily with fork.

(Continued)

Seasoned Coating Mix (continued)

Microwave

In step **1,** rinse fish with cold water.
In step **3,** put coated fish fillets in 8x12x2-inch microwave-safe baking dish. Cover
with waxed paper.
In step **4,** microwave on 100% power 1 pound of fish 5-7 minutes, rotating
dish once.

Spaghetti Seasoning Mix

1 packet

Not only are homemade mixes economical, but they are a great way to
avoid preservatives and be in complete control of which ingredients are used. This
spaghetti sauce mix looks great when packaged in a French bread basket complete
with cans of tomato sauce, tomato paste, spaghetti and can of grated Parmesan
cheese.

1   **tablespoon instant minced onion**
1   **tablespoon parsley flakes**
1   **tablespoon cornstarch**
2   **teaspoons green pepper flakes**
1-½ **teaspoons salt**
¼   **teaspoon instant minced garlic**
1   **teaspoon sugar**
4   **teaspoons Italian seasoning**

1. In small mixing bowl, combine onion, parsley, cornstarch, pepper flakes,
salt, garlic, sugar and Italian seasoning. Mix well.

2. Package in small plastic bag or recycled jar. Store airtight in cool,
dry place.

Attach these directions for spaghetti sauce:

1   **pound ground beef**
2   **(8 ounce) cans tomato sauce**
1   **(6 ounce) can tomato paste**
2-¾ **cups water**
1   **packet Spaghetti Sauce Mix, (above)**

1. Brown ground beef in a medium skillet, drain well.

2. Add tomato sauce, tomato paste and water. Stir in Spaghetti Seasoning
Mix. Simmer to develop flavors.

3. Serve over hot spaghetti. Pass grated Parmesan cheese.

Brownie Mix

Makes 17 cups

Here is a recipe that can be a time saving gift to yourself and also can be premeasured and packaged for giving to home baked brownie fans. It works well to make this mix in a food processor, even if it needs to be done in two batches because of work bowl size. Include premeasured mix, recipe and even a baking pan for a nifty food gift.

6   **cups flour**
4   **teaspoons baking powder**
4   **teaspoons salt**
8   **cups sugar**
1   **(8 ounce) can unsweetened cocoa**
2   **cups vegetable shortening**

1. In a large mixing bowl, sift together flour, baking powder and salt.

2. Stir in sugar and cocoa. Blend well.

3. With a pastry blender, cut in shortening until evenly distributed.

4. Store in airtight container or package cleverly in premeasured amounts for gift giving. Label clearly.

5. Store in a cool, dry place. Use within 10-12 weeks.

6. Attach directions for brownies using the following recipe.

Easy Brownies

Makes 16 brownies

Here is the brownie recipe that you'll need to attach to the Brownie Mix above. This recipe makes the popular fudge-type brownie. If you prefer a cake-like brownie, add 2 tablespoons milk to the batter.

2   **eggs**
1   **teaspoon vanilla**
2-½   **cups Brownie Mix (recipe above)**

1. In medium mixing bowl, beat together eggs and vanilla.

2. Stir in brownie mix. Beat until smooth.

3. Stir in walnuts.

4. Pour into greased and floured 8-inch baking pan.

5. Bake in preheated 350 degree oven 30-35 minutes.

6. Cool, if time permits. Cut into squares.

Taco Seasoning Mix

1 package

Food gifts are welcome in all sizes, shapes, and forms. Homemade mixes are a thoughtful inexpensive way to give a nonperishable food gift. This taco mix is a great idea for the busy person who savors south of the border flavors. Attach clear directions and complete the gift with a can of tomato sauce and packaged taco shells, if you wish.

2	teaspoons instant minced onion
1	teaspoon salt
1	teaspoon chili powder
½	teaspoon cornstarch
½	teaspoon crushed dried red pepper
½	teaspoon instant minced garlic
¼	teaspoon dried oregano
½	teaspoon ground cumin

1. In a small mixing bowl, combine minced onion, salt, chili powder, cornstarch, red pepper, garlic, oregano and cumin. Stir to combine.

2. Package in small plastic bag or recycled jar. Store airtight in cool, dry place.

Attach these directions: Brown 1 pound ground beef in skillet or microwave. Drain well. Add 1 (8 ounce) can tomato sauce and taco mix packet to browned ground beef. Heat gently to develop flavors, stirring occasionally. Makes filling for 8-10 tacos. Top tacos with shredded lettuce and cheese.

Minted Hot Chocolate Mix

Makes 6 cups mix

A sampling of this minty cold weather hot chocolate mix was given to me by my friend Pat Hammerschmidt of East Lansing, Michigan. How thoughtful of her to include the recipe to share with others.

2	cups chocolate-flavored instant malted powder
½	cup white buttermints
3	cups nonfat dairy milk powder
½	cup presweetened cocoa powder

1. In blender, combine 1 cup malted milk powder and the mints. Cover; blend until mints are finely chopped.

2. Turn into medium size mixing bowl; stir in remaining malted milk powder, dry milk powder and cocoa powder. Store in airtight container.

3. Package in attractive recycled jars or decorated canisters.

4. Attach these directions: Stir ¼ cup minted hot chocolate mix into ¾ cup boiling water in mug. Top with marshmallows, if desired.

Harvest Popcorn

Makes 2-½ quarts

Snack mixtures are great gifts from the kitchen. Not only are they fun and quick to create, but recipients welcome a non-perishable snack. Packed in airtight cans this crunchy combination stores well and mails easily.

2   quarts freshly popped popcorn, unsalted
2   (1-¾ ounce) can shoestring potatoes (3 cups)
1   cup salted mixed nuts
¼   cup butter or margarine, melted
1   teaspoon dried dill weed
1   teaspoon Worcestershire sauce
½   teaspoon lemon-pepper seasoning
¼   teaspoon garlic powder
¼   teaspoon onion powder

1. In large roasting pan or aluminum foil turkey roasting pan, combine popcorn, shoestring potatoes, and nuts.

2. In small bowl, combine melted butter, dill weed, Worcestershire sauce, lemon-pepper seasoning, garlic powder, and onion powder.

3. Pour over popcorn mixture, stirring until evenly coated.

4. Bake in preheated 325 degree oven 8-10 minutes, stirring mixture once.

5. Cool.

6. Package in a festive way for gift giving.

Herb Seasoned Popcorn

Makes 6 cups

This popcorn seasoned with herbs instead of salt would make a quick thoughtful gift for a friend who requires low sodium snacks. Seal in an attractive container to ensure freshness.

6   cups popped popcorn
2   tablespoons butter or margarine, melted
½   teaspoon basil leaves, crushed
¼   teaspoon oregano leaves, crushed
        Dash of cayenne pepper
1   tablespoon grated Parmesan cheese

1. Place popcorn in large bowl.

2. In small dish, combine melted butter, basil, oregano and cayenne.

3. Pour herb mixture over popcorn. Toss gently.

4. Sprinkle popcorn with Parmesan cheese; toss gently.

5. Package cleverly for gift giving.

Classy Raisin-Nut Party Mix

Makes 8 cups

When it comes to a first-class gift from your kitchen, this is my choice. Chock full of cashews and almonds with supporting ingredients, this is an easy recipe to create. A quick visit to the bulk food section of the grocery store is an economical way to purchase the nuts. Remember too, this mixture mails very well.

2-¼ **cups (12 ounces) whole almonds, salted or unsalted**
1-½ **cups (7 ounces) dry roasted cashews, salted or unsalted**
1-⅓ **cups (8 ounces) dry roasted peanuts, salted or unsalted**
1 **(5 ounce) can chow mein noodles**
6 **tablespoons butter or margarine, melted**
1-½ **tablespoons soy sauce**
1-½ **tablespoons Worcestershire sauce**
3 **dashes hot pepper sauce**
2-½ **cups (15 ounces) raisins**

1. Combine almonds, cashews, peanuts and chow mein noodles in large roasting pan. (I use an aluminum foil turkey roasting pan.)

2. Combine melted butter or margarine, soy sauce, Worcestershire sauce, and hot sauce; pour over nut mixture, tossing to coat.

3. Bake in preheated 325 degree oven for 15-20 minutes, stirring twice.

4. Cool. Add raisins and mix well. Package cleverly in airtight containers for very special gift giving.

Fruit-Nut Mix

Makes 11 cups

Part of the joy of giving a food gift is the sharing of one's time and energy with others. Here is a delicious fruit and nut mixture that is so quick and easy that very young hands could help prepare this gift mix for thoughtful appreciation gifts. Packed in airtight containers, this mix travels well too.

1 **pound dry-roasted peanuts (3 cups)**
1 **(15 ounce) box seedless raisins (2-½ cups)**
½ **pound dates, cut up (1-¼ cups)**
¼ **pound cashew pieces (1 cup)**
¼ **pound walnut pieces (1 cup)**
1 **cup flaked coconut**
1 **cup dried apricots, cut in bite-size pieces**

1. In large mixing bowl, combine peanuts, raisins, dates, cashews, walnuts, coconut and apricots.

2. Toss to mix.

3. Store in airtight container in the refrigerator, if possible, ready for gift giving.

Snack Attack Party Mix

Makes 6-½ cups

If you know friends or family members that often have snack attacks, then this recipe is for you. This crunchy mix is easy to make and stores well in airtight containers. It can be packaged for gift giving in attractive covered containers or sealed plastic bags.

1   (1-¾ ounce) can shoestring potatoes (1-½ cups)
1-¼ cups bite-size cheddar cheese crackers
1-¼ cups goldfish-shaped crackers
1-¼ cups thin pretzel sticks
1-¼ cups mixed nuts
3   tablespoons butter or margarine, melted
2   teaspoons Worcestershire sauce
½   teaspoon seasoning salt

1. In large roasting pan or aluminum foil turkey roasting pan, combine shoestring potatoes, cheese crackers, pretzel sticks, goldfish crackers and mixed nuts.

2. In small bowl, combine melted butter, Worcestershire sauce and seasoning salt.

3. Drizzle butter mixture over snack mixture, tossing gently.

4. Bake in preheated 250 degree oven for 45 minutes, stirring every 15 minutes. Cool.

5. Package in airtight containers ready for gift giving.

White Chocolate Salties

Makes 1-½ pounds

Can you imagine producing a batch of delicious homemade candy in just a matter of minutes? No one need ever know how easy it is to do. Just follow these directions and give your favorite "sweet tooth" a special gift from your kitchen.

1   pound white candy coating
3   cups pretzel sticks
1   cup Spanish peanuts

1. Melt candy coating in double boiler, over low heat.

2. Stir in pretzels and peanuts.

3. Spread on large piece of wax paper. Chill until set.

4. Break in pieces and package cleverly for gift giving.

Microwave

In step **1,** melt candy coating in 2-quart microwave-safe measurer on 100% power for 1 to 3 minutes, stirring every 30 seconds. Do not over-heat.

Chocolate Covered Strawberries

Makes 20-24 covered berries

This is one of the easiest, yet most spectacular food gifts you can create. The berries are very perishable, so it is best to do the dipping shortly before gift giving time and then encourage quick tasting. For a nifty gift container, I like to decorate the cover of a white foam egg carton with strawberry fabric and then put a chocolate covered strawberry in a small red paper cupcake liner in each egg cup.

1   **quart very fresh strawberries with fresh green stems, if available**
4   **ounces semi-sweet chocolate or commercial chocolate coating**

1. Rinse the berries quickly in cold water and pat dry on paper towel.

2. Put chocolate in double boiler and melt over very hot water.

3. Working as quickly as possible, pick up a berry by the stem, dip it into the chocolate so that it is covered about two-thirds of the way up, shake slightly to remove the excess or scrape it lightly against the edge of the pan. Place carefully on waxed paper.

4. Chill just until chocolate sets. Store at room temperature, but do not try to hold more than 8-10 hours.

Microwave

In step **2,** put chocolate in 1 quart microwave-safe measurer. Microwave at 50% power 2-3 minutes until melted, stirring every minute.

Valentine Crunch

Makes 1-½ pounds

If you're looking for a quick Valentine treat from your kitchen, this crunchy candy is just the idea you need. Commercial candy coatings don't need refrigeration, so candy-filled heart-shaped tins can be sent across the miles.

1   **pound red candy coating**
3   **cups crisp rice cereal, crushed**

1. Melt candy coating in a double boiler or over very low heat, just until melted. Do not over-heat.

2. Stir in crushed rice cereal and stir to completely coat cereal with melted candy coating.

3. Spread mixture on waxed paper lined tray. Cool until set.

4. Break into pieces and package for gift giving.

Microwave

In step **1,** microwave candy coating in 2-quart microwave-safe measurer on 100% power for 1-3 minutes, stirring every 30 seconds. Do not over-heat.

Peanut Clusters

Makes 4 dozen

If you've ever needed an almost "instant" food gift, here is an excellent suggestion. Even very small hands can help make these tasty clusters for a special teacher or friend.

1   **(12 ounce) package semisweet chocolate chips**
1   **(12 ounce) package butterscotch chips**
3   **cups salted Spanish peanuts**

1. In the top of a double boiler, over hot water, melt chocolate chips and butterscotch chips.

2. Stir in peanuts until well coated.

3. Drop by rounded teaspoons on waxed paper lined baking sheets or trays.

4. Chill in refrigerator until set.

5. Enjoy giving to friends.

Microwave

In step **1**, put chocolate chips and butterscotch chips in 2-quart microwave-safe measurer. Microwave on 100% power 2-3 minutes, stirring every minute. Do not over-heat.

Chocolate Easter Nests

24 medium nests

If you need a quick Easter treat for small fry or for the "young at heart", here is a suggestion that always pleases recipients. One batch will create enough nests for several gifts. Enjoy being the Easter Bunny.

1   **(8 ounce) milk chocolate candy bar**
1   **(4 ounce) package German's sweet baking chocolate**
2   **cups crushed cornflakes**
1-⅓ **cups shredded coconut**
     Miniature jelly beans

1. Melt milk chocolate and sweet chocolate in double boiler.

2. Stir in cornflakes and coconut until completely coated with chocolate.

3. Spoon small amount of mixture on waxed paper and form into nests shapes.

4. Decorate with 3 jelly bean "eggs" in each nest.

5. Refrigerate until set. Keep chilled.

6. Arrange on small plates or in flat boxes for gift giving.

(Continued)

Chocolate Easter Nests (continued)

Microwave

In step **1,** put milk chocolate and sweet chocolate in 2-quart microwave-safe measurer. Microwave on 100% power 2 to 3 minutes, stirring every 30 seconds. Do not over-heat.

Home Frozen Michigan Peaches

6 pints

This plan for freezing peaches is a "gift" to students in my Portage Community Education Basic Microwave classes who have sampled frozen peaches during the defrosting lesson. It uses a very light syrup which produces a quality product with wonderful peach flavor.

1	**quart water**
1	**cup sugar**
3	**teaspoons vitamin C fruit protector**
15-20	**fresh ripe peaches**
6	**pint plastic freezer containers**

1. In medium saucepan, bring water and sugar to a boil, stirring occasionally.

2. Chill.

3. Peel peaches by dipping 3 or 4 of them at a time in boiling water for 15-20 seconds or until skins loosen.

4. Chill quickly in ice or very cold water and peel.

5. Add vitamin C fruit protector to cold syrup. Stir well.

6. Fill freezer container ⅓ full of cold syrup.

7. Slice the peaches directly into the cold syrup in the freezer container, leaving ½ inch head space.

8. Completely cover fruit with cold syrup, leaving ½ inch head space.

9. Keep the peaches submerged in the syrup by placing a generous piece of crumpled freezer paper or waxed paper under the lid.

10. Cover, label, date and freeze immediately.

Microwave

In step **1,** put water and sugar in 2-quart microwave-safe measurer. Microwave on 100% power 5-8 minutes, stirring once.

Home Made Egg Substitute

Makes 1 cup

When Millie Vandenburg offered to share her recipe for cholesterol-free egg substitute, I soon phoned her to get the exact directions. I think ¼ cup portions frozen in small paper cups and sealed in plastic bags would be a fantastic food gift for the cholesterol-free cook.

6	**egg whites**
¼	**cup nonfat dry milk powder**
1	**tablespoon corn oil**
6	**drops of yellow food coloring, if desired**

1. In medium mixing bowl, combine egg whites, dry milk powder, oil and food coloring. Stir with fork or wire whisk until thoroughly combined.

2. Store in refrigerator up to one week. Or freeze in 1 egg portions.

3. In recipes, use ¼ cup egg substitute for each whole egg required.

Clever Scented Cinnamon Cut-Outs

Makes 3-4 dozen decorations

There are lots of folks here in this corner of Michigan that will remember Christmas 1985 as the year my sister-in-law, Betsey House from Minnesota, sent me the Cinnamon Bear recipe. I shared the ingredient plan with my students in Portage Community Education and soon the town became cinnamon scented with cut-outs of various sizes and shapes. This non-edible food gift is very attractive tied on gifts or hung on decorations.

1	**cup applesauce**
4	**ounces ground cinnamon (about 1 cup)** **(purchase in bulk, if available)**

1. In large mixing bowl, thoroughly mix together the applesauce and cinnamon.

2. When all the dry cinnamon disappears, knead mixture several times until a smooth ball forms.

3. Sprinkle a pastry cloth or surface with ground cinnamon and roll dough to desired thickness.

4. Dip cookie cutter into ground cinnamon. Cut desired shape and put on waxed paper to dry.

5. With straw or other object make hole as a place for string or ribbon.

6. Let air dry for several days, turning cut-outs over once or twice.

7. Tie on food gifts or hang on decorations.

Special Additions

The next few pages are jam packed with information that's
been developed to assist cooks with menu planning and meal
preparation. You'll find ten wonderful menus for various occasions using recipes found right here in *More House Specialties*.

Both the substitutions suggestion list and the equivalent
chart are designed to rescue the person who ran out of an
ingredient or come to the aid of someone who needs assistance
with quantities. Microwave users will want to review the
memos on microwave cooking as most of us appreciate a helpful
hint or two.

Contents

Menu Planning

Planning menus can be a creative satisfying task or just plain drudgery. Here are some suggestions and ideas that I try to remember when combining recipes to be served for specific occasions. With the use of these pointers, I hope your menu creating is always a happy experience.

When Planning Menus Remember:

Management of Time, Energy, and Skill:

Persons who dovetail family life, careers, volunteerism, and leisure time need to assess their time, energy, and skill management when planning menus. How many foods can be prepared ahead of time? How many foods fall into the quick and easy category? How much time will be necessary for cleanup? What can I serve to guests even if I hate to cook? Try to put your effort into one or two recipes and have the rest of the menu selections be free from last minute measuring and detail.

Variety in Color:

We have all heard the saying "We eat with our eyes." Therefore, it's up to the menu creator to include a bright colored vegetable or salad if the other foods seem to lack eye catching appeal. My old friend parsley has rescued many a blah menu.

Variety in Flavor:

A basic rule of thumb is not to repeat a flavor in a menu. For example we would not suggest serving Pineapple Rhubarb gelatin salad with Honeyed Rhubarb Pie. Try not to have an excessive amount of either strong or bland tastes; rather work for a nice blending of flavors that complement each other.

Variety in Shape:

Remember we have round foods, long foods, square foods and many other shapes, so vary them in each menu. This variety of shape will add interest as you present the food.

Variety in Temperature:

Always serve hot foods hot and cold foods cold. Again, variety is the key. Stay away from repetition like a frozen salad and a frozen dessert.

Variety in Texture

The common pitfall in texture variety is too many saucy items. For example Creamed Chicken and Broccoli with Cheese Sauce in the same menu would be too much. One "sauced" food is usually adequate. Introduce some crispness in each menu too.

Likes and Dislikes of Guests

Along with personal desires of guests, remember their ages and activity level. Attempt to have at least one or two items that most people will enjoy.

Menu Suggestions

Here are some menus that keep in mind the principles described on page 262 using recipes in this cookbook. Hopefully these ideas will be helpful to you as you experience the joys of home cooking.

Family Breakfast
Honey Fruit Delight
Sausage Breakfast Pizza
Banana Coffee Cake
Milk and Coffee

Ladies' Luncheon
Crab Salad
Fresh Asparagus Oriental
Lemon Muffins
Sherbet Bouquet
Tea and Coffee

Low Sodium Supper
Oven Fried Fish Fillets
Green Beans with Tomatoes
Grape Delight Salad
Low Sodium Rolls
Milk and Coffee
Orange Frost

Casual Evening Buffet
Make Ahead Mexican Chicken
Gingered Fruit
Food Processor Vinaigrette
Angel Biscuits
Milk and Coffee
Chocolate Zucchini Cake

Special Dinner for Eight
Hot Cranberry Swizzle
Crab Dip
Roast Pork Orange
Rosy Applesauce
Twice Baked Potato Casserole
Snow Capped Broccoli
Pear Royale Salad
Whole Wheat Yeast Rolls
Milk and Coffee
Lemon Frost

After Church Brunch
Tomato Frappe
Fruit Salad Extraordinaire
Bacon/Egg Bake
Easy Overnight Caramel Rolls
Milk and Coffee

Calorie Counter's Lunch
Dieter's Tuna Salad
Fresh Apple Wedges
Favorite Popovers
Kiwi Ice
Tea and Coffee

Soup Supper
Sausage Chowder
Lime Applesauce Mold
Italian Breadsticks
Milk and Coffee
Crowd Pleasing Tin Roof

Outdoor Barbecue
Sugar Free Punch
Giant Taco Appetizer
Sesame Chicken Kabobs
Carrot 'N Cauliflower Casserole
Romaine and Walnut Toss
Hot Garlic Bread
Milk and Coffee
Fruit Pizza Wheel

Microwave Dinner
Meat Loaf Logs
Sweet Potato Delight
Green Beans 'N Bacon
Cabbage Waldorf Slaw
French Fried Onion Bread
Milk and Coffee
Cran-Apple Crisp

Microwave Memos

Here are some suggestions and ideas that are designed to be helpful as your use of the microwave oven increases. Remember constant microwave cooking is the best teacher.

Consumer countertop microwave opens vary in wattage from 400 to 700 watts. Recipe times in this book are based on ovens ranging from 600 to 700 watts. If your oven is lower wattage, you will need to add extra time to the recipes.

One of the main concerns in learning to use the microwave is to be able to cook food evenly. Here are several suggestions:

Elevate foods on a microwave roasting rack to insure even distribution of the microwaves. Do NOT use the roasting rack with a browning skillet or dish as the two surfaces will adhere together when the browning skillet or dish is preheated.

Rotate, stir, or rearrange foods.

Use a ring shaped container or place a glass in the center of a dish to achieve the "donut shape".

Select round containers rather than square.

Reduce power to distribute energy more efficiently.

The question of whether or not to cover foods in the microwave often arises. Here are some guidelines:

Many foods are left UNCOVERED whenever you want to allow steam created from the heating of the food to escape. In this cookbook if a cover is not mentioned, no cover is needed.

Cover foods with waxed paper when you wish to retain natural moisture in the foods. The waxed paper will allow the moisture to self-baste in the items without creating such a tight seal that it would be steamed.

Cover foods with vented plastic wrap or a tight fitting casserole lid whenever you wish to trap the steam created to help cook the item. At the end of the cooking time, leave the lid or vented plastic wrap on during the "standing time" to allow the food to finish cooking from the steam. Remove plastic wrap carefully to avoid steam burns.

Cover foods with paper towel whenever you want to absorb steam or splatters. Wrap bread products and sandwiches in a paper towel or paper napkin to absorb moisture so the bread will not be soggy.

Try reducing power level to 75% or 80% for reheating foods. This will take a few seconds longer than at 100%, but the results will be a more evenly heated food.

Reheat bread products wrapped in paper towels or napkins on 30% power. The guideline is approximately 30 seconds per roll.

The terms 100% power, High, Full Power and Normal all mean the same thing. In this cookbook the term used is 100% power.

When honey gets too thick, remove the lid from the jar and microwave the jar on 100% power for a few seconds until the honey gets thinner. Be careful not to overheat.

To separate slices of refrigerated bacon more easily, microwave 1 pound of bacon for 30 seconds on 100% power to soften the pieces. Peel off only the slices you wish to cook. Rewrap and refrigerate the remainder.

Keep your microwave oven interior clean. Since spatters and spills don't cook on they wipe up easily with a damp sponge or cloth. What a time saver.

Off-The Shelf Substitutes

All of us have experienced a time when we need or wished to make an ingredient substitution. The question is how do I substitute? Here is a chart that I hope will be helpful in that situation. Swapping one ingredient for another can cause slight variations in texture and taste, but the overall result is the same. All substitutions are approximate.

Basic Ingredients:

1 cup cake flour	1 cup minus 2 tablespoons all purpose flour
1 teaspoon baking powder	¼ teaspoon baking soda plus ½ teaspoon cream of tartar
1 tablespoon cornstarch (for thickening)	2 tablespoons all-purpose flour or 1 tablespoon arrowroot
1 cup granulated sugar	1 cup packed brown sugar or 2 cups sifted confectioners' sugar or 1 cup honey plus ½ teaspoon baking soda (reduce liquid in recipe ¼ cup)
1 (1 ounce) square unsweetened chocolate	3 tablespoons unsweetened cocoa powder plus 1 tablespoon margarine or butter
1 package active dry yeast	2-¼ teaspoons bulk dry yeast

Tomato Ingredients:

1 cup catsup or chili sauce	1 cup tomato sauce plus ½ cup sugar and 2 tablespoons vinegar
1 (15 ounce) can tomato sauce	1 (6 ounce) can tomato paste plus 1 cup water
1 (16 ounce) can tomatoes, cut up	3 fresh medium tomatoes, cut up or 1 pint home canned tomatoes or 1 (16 ounce) can stewed tomatoes

Dairy Ingredients:

1 cup milk	½ cup evaporated milk plus ½ cup water or 1 cup reconstituted non-fat dry milk
1 cup buttermilk	1 tablespoon lemon juice or vinegar plus enough milk to measure 1 cup or ¾ cup yogurt plus ¼ cup whole milk
1 cup cultured sour cream	1 cup plain yogurt
1 cup light cream	14 tablespoons milk plus 2 tablespoons butter or margarine
1 cup whipping cream whipped	1 (4 ounce) container frozen whipped dessert topping, thawed or 1 (1-¼ ounce) envelope dessert topping mix (prepared by package directions)
1 whole egg	2 egg yolks and 1 tablespoon water

Soup Ingredients:

1 (14-½ ounce) can beef or chicken broth	2 teaspoons instant beef or chicken bouillon granules plus 2 cups water or 2 beef or chicken bouillon cubes plus 2 cups water
1 teaspoon instant beef or chicken bouillon granules	1 beef or chicken bouillon cube, crushed

Helpful Hints

Here are some helpful hints that I hope will save you time and energy. Some of these clues can be instrumental in the creation of first class finished products.

Food Preparation Pointers:

Large Grade A eggs weigh approximately two ounces, including the shells. As a rule, five large eggs equal about one cup. The recipes in this book are designed for large Grade A eggs.

When using glass cookware for baking, reduce the oven temperature by 25 degrees. Glass retains heat longer than the average metal baking pan and consequently food may stick to it at a higher temperature. Increase cooking time slightly to compensate.

If you use more than one shelf of your oven at one time, stagger the pans to achieve greater air circulation. Without proper circulation the foods will cook unevenly.

For ease in greasing a baking pan, insert hand in a small plastic sandwich bag. Dip bag into shortening and grease pan without getting fingers messy.

Cookie sheets should be flat and shiny. Pans with sides deflect heat and slow the cooking time (fast baking is essential for cookies) and dark surfaces cause the cookies' bottoms to overbrown. Always start with cold sheets; if you put raw cookie batter on warm sheets, the dough will spread and the cookies will lose their shape while baking.

Most cookies should be removed from baking sheets immediately or they will continue to cook.

If you have only enough cookie batter to partially fill the cookie sheet, cover the unused space with an inverted baking pan. The pan absorbs the heat that otherwise would cause the cookies to bake too quickly.

Oven barbecuing and broiling is usually done in a ventilated oven—the door is left slightly open—for "dry heat" cooking and relatively dry meat or fish. In a closed oven, moisture released from the food itself circulates and leaves the food more moist.

If you need stable whipped cream for decorating desserts, beat a teaspoon of gelatin that has been dissolved in a teaspoon of hot milk into a cup of whipped cream.

Evaporated and condensed milk are not interchangeable. Evaporated milk is homogenized milk dehydrated to one half its original volume. Condensed milk is evaporated milk further reduced and then sweetened.

Equivalents

In the process of planning and marketing, it is helpful to know quantities to purchase and use for desired measurements. I hope this chart contributes to your ease in planning. All measurements are approximate.

Baking Items

1 cup dry bread crumbs	= 3 to 4 dried slices
1 cup soft bread crumbs	= 1-½ fresh slices
4 cups all-purpose flour	= 1 pound flour
1 tablespoon unflavored gelatin	= 1 envelope
1 cup graham cracker crumbs	= 9-12 graham crackers
1 cup soda cracker crumbs	= 18-20 saltine crackers
1-⅓ cup rolled oats	= 1 cup flour
½ cup butter or margarine	= ¼ pound or 8 tablespoons
1 regular marshmallow	= 10 miniature marshmallows
100 to 110 miniature marshmallows	= 1 cup
1 cup chopped walnuts or pecans	= 4-½ ounces
2-¼ cups brown sugar	= 1 pound brown sugar
4-½ cups sifted confectioners' sugar	= 1 pound confectioners' sugar

Cheeses

1 cup shredded or cubed cheese	= 4 ounces chunk cheese
2 cups cottage cheese	= 1 pound cottage cheese

Fruits and Vegetables

3 cups sliced apples	= 3 medium apples (1 pound)
2-¾ cups grapes	= 1 pound grapes
1-⅓ cups shredded coconut	= 1 (3-½ ounce) can
2 to 3 tablespoons lemon juice	= 1 medium lemon
1 tablespoon grated lemon rind	= 1 medium lemon
½ cup chopped onion	= 1 medium onion
2-¼ cups cooked potatoes or 1-¾ cups mashed potatoes	= 3 medium potatoes (1 pound)

Grain Products

2 cups cooked macaroni	= 1 cup uncooked macaroni, (4 ounces)
2 cups cooked noodles	= 1-½ to 2 cups uncooked noodles, (4 ounces)
6-½ cups cooked spaghetti	= 1 pound uncooked spaghetti
3 to 3-½ cups cooked rice	= 1 cup uncooked long grain rice
1-¾ cups cooked oatmeal	= 1 cup quick-cooking oats

Index

Index Cooking With Less

Recipes highlighted with this symbol contain less sugar, less salt, or less fat.